SWEET
AND
SOUR

SWEET AND SOUR

...

ANDREW A. ROONEY

G. P. PUTNAM'S SONS
NEW YORK

G. P. Putnam's Sons
Publishers Since 1838
200 Madison Avenue
New York, NY 10016

Library of Congress Cataloging-in-Publication Data
Rooney, Andrew A.
Sweet and sour / Andrew A. Rooney.
p.   cm.
ISBN 0-399-13774-2 (alk. paper)
1. American wit and humor. I. Title.
PN61612.R63337   1992   92-17753 CIP
814′.54—dc20

Printed in the United States of America

1 2 3 4 5 6 7 8 9 10

This book is printed on acid-free paper.

My thanks to Jane Bradford for her good work on this book and to Neil Nyren for its arrangement . . . although both of them are well paid.

CONTENTS

——— ▪ ▪ ▪ ———

two SIGNED BY HAND

three THE BODY HUMAN

six STRAIGHTENING OUT THE WORLD

seven THE FOLLOWING THINGS ARE TRUE

eight THE ABSENT MIND

nine FIRST THINGS, LAST THINGS

PREFACE: READERS READ, WRITERS WRITE

It is inevitable that, from time to time, a writer thinks objectively about writing. I was thinking, for example, how surprising it is that I can sit down to write without an idea in my head and, come up with something. Quite aside from whether what I've written is any good or not, it surprises me that I can do it at all.

People are always saying to writers, "Where do you come up with all your ideas?" The answer is that ideas are everywhere and the only thing that makes a writer any different is, he's always on the lookout for one. His antenna is up. He recognizes an idea when he sees one. He stops it in midflight and tries to get it into words.

Writing essays is a writing specialty. There is almost nothing that an essayist who knows his business can't write about. In the course of a day, ten thousand thoughts flow through our heads. If a writer can call up and assemble, in a more or less orderly fashion, a collection of thoughts or observations on the most ordinary subject, it's an essay.

Readers take pleasure from recognizing a thought of their own in someone else's words. It makes them feel together with the rest of the world. An essayist doesn't tell people things they don't know the way a reporter does. At best, he shines a light on some of the things in the recesses of the reader's mind that the reader may not have realized were there.

Putting words down on paper and having them printed is dangerous because, once printed they have a kind of immortality that the spoken word does not. The spoken word, no matter how wise, goes up in smoke and is lost forever.

There's no writer who ever lived who hasn't had the presumptuous notion that his words will have some good effect on the world . . . or, short of the whole world, on a few people who read what he writes. I've had that notion and, because of it, if I was forced to choose between never having said a word on television and never having written a word that was printed, there's no question which I'd choose. I'd choose never to have appeared on television.

A writer is relatively oblivious to numbers. I'd just as soon be read by 100 people as watched by a million on television. As long as someone comes up to me somewhere, sometime, and says, "Hey, I liked that!", that's all my ego needs to keep going.

I don't think I could write a novel. I can hardly stand to read one. Being a novelist is as far from being an essayist as being a carpenter is from being a plumber. They work with a lot of the same tools but what they work on isn't the same at all.

A novelist has to know where he's going when he starts writing. An essayist goes where his flighty brain takes him—which is often all over the place. A novel is heavy with action and descriptive phrases. A good essay doesn't have any suspense or drama about it. It's light on adjectives. It simply turns over some little thoughts. While a novelist transports a reader out of his own world into someone else's, an essayist turns a person inside himself for a look at what's going on there.

The essayist starts with nothing but the raw materials, words and ideas and makes them into a form. It's like the story of the ancient sculptor who stood in front of a huge piece of marble and made a bet with a friend that there was a nude woman sitting inside it, playing a lyre. After the bet was made, the sculptor started chipping away at the rock and, sure enough, within a matter of days he had found the woman, sitting there, inside the block of stone.

Essays exist in a pile of words and all the essayist has to do to find one is pick out the right words and put them in order.

There's no subject too big or too small for an essayist. He should be able to turn one out on the head of a pin. By *on* I mean *about* the heads of pins. *An Essay on the Heads of Pins.*

One of the problems an essayist has is an uncomfortable awareness that he's using the first person pronoun "I" more often than becomes a modest person. I overcome any uneasiness I have about this, two ways.

First, I say that it is not really "I" that I'm talking about. The "I" I use in writing is some universal person representing everyone who might read the essay. Readers should associate themselves, not with me but with my "I" . . . which is really them.

Second, if that first explanation doesn't work in my search for modesty, I say to myself that the job of an essayist is to paw through the excess baggage of his brain, looking for old thoughts, bits of information and stories that pertain to the subject matter. The essay is, in part at least, an assessment of what's in the essayist's head and there's no way to avoid the odious "I" word.

Being opinionated is a great help. Fairness does not become an essayist and it makes for dull essays. A little prejudice on the part of the writer is vital, even if it's only a preference for chocolate over vanilla.

There is an obligation on the part of an essayist to spend more time picking at what's wrong with his society than pointing out what's right. It doesn't necessarily indicate he thinks there's more wrong than right. Unbeknownst to most people who read what I write, this essayist thinks there are a great many good things about America, the world and all the people in it.

p a r t o n e

— • • • —

HOME AND AWAY

NOT FOR SALE

The question about selling the house came up again at Christmas dinner. It's come up for forty-one years now but I don't think it will ever happen. You want to know why we couldn't sell the house? I'll tell you why:

Because there are a thousand things I know about this house that no one else would ever know, that's why. You think you know how to open a locked door? Try our back door. You think it's easy because you have a key? Forget it. The lock on that door takes a special little twist and jerk that comes with years of experience. A stranger couldn't get into our house through that door with a ring of keys and a crowbar.

And how would anyone else know how to turn the water for the outside faucet off in the fall and on in the spring? It's a routine I've performed twice a year for thirty-nine years now (I forgot to do it twice).

To turn off the water going to the outside faucets, I go to the back of the basement where the washer and drier are lined up against the wall. The faucet is up between two rafters right behind the washing machine. I turn my back to the washing machine, put my hands behind me and up on the front edge of the washing machine. I give a little jump and boost myself to a sitting position on top of it. My back is to the wall, but by leaning back, looking up over my head and extending my right arm up behind me and between all the pipes, I can reach the valve handle and turn it off.

Who else would know you have to jump up and sit on the washing machine to turn off the outside faucet?

And how would you put your car in the garage if you bought our house? Would you have any way of knowing that if you pull the car forward just to where the divider between the front and rear door of the car is exactly opposite the leaf rake hanging from a hook, that you won't bump into anything at the front of the garage but will still be in far enough so you could close the door? Would you know that?

And, by the way, don't open the garage door early in the morning if someone's sleeping in the little guest room over the garage. The door makes a loud rumbling sound right under that bed.

Would you know that the fan in the attic lets in too much cold air when it isn't working in the winter and has to be stuffed with insulation? And if you knew that, would you know the best way to climb up into the attic through the small entry over the upstairs hallway? I'm sure you wouldn't. It's by using the little ladder I keep under Brian's bed. You wouldn't know that, would you? And anyway, if I sold the house, I'd take that little ladder because I made it in 1957.

You certainly wouldn't know that when it rains steadily for a couple of days, the front part of the basement gets damp unless I put a sheet of plastic on the ground under the downspout where all the water pours out off the roof. While I'm basically an honest person, it is quite possible that if you were interested in buying my house, I wouldn't go out of my way to tell you about the damp basement.

If you don't jiggle the handle on the downstairs toilet just a little after you flush it, it keeps running. It takes a special touch to jiggle it just right.

When I come downstairs in the dark and want to turn the light on, I can put my finger on the light switch halfway down the hallway leading to the kitchen nine out of ten times without feeling for it. It's nothing I could teach anyone how to do. After forty-one years, I just know where every light switch is in the whole house. Every time I turn on a light, I think what it must be like to be blind and still be able to find things.

I know our house too well to sell it. I know it's the seventh step from the top coming downstairs that creaks the most. And if, by any chance, you did buy our house, you couldn't move in right away because it would take us at least a year to empty out the closets.

FOXHOLES

When I go into someone else's house, I'm always pleased that the owners don't know what I'm thinking.

I come in the door, say hello and right away I start making changes. In my mind, I move the furniture around, throw out some stuff, take down some pictures and often paint the walls. Sometimes I wonder how they stand the place. I'm certain the silent insults are mutual when they come to our house.

The fact is, we all like our own place best. It's why all those old sayings about home are true. "Be it ever so humble . . ." "Home is where the heart is," etc.

I'm suspicious of anyone who likes to travel a lot. Being happy at home is better than being happy anywhere. It's cheap and readily available. Kids playing in the backyard sense how good their own home is when they make a treehouse or build a hut in the woods.

Even the homeless make homes for themselves. This morning, walking to the office in New York, I passed three homeless men. It was shortly after seven A.M. and they were still asleep on the street but their homeless homes were very individual.

One of these men had folded a huge piece of cardboard that had been the container for a new refrigerator, into a peaked roof so the rain would run down the sides onto the sidewalk instead of onto him. Another man had tied a heavy string from the doorknob of an empty building and run it to a heavy wire mesh screen covering a window eight feet away. He had put several old blankets over the cord and made a half-tent for himself by stretching the bottom of the blankets out from the wall and holding them there with four bricks.

American soldiers overseas are great homemakers. They make nests for themselves wherever they go. Just a couple of years ago, GIs made homes for themselves in the sand in Saudi Arabia. They dug out underneath their truck or their tank looking for protection from the sun. They used discarded food and ammo containers and made themselves a place to be whenever they were in one position for more than a few days.

There are always long pauses in the action in any war while the commanders decide what to do and before they tell the soldiers or the sailors to do it. In Normandy, after the D-Day invasion of WW II, the guys hunkered down behind the hedgerows and dug foxholes for themselves as protection against the blast of mortar shells. You'd think that once you'd seen one foxhole you'd seen them all, but it was always a surprise to see what a foxhole looked like after an American soldier had been in it for two or three days. No two were alike.

A few years ago, I spent four days on a Navy ship, the *Guam,* off the coast of Beirut. Sailors are special homemakers. Those of us with three- and four-bedroom homes with three bathrooms and a two-car garage for storage could take lessons in homemaking from them.

Each sailor is assigned a space not much bigger than a coffin, and as a person with a claustrophobic psyche the idea of spending hours in a space that small, three decks below the waterline, scared me to death. It didn't seem to bother the sailors. They made themselves a nest and were content inside their cocoonlike bunk space.

An old house makes the best home because after a house has been lived in for fifteen or twenty years, it's got the bugs worked out of it. If the roof leaked, it's been fixed. If there was a plumbing problem, it's been repaired. The worst problems are with new homes, not with old ones. The old ones are slow to fall apart, but the new ones have problems built into them that can only be discovered and worked out over a long period of day-after-day living in them.

STILL HANGING AROUND

Every so often, the pictures we have hanging on the walls in our house begin to irritate me. What IS that damn picture, anyway, and what's it doing hanging there year after year?

I remember my mother had pictures hanging in the house when I grew up. They weren't very pretty, they weren't really *of* anything, they were just there, year after year, and they stayed there until I left home and went to college. They weren't anything my mother particularly liked, they were simply pictures on the wall.

Now, the same thing has happened in our house. If I didn't like our house so much, I wouldn't have lived in it for forty-one years, but there are some things I don't know why we haven't changed. The pictures on the wall are among them. They may be good but not for forty-one years they aren't.

Over the television set in our living room hangs a black and white photograph, 18″ × 24″. It is very arty. It shows, in the grainy black and white detail that is the mark of an arty picture, a woman dancing. She isn't just any woman dancing, she's a ballerina bent in the shape of a capital C with a flowing robe that looks as if there was a huge fan directed at her from offstage.

I liked the picture when it was first hung, but to be honest with you—and to my wife—I've had it with Miss Tipsy Toesel. I'm ready for another picture. Every time I watch television, there she is in the background, a constant reminder to me of everything I'm not. Her lithe body exudes culture, art and the promise of imminent action. She stands lightly on one foot with the other toe pointed forward, ready to go. I, on the other hand, am a clod, slumped in my big old chair, ready for nothing, watching some bad old television show that has no artistic merit whatsoever. Do I have to be reminded of my shortcomings so constantly?

I suppose if we start changing pictures in our house, we're going to have to paint the walls, because the color behind the pictures will be different if we don't. It won't have faded as much as the paint that's been exposed to the light all day.

There's a picture of me, in a small frame, on the shelf in front of the bookcase. It's in with several pictures of our children but there it is, me. What in the world is a picture of me doing in our own living room? I don't really think the picture is there on purpose. It was put there one day for no special reason and, in all these years, no one has bothered to take it away. When I'm away, I don't have any feeling that other members of the family look longingly over at it, counting the hours to my return. It's another picture that should go to the attic, along with Miss Tipsy Toesel.

We have several small still-life oil paintings . . . flowers in bowls, mountains in mist, and a seascape. Things like that. Oil paintings often look to me as if the artist got too much paint on them by mistake. I like them okay. I just don't like them so much that I want to live my whole life with them. If our house were a museum in which there were fifty Van Goghs hanging, we'd leave them there for a while and then we'd take them down and put up the Picasso exhibit for a few months. Not in our house. Once a picture is hung, that's it, in perpetuity. It's as permanent a part of the house as the kitchen sink.

We have a few good paintings but I can't tell the good ones from the run-of-the-mill ones, and I don't think anyone else looking at them would, either. The difference between a great painting and a poor painting is noticeable to almost anyone, but the difference between a good painting and an average, professionally-painted picture cranked out by a workaday artist isn't apparent to me.

The whole business of reproduction has become so efficient that it's difficult, even for an expert, to tell when something is a reproduction and when it's an original. The only joy in owning an original work of art is the knowledge and pleasure of possession you have in your own heart.

In our dining room, we have a picture painted by Degas of a scene on the French Riviera. I like it because of the shape and colors. We paid thirty-five dollars for it many years ago so I suppose it's worth forty-five dollars today, but if it were wallpaper, we'd have taken it off the wall, thrown it out and replaced it years ago. It's a picture, and pictures are protected by some unwritten rule in our house that you don't ever take one down and throw it out.

HOUSEKEEPING

Anyone who lives in a house does a certain amount of housekeeping. I do very little—but a certain amount.

There's a stigma attached to housework which accounts for why it's called "housekeeping." The people who don't do it try to make the people who do feel better by using a friendly name to describe it. If this were not true, it would be called "housecleaning."

In the fairly recent past, there has even been an effort to improve the sound of the word used for this chore by calling the people who do it "homemakers." No matter what you call it, it's dull work. Over the holidays, I've been home a lot and inevitably have been pressed into some housework. The following things are true about housework:

• Vacuuming a large rug is the easiest housekeeping job. Anyone doing it gets more credit than he or she deserves. This is partly because the vacuum cleaner makes so much noise it gives the illusion that someone's working hard.

• Putting away the vacuum cleaner is harder than vacuuming.

• The single easiest thing to do in exchange for the most credit, is mopping the kitchen floor. It sounds like a big deal but it isn't.

• Forgetting to put the trash out by the curb on the day it's picked up is the single worst mistake a housekeeper can make.

• No matter how many times it happens over the years, it's always a big surprise when a fuse blows, or a circuit breaker breaks.

• There are parts of a stove where grease collects that I don't want to know about.

• No soap, detergent, scouring pad, brush or grease-remover that claims to make cleaning easy makes cleaning easy. It's hard no matter what you use.

• An easy way to get out of housework is to go get something at the store.

• Certainly there's someone somewhere in the world smart enough to make an automatic bedmaker. I can't actually design it myself but I have the outline of it in my head. It's a tubular aluminum frame that's fixed to the ceiling above the bed, except when it's lowered to do its job. It rolls the sheets and blankets onto a wide drum, smooths them out and then lays them on the bed. I haven't quite worked out how it tucks the blankets in or fluffs up the pillows.

• Whenever I iron something, I think of my mother. Every time she ironed, she said, "I enjoy doing a little of it." I realize now that what she was really saying was, "I hate to do a lot of it."

Ironing a pair of men's pants is the hardest for me. The pant legs never fold exactly in half, so you can just lay them flat and run over them with the iron. I invariably end up with at least two creases in each leg.

Shirts would be easier to iron if it weren't for having to steer the iron around the buttons. My dress shirts go out to the laundry but ever since I found out it costs about a dollar to have each one washed, I'm more careful about wearing them. If I put on a clean shirt and go out to dinner, I wear the same shirt again the next day.

• If you've ever simply soaked dishes in the sink with dishwasher detergent, you realize that it's dynamite. It does more to wash the dishes than the dishwater does.

• After I finish inventing the bedmaker, maybe I'll invent a robot housekeeper. When I come home from work, it will say, "Is that you, dear?"

SMART KITCHEN, DUMB COOK

You know progress has passed you by when your new kitchen is smarter than you are.

Over the winter we had the kitchen done over in our house in the country and my inclination now is to go out for dinner more often.

My advice to people about to do a kitchen over is this: Figure out how much the new kitchen is going to cost, then double that figure. First have the kitchen done over, use it for a month and then tear it out and start over without the mistakes. There is simply no way that anyone, looking at a piece of paper, can do it right the first time.

There are kitchen-design experts who'll plan one for you but to do it right they'd have to live with you a month in your old kitchen. No two families use a kitchen the same way. The builder who did our kitchen is a fine craftsman. The workmanship is great but he has one shortcoming: he doesn't cook. A kitchen doesn't come naturally to him.

One problem with kitchens is that everything can't be right next to everything else. You may like your stove near the refrigerator but if it is, it can't be next to the sink.

The kitchen table should be handy so you can put things on it but it shouldn't be in the way. If it's handy sometimes, it's in the way others.

Our kitchen was designed, but we can't blame the designers. We made changes and most of the mistakes are ours. Mistakes? Let me count the ways:

• We moved the refrigerator from where it was planned to be, to a place next to the wall. Now the door will only open to slightly less than a right angle, and as a result, the vegetable drawers at the bottom cannot be pulled all the way out.

• We have a double stainless-steel sink with a garbage disposal–grinder-upper in the sink to the left. It should have been put in the sink to the right because the board on which we cut up vegetables is to the right. It should be easy to sweep the hard ends of asparagus and other vegetable cuttings into the grinder. Now we have to lift them over one sink to drop them in the other.

I know I should have studied all the manuals first, but you get impatient with a new toy. You want to play with it, you don't want to read about it. You may not believe this, but the dishwasher, the garbage-disposal unit and the oven all came with half-hour instructional videotape cassettes. How would you like to settle down to a nice quiet evening looking at a tape of how to use your dishwasher?

I looked for a place on the garbage disposal to play the tape but there was no screen for viewing it.

There are two ovens, one above the other, which is very handy. It's difficult to get a big dinner with just one oven. If you roast a leg of lamb, you can't heat rolls or warm the plates.

Our top oven is a state-of-the-art combination regular, convection and microwave. We've never had a microwave before and it's still not clear to me how a microwave heats things or why it isn't dangerous when you get near it. I can't get over the fact that you can't use a metal pan because it might melt so you use plastic, which doesn't. Why's that?

The first day, I put a loaf of good homemade bread that had been frozen in the oven, and turned the microwave on for three minutes. When I took the bread out, it was one big crouton, hard as a rock throughout. I bought some popcorn in a bag designed for the microwave oven. The directions said it might take from two to five minutes. I put the microwave on medium-low instead of high and when I took the bag out at five minutes and opened it, I had more unpopped kernels than popped corn.

We're going to the country this weekend. I think I'll buy a steak and cook it on the grill outside the kitchen door. It's a new door and I want to use it. There's such a thing as having a kitchen more modern than you are!

THIS NEW OLD HOUSE

We've bought a dilapidated old house near our home and we're having it fixed up. It seemed like an interesting project that would give us some satisfaction, and maybe even make us a little money if we can sell or rent the rebuilt house. Our house has been paid for since 1974, and being without a mortgage makes me feel like an outsider.

The new old house was built in 1885. If this brings to your mind visions of some grand old mansion, sturdily built of heavy, hand-hewn timbers mortised-and-tenoned and held together with wood pins, turn off your mental television set with that picture on it. That's not the way it is.

This house was poorly built 107 years ago and has been deteriorating ever since. The floor in the living room slopes toward the center of the house because the beams in the cellar that had supported the floor were partially removed when a chimney was added for an oil burner.

The roof is laid on 2 × 4s that are thirty inches apart. If you were putting up the house today, the building code insists on 2 × 4s only sixteen inches apart for strength. I asked an architect if he thought it was safe to put a new roof on those old supports.

"Well," he said, "you wouldn't think it was safe now, but the house has stood that way for more than one hundred years. I guess it won't fall down tomorrow."

The only interesting thing about the 2 × 4s in the old house is that they actually measure two by four inches. If you've ever used what are called 2 × 4s in a lumberyard today, you know that they're actually only one and a half inches by three and a half. "Two-by-four" is just a name, not a measurement.

An old house reminds me of the progress we've made in the homes we live in. I remember in school reading what a hard time the Jamestown and Plymouth settlers had when they came here, because they didn't realize how hot the summers were going to be or how cold the winters were. They hadn't thought much about housing.

Those early Americans had been soldiers or sailors and they didn't know how to build anything. A lot of them died because they were wet and cold so much of the time that they got sick easily. Imagine trying to get through a winter in Massachusetts living in a tent with a dirt floor. That's how a lot of them lived the first few years.

The house that made colonizing America possible was the log cabin. All the men needed for a tool to build it was an ax. They cut a notch near both ends of four trees and fitted them together at right angles to make a rectangular structure. Then they did the same to four more trees. Nails were too expensive. They just kept laying one log on top of another until the shelter was tall enough. Then they put a roof on it, cut a door in one side, and called it home.

The log cabin became an American symbol. As some schoolchild wrote: "Abraham Lincoln was born in a log cabin he built with his own hands."

We've come a long way. Even the log cabins built today have a polystyrene foam sprayed between the layers of logs to keep the drafts out. Even this old house we bought was set up on stones so that the beams the house rests on wouldn't stay wet and rot. The builder now takes that one step further. The base of the new addition is on concrete blocks covered with tar to keep moisture out of the basement, and the heavy beams are of lumber that has been pressure-treated to preserve them against rot.

The redone house will have fiberglass insulation, central heating and air conditioning. Americans profess to like the outdoors but they like their indoors just the right temperature.

The half-finished addition looks good now. The siding is redwood but it isn't red, it's a beautiful nut brown. I'm going to hate to see it painted but I suppose it will have to be.

I feel great and terrible about the redwood. We're cutting down all our great forests and here I am contributing to it by paying to have a house built with redwood.

I am a little uneasy about building a home I don't need when there are so many homeless. Still, I think it's the right thing to do. The house will be better than it was and someone will live in it.

HAVE A NICE WEEKEND

"**H**ave a nice weekend," Jane said to me as I was leaving the office Friday, and subsequent events affirmed my suspicion that having someone wish you one doesn't help.

Saturday morning I looked forward to the small pleasures that accomplishing some easy jobs gives me. I planned to go to the dump with some junk, take a lamp to have the switch fixed, go to the lumberyard, and take the small television set in the kitchen to the repairman. While I was out I was also going to pick up a 20-inch inner tube for a bicycle wheel.

I swept out the garbage and washed the car and it was almost noon before I got started. It's hard to decide which errand to do first on Saturdays. The dump has always been open until three P.M., and I had plenty of time for that, so I headed for the man who knows how to fix lamps. I parked nearby and, as I walked toward the shop, I saw the dreaded cardboard sign in the window: CLOSED NOON SATURDAY. It was five after.

The lamp went back in the car and I drove to the lumberyard. I wanted half a piece of treated plywood. The lumberyard was awfully sorry but they don't cut anything on Saturdays. I left without the plywood. The bicycle shop had just sold its last 20-inch inner tube.

It was 1:45 and I decided I'd better get rid of the junk in the back of the car, so I headed for the dump. As I turned into the entrance, a man was swinging the huge wire entrance gate closed. It was a minute after two P.M.

"Closed!" he shouted. "New hours. We close at two Saturday."

I idly wondered, as I drove away, whether I should put the junk back in the garage or leave it in the car until I got to the dump again next Saturday.

The door of the TV shop was locked and my heart sank, but I knocked and a young man came to the door.

"We're closed," he said. "But come on in." I thought I was finally having some luck.

"I got this little Sony," I said. "The channel selector doesn't work."

"How old is this thing?" he asked. I could tell by the disparaging way he said "thing" that the news wasn't going to be good.

"You mean I should get a new one?" I asked.

"Probably," he said, "unless you're really sentimentally attached to this one. It needs a new tuner and it's gonna run you $200."

I left with my TV set.

It was good to have Saturday over with. I had a terrible cold and went to bed early. I hoped Sunday would be a better day.

Don't ever have the rubber hose behind your washing machine burst at three A.M. Sunday morning if you're planning to have a nice weekend.

At about three-thirty I'd been up to go to the bathroom and take an aspirin and I thought I heard water running. You know how noises are in a house, though. You can't be sure. "Maybe it's something else," I thought to myself, and went back to bed. Big mistake.

When we came down for breakfast, we discovered three inches of water in the basement and rising. The black rubber hose had split open and water was spewing all over the boxes of washing machine soap, the electrical panel, the radio and some of my tools. Everything was awash. Bits of wood were floating around. The base of the furnace was in water and, by the time we finally got the main valve turned off, water had seeped into the front part of the cellar where my office is.

The wall-to-wall carpet squished as I walked on it. The file cabinets were in water, the couch was wet and various pieces of equipment like the slide viewer and the camera tripods were ready to start rusting.

We called the plumber and by the time he got there, I was using my wet/dry vacuum to get some of the water into two large garbage barrels. The plumber quickly replaced the broken hose, presented his bill for $150, and left.

A plumber who comes early Sunday morning when you need him is worth $150. It just wasn't what I was looking forward to when Jane said to me, "Have a nice weekend."

AN APPRECIATIVE HUSBAND'S GRATITUDE

Wives do a thousand little things for their husbands that they don't get credit for.

Right here I want to give credit where credit is due. A few weeks ago, while I was away, Margie did something for me I'll never forget. She cleaned up my shop in the basement. She got our friend Joe to come in and help and between them they tidied up everything. It must have taken several days because it would have been impossible to put that many things in places where I can't find them in less than several days.

I confess that the shop would have looked as though it was a mess to anyone but me. To me, everything was in its place. I had little scraps of wood everywhere. If I use six feet of a seven-foot piece of maple, I don't throw away the leftover foot. I save it. I don't always put my scraps of wood away neatly in a pile of other scraps, but I know where they are. Now my scraps of wood are in neat piles. I can't find them, but they're neatly piled.

I would be the first to admit that I'm not neat. (Come to think of it, I was not the first to admit it. Other people have said it several hundred times before I ever did.)

My wood treasures, pieces of lumber, were leaning against the basement walls or were stashed up in between the beams under the dining-room floor upstairs. Because there were years of accumulated sawdust everywhere, Margie and Joe moved everything. Margie said she was afraid of fire, but if the house had burned down, it wouldn't have disrupted my shop any more than the cleaning job did.

There were dozens of different sizes of nuts, bolts, nails and screws on my workbench. When I wanted one I pawed through the pile until I found the size I wanted. No longer. Now only the three of them—Margie, Joe and God—know where anything is. Margie's out shopping, I don't know where Joe is and God has more important things to do than tell me where they put my dovetail jig.

All those nuts and bolts and screws are in dozens of little jars with tops on them now. When I want one, I dump them out of the jar onto my workbench and paw through them just like before.

Tools like chisels and screwdrivers were lying helter-skelter on my workbench. No longer. Margie put each and every item somewhere. That's the key word. Everything is "somewhere."

I go to the bottom of the cellar steps and yell up, "Hey, Margie! Where did you put the chuck key to my drill?"

"I put it right there somewhere," she yells back in obvious irritation over my lack of appreciation for the work she did.

She hung hammers, saws and extension cords. She put two tri-squares down behind some cans on a shelf. I found my level in a box over by the shelves with the paint. Margie and Joe piled my lathe chisels under my workbench and put my drill bits—well, actually I don't know where they put my drill bits, because I haven't found them yet.

Listen, it's just another reason to thank her. Most of those bits were dull anyway, so I went out and bought a set of new ones.

How can I ever express my appreciation for the job Margie did? I've been considering some ways. Margie does all our bookkeeping in what used to be the twins' room. Her papers are spread out all over several tables and desks and piled on the little couch that pulls out and turns into a bed at Christmas when everyone's home. I think that one of these days I'll repay Margie's kindness. I'll pick up her workroom the way she picked up mine. I'll pile all her papers, government forms, tax receipts and bank records, and put them in boxes. I'll tidy up. I'll try and make that room as spick-and-span and free of anything out-of-place as Margie made my shop.

There must be a rule of life here somewhere. I think the rule may be, "It may be a mess, but it is MY mess."

FEEDING CYCLES

There are five baby birds in the small nest above one of the posts holding up the little roof over our back porch. We use the dining room door to go out back now, because if we go out the kitchen door, the mother bird goes bonkers.

She's plenty busy, flying in about once every two minutes with a mouthful of food for her babies. One of the young ones is more aggressive and must be a pain in the neck to the others. It's bigger and louder, moves around more and is probably getting more food. I hope the mother is keeping track of which one she gave the last mouthful to or this pushy one's going to get all of it.

We aren't the only ones who know the baby birds are there. This morning I came out the dining room door, and sitting on its haunches in the grass ten feet off the porch was the big, mean yellow cat, the one that kills chipmunks.

I'm really fond of those birds, and I'd hate to see the cat get any of the babies after the mother has gone to all that trouble of getting them this far in life. It's been a tough spring for her. The eggs were already in the nest when we first came to the country in May and she was sitting on them then. There were some very cold days and I don't think she dared stray far from the nest for fear the eggs would get cold.

Of course, that's sexist talk. I have no idea whether it was a mother or a father bird sitting on those eggs. Neither can I say for sure that the bird going in and out from the nest with food at regular intervals is a female bird. For all I know, those baby birds got a bad mom who abandoned them and the father bird had to take over. I mean, it's possible, isn't it?

These birds bring more questions to my mind than I have time to find the answers for. I think of birds as eating worms because I see the robins on the front lawn going after them. These birds are eating something else, though. It must be mosquitoes or some kind of small, flying object, because the mother seems to collect food on the fly. Is it any crueler for that yellow cat to kill a baby bird than it is for that mother bird to kill a baby fly or mosquito?

Are baby birds ever mistreated by their parents? Why would it only be humans who abuse their young? Don't you get a bad bird once in a while? One who loves to fly but hates kids?

I don't even know whether these are the same parents that built a nest there last spring. Do birds have memory enough to recall that they liked that little spot on our kitchen porch? And if it's the same mother bird, did she stick with the same father bird?

Nature seems unnecessarily cruel. I know that cat is part of the natural cycle but I don't like it, even though if every two birds flying around here had five young who survived every year, we'd have too many birds. Nature knows that and arranges for some of them to die or be mauled to death by yellow cats.

Our concern for these little birds is a puzzle to me, too. They're nothing to us and yet we actively don't want anything bad to happen to them, annoyed as we are that they've taken over the back porch. The cat left this morning when he saw me but I attached the hose to the outside faucet near the kitchen. If I see the cat again, I'm going to douse him with the hose to discourage him from hanging around. Or her. I'm never sure about cats.

But if we're so concerned about the survival of these birds, how do we reconcile our kind-heartedness toward them with the chicken dinner we had tonight? Presumably some mother chicken felt the same maternal concern for our dinner as this busy mother bird feels for her young but we didn't give the mother of the bird we ate for dinner a second thought. To tell you the truth, I didn't give her a first thought until this moment.

Maryann lives in the country, close to the birds and the bees all year long. She said that our birds might die in the nest this year. That idea didn't appeal to me at all. She said seven bluebird eggs had hatched in a birdhouse that Dick built in their backyard but they all died. You could blame this on some predator like a red squirrel or a bluejay or environmentalists could blame it on people by saying the surrounding fields had been sprayed with something poisonous that got into the birds' food system.

Maryann had a simpler explanation. At this time of year we are plagued with tiny black flies, known locally as May flies. It had been windy and colder than normal the year her bluebirds died. The black flies like it muggy and still, so they hadn't been flying round where the mother bluebirds could catch them to bring back to the nest. It was Maryann's conclusion that the baby bluebirds starved to death because of a shortage of black flies.

I had never known there was anything good about black flies and I'd been very pleased to be free of the dreaded little devils. I hadn't known that my comfort was at the expense of dinner for the birds.

Last week, the black flies were out in force again, so I don't think Maryann's suggestion our birds might starve will come to pass. Some of the black flies were being fed to the birds in the nest on the back porch and the rest of the flies were feeding on us.

Now, what does God have in mind here, if God's the one at work? Why no flies last week and too many this week? You have to suspect there's some master plan but if so, what is it? God could hardly be expected to take into consideration people's attitude toward birds and black flies . . . or flies' and birds' attitudes toward each other.

I confess that I bought a barn fogger several years ago and have been known to spray the area around our house when no one's looking, so we can sit outside and have a drink before dinner without being drunk and eaten alive. I say "drunk" because these little devils draw blood and I assume they drink some of it after they've opened you up. Being eaten by a bird is too good for a black fly, as far as I'm concerned.

No one in the family approves of my spraying so I don't do it often, but I think people, and especially the environmentalists, take an untenably egotistical position. When they refer to nature, they specifically exclude human beings or any human action as being part of the "natural" process. If there is a God at work here, does God think of human beings as separate from nature? I doubt it.

And why do environmentalists assume that the natural process is always best? Best for whom and to what end? Nature seems unconcerned about the welfare of species. The mastodons and the dinosaurs were not wiped out by man and I don't think they'd endorse the evolutionary process that led to their extinction, "natural" as it was.

If science has invented a spray that kills black flies, might this not be simply another natural phenomenon . . . like a cold, windy day?

WATER ON THE BRAIN

It's a funny thing about water—either there's too much of it or too little. If there isn't a flood, there's a drought. The waiter in the restaurant either doesn't bring you any water at all or won't stop filling your glass. What is it with water anyway?

We visited two places last week and the problem in both houses was water. In one house there wasn't enough and in the other, there was too much.

The water in the first house was supplied from a deep well. The problem was that the flow was three gallons a minute. Three gallons a minute would be a lot of water if you were living in a tent one hundred miles east or west of Cairo, but in this house there were two bathrooms and eight people. Between cooking, baths, laundry and toilets, three gallons a minute isn't much. In any big American city, water comes so easily, you forget what it can be like without that torrent that comes with a twist of any faucet.

In this house, anyone about to take a shower had to check to make sure no one was about to take one in the other bathroom because the well didn't produce enough water for two simultaneous showers. The pump at the bottom of the well shuts off automatically if it goes dry. When that happens, you have to wait ten minutes, then restart the pump.

The other place we visited was a cottage on a big lake. Water was drawn from the lake for the cottage, so there was plenty of it but, unfortunately, the septic tank was small and on rocky ground, so everyone had to be very careful about letting the water run lest it overflow. An overflowing septic tank is one of the worst experiences known to man.

In the cottage, you couldn't turn on the water and let it run when you were washing dishes, because of the septic tank. Showers had to be brief because the tank wouldn't take much runoff. Even flushing the toilet was a sometime thing. Anyone who grew up with a septic tank and has experienced an overflow knows how it can take the fun out of a day.

I don't know whether I'd prefer living in a house with limited water and a good sewer system or a house with lots of water with a poor sewer system. What I prefer is a home where neither is a problem.

In the cottage by the lake, we were often in the dark because almost any rainstorm produced a power outage and we had several rainstorms. When a branch falls from a tree and hits a line or a telephone pole with a power transformer, the lights go out in the house. It happened twice in two days. The flashlight was never where I'd left it and I groped in the dark. When the power went out, the electric pump down in the lake went, so there was no water. When there's no water, there's no way to cook, no way to use the bathrooms. With no lights, you can't even read.

At the lake, we spent a lot of time out on the water in a 21-foot powerboat. Boats don't work. Cars work but boats don't. It must be because of all the water. There is almost always something wrong with a boat. If the boat doesn't leak, the engine won't work. If the boat does leak, there's usually something wrong with the automatic bailer. Sailboats aren't much better than powerboats.

I've had trouble with every boat I ever had anything to do with and I can't think of any explanation except water, for why boats can't be made as reliable as automobiles.

In many parts of the country, boats spend 75 percent of the year pulled up out of the water and they're no trouble when they're on shore. They spend 99.9 percent of the 25 percent of the time they're in the water tied to a dock, not going anywhere. About 15 percent of the one-tenth of one percent of the time the owner wants to use a boat, he can't because there's something wrong with it. Not only do boats often fail to work properly, but people who know how to fix boats are almost nonexistent. What boatyards are good at is storing boats because there's no water involved in that.

ON THE ROAD

I'm going somewhere.

It doesn't matter where. The idea of leaving where you are for someplace else takes over. I have some things I absolutely must do before I leave but I know what will happen. In the enthusiasm that comes with departure, I'll find reasons not to do them. Their importance will fade in my mind. Leaving is the important thing and everything in life is directed toward that end.

I got out my suitcase last night, even though I'm not going to pack it until tonight. I always take more than I need. For instance, I often take a suit I never wear. I pack as many shirts as there are days I'll be gone, but I almost always wear one shirt for part of two days so I come home with one or two clean shirts. You never know what the temperature's going to be, so you take both warm and cold weather clothes.

It's hard to know exactly what you'll need for clothes no matter what the temperature is. I take a big suitcase because it isn't much harder to carry than a small one, and I can get all the little stuff in it. I'd rather have one big suitcase and my briefcase than a small suitcase and several little bags . . . in addition to my briefcase. I have no patience with people who bring more luggage than they can carry. There ought to be a law at airports. If you can't lift it, you can't take it.

Travelers who carry their bags on board an airplane are trying to save time at the other end, I suppose, but I resent the ones who take up all the room in the overhead compartments.

There are always people three rows back of me who boarded early and filled the compartment over my head with their luggage so there's no room for my coat. Sometimes it seems as if those overhead compartments were built full. I've never seen an empty one. That's partly the airline's fault, of course. People carry on their luggage because it takes so long to recover checked bags at the other end of the trip.

I'm flying first class. I only do it when someone else pays. Normally I wouldn't dream of paying the ridiculous price they get for first class. First class is a joke on most planes. You get a few more inches of room and the attendant is more apt to wake you when you're sleeping to ask if there's anything she can do for you, but that's about it.

It is nice, though, having your own seat up front with a little extra room instead of getting the center seat on a crowded plane in back alongside a mother with a crying baby. Anyone sitting near a crying baby on a plane should get a partial refund.

It's always a little embarrassing being in first class on the infrequent occasions I travel that way. I board late so a lot of people won't pass by and see me sitting up there like a big-shot company executive, as they make their way back to tourist. I think, by the way, that they ought to abandon the words "tourist" and "coach" and revive the classification on the old ocean liners, "steerage." The space they give you on planes suggests the word.

I'm traveling alone and that's a help. It doesn't matter how much you like the person you're traveling with, it's more than twice as hard. It isn't just getting from here to there with someone else. It's the decisions. Alone, you consult no one. Right or wrong, you do it.

The group I'm joining in Palm Springs wanted to meet me at the airport but I don't want to be met. Tell me where I have to be and what time and I'll get there. Being met is a nuisance. I'd rather rent a car and get lost on the way to where I'm going or take a bus or a cab, than be met and driven by a stranger I don't want to talk to. Getting lost on the way into town from the airport, I learn a lot about a strange city.

Travel is an escape from all your pressing problems. That's why we're so willing to give it our complete attention. The need for being someplace on time to catch an airplane before it leaves creates a false sense of urgency that temporarily overrides any real problems we ought to be solving. Temporarily, at least, it gives us a reason for setting our worries aside. That's why the idea of going someplace takes over our lives.

MY GRANDMOTHER'S TRUNK

My parents always had a trunk in the attic of our house. Houses often don't have attics anymore, and if they do, there aren't trunks in them.

We were packing up for a summer vacation this week and I got to thinking how handy it would be if we had a trunk. You would need ten big suitcases to hold as much as you could pack in one of those old trunks. Uncle Bill and Auntie Belle had three trunks in their attic in Ballston Spa, New York. The trunks held family treasures for generations back.

I don't know what happened to those trunks or to the family treasures. That's what happens to family treasures . . . no one knows what happens to them. They vanish. You get one thrower-awayer in the family, like my mother was, and that's the end of the line for all the vestiges of the family past. Out go the old letters, the tattered lace tablecloths, the photos of unidentified friends of relatives long gone. And, of course, out goes a lot of useless, sentimental junk.

The biggest trunks were called "steamer trunks" because that's what you took on a steamship if you were going to Europe before there were airplanes. Uncle Bill and Auntie Belle had steamer trunks even though they never went to Europe. I suppose the steamer trunks were leftovers from my grandparents who came from Scotland after stopping there for a generation, on the way from Ireland. I wish I had those three trunks today with everything that was in them. Going through them now would be like a family archaeological dig.

If you think everything that's happened with cars and airplanes is progress, consider how people used to go away for the summer. They'd pack their trunks, call Railway Express, I think it was, and Railway Express came and picked up their trunks, took them to the railroad station and turned them over to the baggagemaster. Trains actually had something called a baggage car.

If you're young, you're not going to believe this, but when you took a lot of baggage on a train with you, you didn't have to go through a metal detector and no one inspected your luggage for explosives. It sure would be handy to ship in a trunk on a train some of this stuff we're taking with us instead of carrying the whole mess in the car.

Instead of a trunk, I've been putting things in suitcases, cardboard boxes, old shopping bags, and then I've been stuffing a lot of stuff in different parts of the car. If we ever had a flat tire en route, it would take two hours to unload the trunk, twenty minutes to change the tire and another two hours to load up the car again.

All the space inside one of those old trunks was usable. The trunk of a car is not nearly so good. Something's always in the way in the trunk of a car. There are structural members, pipes and wires and jack handles sticking out all over the place and it's difficult to judge how much you can put in the trunk and still slam the lid closed. If you overestimate the trunk's capacity and put in too much, it can often mean starting over. I could use a car with two trunks.

It's that "miscellaneous" that takes up so much room when you pack. Anything that's a regular shape and flat is easy, but shoes, a typewriter, or kitchen equipment like a food processor are tough to find a place for.

I have a lot of duplicate tools I leave in the country but I cart a lot back and forth, too. Tools are hard to pack. Margie wants things like her hair dryer and I suggest she let her hair dry naturally during the summer, but I can't argue much when I'm taking a lot of cumbersome tools myself.

The only thing I hate worse than packing up the car is getting there and having to unpack it. I just want to turn it over and dump it out.

RESTING IS HARD WORK

This is it. I'm what's known as "off."

It's the time I've been dreading for months. I'm on vacation. I like some of the things I do on vacation, but I always have the nervous feeling everyone back at work is getting ahead of me while I'm gone.

A lot of people have my problem. They try to get too much in on vacation. They know they ought to be having a good time. They know they ought to be resting and relaxing but it doesn't come easily to them and they get tense and upset trying to relax.

One of my problems is that I'm relaxed at work. When I try to make a change on vacation, things go wrong. I know I have to enjoy myself and have fun and take it easy, and the pressure is too much. I get tense. I get to counting the number of vacation days I have left and wondering whether I'm going to get in all the fun I'm supposed to.

This year, I'm going to try to do it differently. There are some things I'm determined not to do. If I cannot do them, I think everything's going to be okay.

1. I'm not going to try to have a good time. If a good time comes along, I'll take it but it'll have to be by accident. I'm not planning to have one because whenever I do, my plans go wrong.

2. There's a lake near our summer home but I'm not going to swim in it. I swam half the day when I was a kid and I liked it, but swimming no longer interests me. It's like walking. I know how to do it now but unless I have to get somewhere doing it, I don't do any more of it than is necessary. There is no place I could swim to that I couldn't get to quicker some other way. Anyway, I'm no longer excited about how I look in a bathing suit.

3. We have a hammock slung between two trees on the front lawn, but I'm not going to lie in it and read. I'm not going to get a good tan, either. I don't like lying around and I particularly hate lying around in the sun. Not liking to be out in the sun is one of the few healthy preferences I have. The word sunbathing is loathsome to me. I wear dark glasses when the show on television was shot in Hawaii.

4. I'm not going to relax and catch up on my sleep. I get plenty of sleep when I'm working. I don't need to catch up. As a matter of fact, I'll be getting up earlier during my vacation because the sun hits the bedroom window between five and five-thirty A.M. during July and I'm going to get up about then so I don't sleep through my vacation.

5. I have no intention of losing some weight. Eating is wonderful entertainment after a busy day on vacation and I plan to do a lot of it. We cook out most nights when we're at our summer home and I often make ice cream. Fresh peaches and fresh raspberries make some of the best homemade ice cream. If I want to lose weight, I'm going to do it some other time. I'm not going to spoil my vacation by trying to do it then.

6. During the regular working part of the year, I'm always worried about being way behind on answering letters, paying bills, sending in registration forms for stuff that comes with a guarantee, renewing my license, writing angry letters and phoning people I should have gotten in touch with a long while ago. On my vacation that's all going to change. I'm not going to catch up on any of it then, either. The difference is, I'm not going to worry about it.

7. There are a lot of odd jobs I've been meaning to do. The doorknob on my closet is just turning around so I don't dare close the door. The two front windows in the living room are stuck shut. The doors leading down into the cellar from outside need painting.

Someday, during my vacation, I'm going to sit down and make a list of all the jobs I should do and then not do them.

8. I've often thought of taking a month off from writing. I'm not going to do that, either. Somedays, working is the most fun I have on vacation.

"LOVE, ALICE FAYE"

I f you wanted to give a first-time visitor to the United States an honest but favorable look at a typical American city, you could fly him to Minneapolis and then drive across the river to St. Paul.

I can't imagine why St. Paul would want to be the tail end of the hyphenated designation Minneapolis-St. Paul, but that's the way it is. An airport may be called "Minneapolis-St. Paul," "Dallas-Ft. Worth," or even "Albany-Schenectady," but it gives a place a small-town air. A city should have a name all its own.

It's a great city, though. Even the passengers flying to Minneapolis-St. Paul look like nice people. When I flew out there, I put my briefcase and coat down on a chair in the area by the gate at the airport in New York and went back to the main lobby to get a newspaper. I had judged that there was no one going to Minneapolis-St. Paul who was likely to steal my briefcase.

Parts of the grand old city of St. Paul are beautiful and there are things about it I knew but had forgotten when I visited it. Driving through town one morning, I made a turn, and there, looming bigger than life on top of a hill, was the imposing white marble State Capitol.

"Of course" I thought to myself as I reached back into my mind for some fourth grade geography. "Lincoln is the capital of Nebraska, Salem is the capital of Oregon and St. Paul is the capital of Minneapolis . . . I mean, of Minnesota. Milwaukee is in Wisconsin."

"What brings you to St. Paul?" everyone wants to know. They like their city but they all seem a little surprised that anyone else would have a reason to come there. I had come to make a speech. My habit is to come a day early, lock myself in my hotel room and write what I'm going to say.

The first evening there, I ate alone in a place that called itself a "four star" restaurant. It was about as close to a four-star restaurant as Paris is to North Dakota, but still it was pleasant and not bad.

The menu was elaborate and I looked, as I always do, for some sign of a local specialty. There was "New York-cut steak," Maine lobster", and "Norwegian salmon." I don't go to St. Paul, Minnesota, for any of those. The only thing that seemed as if it might be local was the "wall-eyed pike."

"I wouldn't have that if I were you," the waitress said in the friendliest possible way when I ordered it.

"I was looking for a native dish," I said. "Is the pike from Minnesota?"

"Well, yes, I guess so," she said. "But don't have it. It tends to be bony."

I told her that unless the person doing the cooking advised me against having it, I was going to have the pike in spite of her advice.

Shortly thereafter, I saw the waitress and the headwaiter conferring in subdued voices over near the pastry cart. The captain disappeared into the kitchen and came out shortly thereafter and approached my table.

"Don't have the pike," he said firmly.

It was advice I could not ignore and it ended my search for a native dish in St. Paul.

The second day brought the highlight of my stay in St. Paul. I entered my room late in the afternoon and found a bottle of wine in an ice bucket on the table. There was a note with it, which I ripped open, expecting to find a perfunctory greeting from the hotel manager.

"I look forward to seeing you at the meeting," the note said. "I am in room 925. Love, Alice Faye."

If you are too young to have known Alice Faye in her heyday, let me tell you that she was one of the all-time beautiful women ever born. I sat, enthralled, through a half-dozen of her movies, as she danced, sang and acted her way through them.

Me? A note from Alice Faye? Visions of a stage full of beautiful girls dressed in spangled costumes in a Busby Berkeley musical danced in my eyes, as the star Alice Faye, the most beautiful of all the beautiful girls on the stage, came to center stage and stole the show. I couldn't have been more excited if I'd had a note from Katharine Hepburn, Ginger Rogers or Marilyn Monroe.

Alas, though, the story has a sad ending. Alice and I never met before we both left St. Paul. I'll never know for certain why I feel so warm toward the city, but I'm probably the only man in America who will always think of Alice Faye when I hear the name St. Paul.

Imagine. Me. "Love, Alice Faye."

SURRENDERING TO PARIS

Paris is a special city in my life, considering I'm not much of an international traveler. I first saw Paris on August 25, 1944, the day the city was liberated from the Germans by a combination of French and U.S. troops. I entered it across the bridge at St. Cloud. We had reached St. Cloud the night before, and the tank commanders decided to wait until morning to make their final drive into the city.

Two German Army trucks, loaded with soldiers, tried to cross the bridge in our direction in the middle of the night, not knowing we were there in such force. They ran into the barrage of fire from the 75mm guns mounted on the tanks of our armored division sitting there on the other side of the river.

The bodies of the Wehrmacht soldiers, riddled by machine-gun bullets, lay askew in the trucks and on the grated bridge roadway where some of them had fallen, their blood dripping into the Seine below. That was my gruesome introduction to what has been, ever since, an almost idyllic relationship to one of the world's great cities. (I suspect that if there were a poll taken among all the people who have been everywhere to determine their favorite city, Paris would win.)

Paris is too expensive for an American to visit now, of course, but a lot of Americans go there anyway. We try to save some money and take the trip once every few years. I'd rather go to a foreign city I'm sure I like than take a gamble on a place I don't know.

Two of us went to one of the good restaurants in Paris for a birthday celebration in 1991 and dinner cost almost two hundred dollars apiece. That included one of the least-expensive bottles of wine. French wine is as expensive in France as it is in the United States. You could say that about California wine and California, too.

When you enter a restaurant in France, an American is struck by how many people are puffing cigarettes. The French don't have no-smoking sections. Morley Safer attributes the relatively good health of the French to the amount of red wine they drink. Some people are always looking for reasons why a vice of theirs is actually good for them. I accept Morley's word on this myself.

All French restaurants add 15 percent to the bill for the waiters. Service is as good or better than in the U.S., where we assume waiters try harder to get a better tip. They don't, and we should abandon tipping and add a service charge. There's a restaurant I go to in New York that gets a lot of French tourists and one waitress told me they often don't get tipped by their French customers because the French assume it's included on their bill.

The French always seem to be having a good time when they eat. When a man and a woman sit together in a cozy restaurant, it's as if they were dancing. I don't understand what French women see in French men, though. I do see what French men see in French women. Even the women who are nowhere near beautiful have an attractive, sexy way about them.

French men, on the other hand, are as a whole and by my own standards not as good-looking as the average American man.

Before I left home for Paris, I bought a new pair of white pajamas, because I didn't want to be in my old, tattered ones when the maid came in every morning with the traditional French hotel breakfast of coffee, hot milk, a crusty loaf of their great bread and several croissants and jam.

I think, by the way, that the French ought to sue some of the bakeries making what they call "croissants" in our country. A soft, soggy roll is not automatically a croissant just because it's made in the shape of a crescent.

The third night I was there, I was getting ready for bed but I couldn't find my pajama bottoms. I know I'd hung them on the back of the bathroom door and it was apparent that the maid had picked them up with the white towels and bedsheets and put them in the laundry.

I didn't know whether to spend the money on a new pair, which probably would have cost as much as the expensive dinner, or sleep in just the tops for the rest of the trip. It occurred to me that it seemed almost impossible to surprise or shock the maids who brought breakfast, no matter what you were wearing, if anything at all. You can guess what I did.

I drove eighty miles from Paris to Reims, the heart of champagne country, and stopped for gas just outside the city. The superhighway gas station had everything one in the United States would have, except unleaded gas. The French don't have much unleaded gas yet. The gas station sold candy, junk food, Eiffel Tower ashtrays for tourists and trashy magazines, but, unlike any gas station I'd ever seen, it had a huge selection of expensive champagne for sale. I was tempted to buy a quart of oil, a bag of potato chips, and a magnum of Moët and Chandon.

We went to Reims, or "Rheims," as it's spelled in English, because I wanted to see where the Germans surrendered on May 7th, 1945. They've made the building into a museum, but it's not very good. The French are not much interested in making a big thing of a German surrender to U.S., British and Russian troops. They seem to be vaguely embarrassed about their role in World War II.

On the way back to Paris, we came over the same bridge I had crossed forty-eight years ago when Allied forces entered the city. It's one thing I know more about than the Parisians know about their city. It gives me a kind of smug satisfaction when they're impatient, because I don't speak French very well.

I just smile quietly and think to myself, "I know something about this city you'll never know."

HEADS THEY WIN,
TAILS YOU LOSE

There are five or six cities in the world that I would enjoy living in but Las Vegas is not one of them. Las Vegas depends for its success on what's wrong with America. It depends on people who want to get something without working for it.

The permanent residents of Las Vegas—those who aren't there because they were trapped years ago by their gambling habit—seem to work hard and think that visitors like myself misunderstand their city of over a quarter of a million.

As much as I dislike everything about Las Vegas, I confess to being fascinated by it. I usually have a good time on the rare occasion I get there.

I didn't get to see any of the shows featured at the big casino hotels last time. Many of the entertainers who are big attractions in Las Vegas are relatively unknown elsewhere. George Carlin and Dennis Blair were at Bally's, but I didn't go because I never heard of either of them.

Engelbert Humperdinck's name is in lights ten feet tall, but I wouldn't recognize Engelbert if he came up to me and asked what time it was.

One of the casino hotels advertised a NUDE ICE SHOW. All I could think was that it must be cold when they fall.

The Sahara advertised a show called "Boy-lesque."

Vic Damone and Diahann Carroll were playing the Golden Nugget. I haven't heard Vic Damone sing since he won the Arthur Godfrey Talent Scout Show in 1949, which I was writing at the time.

The entertainers, like everything else, are there to attract customers into the gambling halls. Huge signs outside the casinos read "BREAKFAST SERVED MIDNIGHT TO NOON. BACON AND EGGS OR SAUSAGE, WAFFLES $.99."

They just want you in there. Whatever it costs them to serve you breakfast for ninety-nine cents is petty cash compared to what they take away if they can get you to the slot machines or the gambling tables.

You couldn't put up buildings as ugly as the buildings are in Las Vegas cheaply. They are not just your average everyday ugly. They are in monumentally bad taste.

The hotel that cost the most money to build and is in the worst taste of all is usually the "in" place. Years ago it was The Sands. In the recent past it's been Caesars Palace. Now it's The Mirage. The Mirage has a waterfall out front that turns into a volcano at night. One cabdriver said it cost them $15,000 every time they turned it on. This is the kind of statistic that interests people in Las Vegas, whether it's true or not.

There were maybe 10,000 people like me, wandering around The Mirage the night I was there. They were gaping at the man-made tropical forest and the enclosure with the two handsome white tigers. Most of the people were tourists in white ankle socks, right off the bus, and I wondered if The Mirage hadn't done itself a disservice by attracting the kind of crowd that comes to look, eat The Mirage's equivalent of the ninety-nine-cent breakfast, and leave without ever dropping a few hundred dollars in the casino.

In my own hotel, I listened to three men talking in the elevator. You have to be able to translate what they say.

"I had a pretty good night," one of them said. That means he didn't lose much.

"I'm playing with their money," said a second. That means he won a little which he lost again almost immediately. Now he's lying because it makes him feel better and thinks it makes you feel better for him.

"One night I lose, the next night I win," said the third man. "It all evens out."

It doesn't even out. There is no way, over a long period, to do anything but lose in Las Vegas. And chances aren't very good for the short period, either.

SODOM, GOMORRAH AND NEW YORK CITY

The two biblical cities of Sodom and Gomorrah were supposedly destroyed by an angry god for having displayed "arrogant pride and haughtiness" and for having "lived in prosperous luxury while ignoring the poor and needy." That was in addition to other acts frequently committed there which now borrow their name from Sodom.

New York City is always being compared to Sodom and Gomorrah. *Time* magazine, whose headquarters is in New York City, says New York, "the Big Apple," is getting worse. "Rotting" is the word *Time* uses. Critics of *Time* have always said the same thing about the magazine, of course.

Like the world going to hell, New York has always been going there without ever having arrived. I don't know whether or not New York will survive as the greatest city on earth, but I know New York is a microcosm of the United States and if New York does not survive and prosper, the United States will not. Everything that happens in New York happens in the rest of our country, but later.

New York is a place people come to from somewhere else. They are doing what our ancestors did when they picked up and left Europe. New York is a magnet for adventurers because it offers both opportunity and danger in great abundance. As a group, these New Yorkers have a restless, creative energy in common. It is they, not the criminal who murders a tourist from Utah, who give New York its character.

The small towns of America are populated by good people who like things the way they are and choose to stay put. They're content with the security of knowing what they're doing and where they're doing it. Those who come to New York are less satisfied with the way things are in their lives.

There are, for example, a great many bright, educated women who have come to new York because the opportunities for bright young women are far greater in New York than elsewhere in the country. The writer and two of the three reporters who worked on the article for *Time* are women who almost certainly belong in that category. Writing about how bad New York is has always been a favorite theme of writers who wouldn't live anywhere else.

Time deplores the estimate that one out of every hundred people in New York is homeless, but New York is the opposite of Sodom in that regard. It does not ignore its poor and needy. It has put itself in debt trying, often unsuccessfully, to take care of more than its share of the homeless of America.

New York has a lot of homeless because you can *be* homeless in New York. You can't be homeless in a lot of cities and small towns in America, because if you try to sleep on a park bench you'll be prodded or poked or picked up by police and ordered to move. Never mind that you don't have a place to move to.

At every level, including leaving them alone, New York does more for indigent people than most cities, and it is ironic that, because of its relative hospitality toward the poor, the mentally ill and the homeless, New York has attracted more of them than any other city. It doesn't seem fair.

Not only does New York do *more* than its share for the poor and the homeless, it has had less help from Washington during recent administrations because New York is not a city that votes Republican.

If New York City's financial condition continues to deteriorate and the city rots, as *Time* says it is, then the homeless whose home is New York will leave because the city can't take care of them any longer, and other towns and cities around the country will get them. And if New York declines, so will the artistic, cultural, financial and creative life of the whole nation.

Wherever you live and whether you love New York or hate it, take no pleasure from predictions of its decline.

For all that's wrong with it, I'm not about to leave New York City . . . and neither is *Time* magazine.

THE CASE FOR NEW YORK

A great many Americans don't understand how anyone could like living in a city whose police chief announced that there were 2,000 murders in town in 1990. Let me give you one small reason why some of us like New York anyway.

Yesterday I picked up two pair of shoes from Jim's. Jim's is a shoe-repair shop on East 59th Street. There's heavy traffic because, among other things, the street leads to one of twenty-eight bridges or tunnels that take a million and a half people onto or off the island of Manhattan every day. (Out-of-towners don't understand how important it is that Manhattan, what they know as New York City, is an island.)

I bought the two pair of identical shoes nine years ago. They were honestly made and this was the fourth time I'd had them soled and heeled, a record for both me and shoes.

For a long while, I knew the difference between the two pair, but after the first few years I lost track of which was which. I wear them interchangeably now, although I have never, to my knowledge, worn one of each.

Jim's shop is narrow, no more than fifteen feet wide, but it must be one hundred feet deep because you can hear the hum of heavy machinery in the back. There are always at least ten customers bringing or retrieving shoes and Jim and his helpers turn out a lot of work.

The customers with minor repairs wait in small stalls so they can walk out in the same shoes they came in wearing. Leaving shoes to be fixed is as inconvenient as leaving a car to be fixed and if you can have either done while you wait, it saves time and trouble. Jim knows that.

The shops called "shoemakers" don't actually make shoes. They fix them and they're a dying breed—although there are 202 shoe-repair shops besides Jim's listed in the New York Yellow Pages.

If a community doesn't have a doctor, there are government agencies that help find one, but there's no government agency that finds a shoemaker so many communities don't have one. People go around with heels run over or they wear sneakers. When sneakers get down at the heels, they don't have them repaired, they throw them away and buy a new pair. That's the American way.

I paid and walked out of Jim's with my shoes and threaded my way through traffic to my car across the street. I was double-parked but trapped, with a truck in front of me, a truck in back of me, and a Mercedes-Benz triple-parked on my right. I couldn't wait to look at my shoes so I took them out of the brown paper bag as I sat there waiting for the Mercedes owner to return.

The shoes looked just the way good old leather should look. After putting on the new bottoms, Jim had burnished them to a beautiful, soft dark brown luster. New shoes could not have looked so good.

Staring at them, I was taken out of New York for an instant. I had been to Ellen's wedding in London in those shoes, twice traveled to Moscow in them and they once trod the decks of the USS *Guam* for five days off the coast of Beirut. I had been to countless Giants games in them. My feet and those shoes have a long, close relationship.

I turned the shoes over and over, inspecting the job Jim had done. I always try to use a shoe horn when I slide into them, but sometimes, in a hurry, jam my foot in, bending down the back in a way shoes should never be treated. After all these years, the tough thread holding the piece of leather across the top of the heel had begun to unravel. Jim restitched that on all four shoes and added a small piece of leather on two of them.

I was still admiring Jim's work when the woman who had parked the Mercedes pulled away. I put my shoes on the passenger seat and joined the flow of traffic with a smug smile on my face.

"Let them knock New York," I thought to myself. "They don't know Jim's."

p a r t   t w o

SIGNED BY HAND

SIGNED BY HAND

The other night I was sitting looking at a brick wall in the living room of some friends. It has become popular to tear the plaster off old brick walls of houses in downtown areas of big cities, and leave the mellow, irregular shape of old red brick exposed. It adds warmth and charm to a room.

The house was something like 125 years old and the wall must have gone up with the house. Many of the bricks weren't perfectly oblong, being handmade, and you could see that the bricklayer had a problem getting the whole thing plumb and square.

It was a great brick wall though, and the people who owned the house had derived a great deal of pleasure from it over the years. There were pictures hung on it, a mirror, pieces of brass and some cherished old family china plates. They loved it.

Who built the wall? I wondered. Who spent months of his life putting up that wall, trying to make a perfect wall out of bricks that were not perfect? Who did this laborer's work of art? I asked my friends if they knew.

They beckoned me to come to a remote corner of the wall over by the door and near the baseboard. There, scratched in the ancient mortar that still held the bricks together, was the name "T. Morin."

Maybe signed work is the answer to getting better workmanship again. Everything that anyone makes should have his or her name on it for praise or blame and reference. Work is frequently so anonymously done that the workman has no reason to identify with it and be proud of it. If everyone is going to know who made it, the person making it will be more careful.

I can understand why people don't always put their names on their work. The workman is seldom completely satisfied with what he's done. The man who built the brick wall in my friends' house was proud enough to want his name there for the life of his wall but modest enough not to want it in a prominent place.

During World War II, I stayed in the home of a British aircraft worker in Bristol, England. The British aircraft engines had a reputation for being the best. When the man came home from work one night, we talked about what he was doing.

"Me and my buddies are making an engine," he said.

And that's what he meant. He and two other men were actually assembling from scratch, an engine for a Spitfire fighter plane. They were intensely proud of their work and you can bet the RAF fighter pilot who sat in the cockpit with a Luftwaffe FW 109 in the sights of his guns had confidence his airplane wasn't going to let him down.

Each Rolls-Royce, the best automobile in the world, is still made by hand by just a few men, not on an assembly line. The work on that airplane, or on a Rolls-Royce, is a long way from the work on the U.S. planes that are reported to have been made with bogus parts. Fake parts might get past an assembly line worker. They wouldn't get past one man making an engine.

Everything should be signed by the people who make it. We live in a house that was built about one hundred years ago. We have raised four children in it. I know every nook and cranny, every strength, every defect it has. I know the beams in the basement, the rafters in the attic. I know the crack between the foundation and where the cellar steps lead down into my workshop—but I don't know who built the house. This is wrong.

Every builder of every house should be compelled to attach his name, in some permanent but inconspicuous way, to that house . . . for better or for worse.

What we need in our country is fewer mile-long assembly lines turning out instant junk and fewer "project" builders turning out ticky-tack houses by the hundreds. We need more builders of solid brick walls willing to put "T. Morin" on their work.

TWO GUYS WHO KNOW HOW TO DO IT

I got to the office at seven this morning, half an hour earlier than usual.

I walked past the elevators I usually take to the seventh floor and went into the newsroom to see if I could find a copy of last Wednesday's paper. Any but today's paper is always hard to find.

Charley and George were sitting in the office that George shares with several other people in the traffic department. The word "traffic" in the news business refers to all incoming and outgoing material related to the news. "Traffic" makes frequent runs to all the airports, expedites the shipment of videotapes from around the world, and generally controls the flow of what makes a television news broadcast.

Charley is the hands-on computer expert. He's not a theoretician. He can take them apart. Almost anyone can take a computer apart, but what makes Charley special is he can get it back together again. You call George if you have to get something from here to anywhere in a hurry, and you call Charley if you've got a computer problem.

They yelled hello as I passed the door, so I stopped and went in. It was before-work conversation. They were talking about dental work they'd had done in the Army. Almost anyone who ever spent time in the Army has had an Army dentist, so I joined in with a story of my own. I remember a dentist, a captain, had some new piece of equipment. If there's anything I don't want when I go to a dentist, it's to have him use something he's never worked with before. You don't have the choice of going to another dentist in the Army, but I was lucky. Everything worked. Wartime Army dentists were probably better than peacetime ones.

We finished with Army dentists and I left and walked back to the elevator.

I should have dismissed George and Charley from my mind at that point, but I got thinking about them. I hadn't even known they knew each other. What George does for the company has nothing at all to do with what Charley does and I wondered what drew them together for that early morning cup of coffee.

I decided I knew why they were friends. George and Charley are both good at what they do. That's what did it.

We all bitch about people who don't know what they're doing. Here are two guys who give the company its money's worth. Just offhand, I can't think of two more competent people I deal with. That must be what made them friends. They recognized competence in each other.

Several years ago, I flew back to New York from London and lost or left my briefcase somewhere along the way. I went into the traffic office to tell George my sad story. I didn't really expect him to be able to do anything about it.

"Lemme work on it," he said.

Several hours later, he called my office. "Your briefcase is coming into Kennedy at four o'clock," George said. "We'll have a courier pick it up and you should have it before five."

I had my briefcase before five.

When I travel now, I carry a small laptop computer. I don't know why they call them "laptops," because you can't type with one on your lap very easily, but I do use mine on the tray table on an airplane.

A few weeks ago, I let the battery run down so far that all the programs on the computer's internal memory were destroyed. I can type on the thing, but once they start talking about RAM, ROM, DOS and Database, I'm lost. Charley is not lost. He sits there hitting keys in some mysterious series until . . . presto! My laptop is up and running, life restored.

There's nothing more satisfying than to work with capable people. You hope you fit in as one of them. Come to think of it, those two fillings that Army dentist put in my mouth forty-five years ago are still there and chewing. If I could find him, I'd like to have him join George and Charley and me for a cup of coffee and a little conversation some morning.

THE "WORK" ETHIC

The word "work" doesn't mean physical exertion, toil, manual labor, as much as it once did. Now, when people "go to work," it may mean doing something that doesn't call for any muscle at all. When I sit down at my typewriter, I say I'm working.

. . .

The word "work" is complex. For instance, even though we associate work with muscle and sweat, a book is called a "literary work." A painting is a "work of art." Well, sometimes, anyway.

. . .

There was a small, dirty body of water called "Raft's Pond" near where I grew up and late in the summer, when the green algae started bubbling, the adults would say, "The pond is working."

. . .

Ogden Nash once said that "people who work sitting down get paid more than people who work standing up." Nash wouldn't say that these days if he hired someone to dig a trench from his house to the street with a shovel.

. . .

The Bible says, "Six days shalt thou labor . . ." but not many of even the most religious people work more than five anymore.

. . .

Of course, the Bible also says, "If any would not work, neither should he eat." We don't live by that anymore, either. We're kinder. We feed the hungry even if they're lazy.

. . .

I'm impressed with someone who can stick at a dull job until it's finished. I can't. I stop and get something to eat or take a nap.

. . .

I can't work in my pajamas. Sometimes I get up early Sunday morning and go down to my typewriter without getting dressed but it never feels right.

Years ago, a doctor friend said to me, "You're lucky. All you need is your typewriter. You can work anywhere, any time."

He didn't say so, but he probably would have included "even in your pajamas."

He was wrong, though. I might just as well have said to him, "You can work anywhere, any time. All you need is your stethoscope."

. . .

It's easy to make sweeping statements about someone else's work. Viewed from a distance, everyone's work looks easier than your own.

. . .

Everyone ought to have a hard job he hates once in his life. It makes any other job you get seem good by comparison.

. . .

Whenever anyone gets fired, he or she always says, "They didn't give me any reason." The reason's usually obvious to everyone else, though.

I've only been fired once. It's not a good feeling. It isn't so much the money as the idea that you're an outsider now. Everyone else has a place to go in the morning and you don't. If you leave your house, all you can do is wander. I went to the movies just to hide.

. . .

When you work for a boss you don't like, it's a good idea to remember that he has a boss, too. He is as apt to get fired as you are. And so is *his* boss.

. . .

I hardly ever do any kind of repair work around the house when I don't wish I had another tool to do it with.

. . .

When you're looking for work, it's always a bad time for the business you're trying to get into. They've had a lot of layoffs lately.

. . .

Exercise is the same as hard work, except you can quit when it isn't fun anymore.

. . .

The day of the week is crucial to how you feel about working. On Monday, I always feel as though I can get it all done. On Friday, I have a feeling of relief at the end of the day, no matter how much I've left undone.

THE ELUSIVE MR. FIXIT

It doesn't happen often, but every once in a while you run into someone who knows what he's doing.

If you're talking with someone about politics, abortion, the Middle East or interest rates, it doesn't matter whether either of you knows what he's talking about because neither of you has any influence on the matter, but if you're talking to someone about fixing something, you want to be sure the person knows what he's doing. I'm referring to repairmen as men because I've never seen a repairwoman.

It's not hard to find people who talk as though they know how to fix something and occasionally you find someone who really does know how. He's too busy. The hard thing is to find someone who both knows how and can come today.

I don't want to go into the ugly details, but I left my computer under a leaky window the other night and when I turned it on the next morning, I shorted out the screen on which I read what I'm writing.

I called five places in town before I got hold of a man who sounded as though he knew what he was talking about.

You frequently don't get the repairman on the phone when you call. You get someone who doesn't know anything about anything except how to answer the phone.

You can tell almost immediately whether the person you're dealing with is any good or not. There are certain questions people ask when they're stalling:

—"What seems to be the trouble?" (It doesn't work, that's what the trouble is. If I knew what was wrong, I'd fix it myself.)

—"How old is the machine?" (They're not asking a question, they're saying, "Boy! You really got an antique there." People who fix things have a way of making you feel cheap for not having bought a new one recently. I'd like to see the homes of some of these repair people. Do all of them have brand-new everything in their own homes? Do all mechanics drive expensive, late-model cars? Do television servicemen throw away their old sets and buy new ones every few months?)

—"Is it under warranty?" (I never want to answer that question because some places don't want to fix something if it is and others won't touch it if it isn't.)

—"How long have you had this problem?" (Is he a doctor or a repairman? What difference does it make whether I've had the problem with the machine for five seconds or five years? It doesn't work and I want it fixed.)

If the repairman comes to your house, whether it's a refrigerator, a television set, or the hot water heater, he'll invariably look at it, shake his head and say, in a disapproving sort of way, "Oh, boy! You got a problem here."

You already know you have a problem or you wouldn't have called him. Service people never act as though fixing things is what they do for a living. You'd think they were all brain surgeons on their lunch break. They act as if they're too busy for this kind of a job and they're doing you a big favor by showing up.

I've never understood why you have to wait three weeks to get something back when you take it to have it fixed, either. If it's working but not very well, you want to keep it until the last minute. You know the service people are going to spend only about twenty minutes actually fixing it once they get at it. Why don't they give you a ticket, let you take the thing home, and bring it in to them the day they're going to work on it? Why should it sit in their shop for three weeks?

One of the biggest hurdles you have to overcome when something doesn't work, whether it's your dishwasher, your car, or your computer, is the feeling that it's a piece of junk that you ought to throw away. The temptation to buy a new one is great among all of us even when the problem is simple—if you can just find the person who knows what that simple problem is.

THE UNHANDY MAN

When it comes to doing jobs around the house, there are five categories of people.

1. The person who knows how to do it, likes to do it, and proceeds quietly and efficiently to get the job done right, alone. This is a rare species.

2. The helpless. This person can't do it, won't try to do it, and has no interest in learning how. At least his or her position is clear. Nothing is expected of this person.

3. The good helper. There are people who won't tackle a job alone, but who are good and willing helpers. Very valuable.

4. The person who does jobs around the house but always needs help. "Helen, hand me the hammer."

5. The bystander. This is the person who doesn't ever do a job but is always there, commenting on how it should be done.

Let's review the people in some of these categories in more detail:

The Category 1 fixers never seem to run into as many obstacles as other people do. They don't ask for help, they don't ask where anything is, they don't have to go to the hardware store to get something they don't have, and they don't need anything held for them.

Of the five categories, people in Category 4 and Category 5 are by far the most annoying.

The Category 4 people's constant demand for help may come out of some deep-seated need they have to be recognized. They may need psychiatry. They want to make sure everyone knows they're doing the job and that it's hard. This person wants someone around, in attendance, getting things and holding things so the work they're doing will be apparent.

He's up on a ladder or down on his knees doing the important job and needs a flunky to do the dog work.

"Do we have any screws about this long?"

(By asking the question this way, he has established the fact that, if there are no screws the right length, it is the helper's fault.)

"Here, hold this for me, will you, while I get this started?"

(I put a question mark after those sentences spoken by Category 4 people although none belongs because the person isn't really asking. He's telling the other person what to do.)

Category 3 people, the good helpers, are most underrated. A good helper doesn't talk a lot even though he or she may see how the job should be done better than the person doing it.

The helper is encouraging and willing to do menial jobs, like sweeping up afterwards.

The helper admires the work being done, loud and often. When the job is complete, the helper steps back and admires it again. Don't ever underrate a good helper.

Category 5 people are a real pain in the neck, to put the pain above where it belongs.

If they are so dissatisfied with the work being done, it is never clear why they don't do it themselves, but they never do.

"Couldn't you move it just a few inches to the right? Now down."

The other thing Category 5s do is add on.

"Oh say," they say, "while you're doing that, could you just . . ." And then they think of three other jobs for you to do that have nothing to do with the original one. They won't let you finish. If you do one job, it reminds them of another. They're never satisfied.

It's interesting that gender doesn't seem to be a big factor in what kind of a fixer a person is. Men most often do the handyman jobs around the house, but there are more and more women who know how to change the washer in a dripping faucet. Quite often now, it's the woman in the house who knows which fuse in the fuse box controls the lights in the upstairs bathroom or in the kitchen. When a fuse blows, she also knows where the flashlight and the extra fuses are.

I think of myself as a Category 1, but notice a good many characteristics of the Category 4 in me.

HELP WANTED: NO ONE NEED APPLY

I was looking at the classified section of a Philadelphia newspaper, and I'm glad I'm not looking for work in Philadelphia, because there are no jobs in town that I know how to do.

Come to think of it, I've never seen a job in a HELP WANTED ad that I *could* do.

There are hundreds of openings for accountants: SR. ACCOUNTANT, ACCOUNTANT JR, STAFF ACCOUNTANT, COST ACCOUNTANT,

ACCOUNTANT TAX, ACCOUNTANTS RECEIVABLE. I just don't count very well.

There are endless openings for nurses. All the hospitals are trying to steal nurses from each other. If you're an accountant who has also graduated from nursing school, you could name your own price. Obviously, what America needs is nurses and accountants. Most accountants are men and most nurses are women, so it would make a great two-income husband-and-wife team.

A good nurse is a saint, and the reason there aren't enough nurses is, there aren't enough saints. Good accountants are not saints.

The Germantown Hospital, near Philadelphia, wants this: "NURSING LEADER. EXCELLENT INTERPERSONAL AND FINANCIAL MANAGE-MENT SKILLS AS WELL AS A STRONG CUSTOMER SERVICE ORIEN-TATION ARE NECESSARY." Translated, that means they want a nurse who gets along with people, keeps good records, and changes bedpans.

Most HELP WANTED ads are sneaky. They don't mention money. The ad will say: "OFFERS EXCELLENT COMPENSATION." Oh yeah? If it's so excellent, how come you don't say how much it is?

"SALARY COMMENSURATE WITH ABILITY" is a favorite. Here's one, "SALARY $28,000 TO $40,000 DEPENDING ON EXPERIENCE." What chance do you think anyone would have of getting the $40,000? They'd want someone under thirty with twenty-five years' experience.

Pharmacists are in demand. The only drugstore I ever got to know really well was Graves Drugstore on the corner of Madison and Ontario, and all I ever bought in there was an ice cream cone with a glass of carbonated water. Drugstores phased out their ice cream soda counters years ago and I think it was a mistake. It humanized them. If someone saw you going in the drugstore, they didn't know whether you were going to get something sneaky or an ice cream cone.

There are a couple of good HELP WANTED ads in this paper for the right person: "WANTED: SWIMCOACH, BAND DIRECTOR." If you can teach several musical instruments and also show backstrokers how to do a somersault turn, that's the job for you.

Bryn Mawr, the women's college, needs skilled help: WANTED: DE-PENDABLE, HARDWORKING DISHWASHERS.

That's an ad for a professor, not a dishwasher. The chances are that if someone is dependable and hardworking, he isn't looking for a job washing dishes.

The most attractive bonus came with a teaching job: "OFF STREET PARKING AVAILABLE."

The fast-food restaurants are looking for help. They try to make the job of handing out hamburgers sound better with ads like: "HELP WANTED: FAST FOOD ASSISTANT MANAGERS." "Assistant Manager" is probably the entry level in a Burger King.

The Banana Republic stores are seeking "ASSOCIATE MANAGERS." I don't know where associate managers stand in the chain of command in relation to assistant managers.

The job I wanted least was this: "AVIAN VIROLOGY—CONDUCT RESEARCH IN DIAGNOSIS AND PREVENTION OF VIRUS DISEASE OF POULTRY. WILLINGNESS TO HANDLE AND WORK WITH POULTRY REQUIRED."

Is chicken poultry when it's alive or only after it's dead?

Looking at HELP WANTED ads makes me aware of how lucky I am to be gainfully employed as a writer.

I BECOME A BUSINESSMAN

Those of you who really love me will be pleased to learn that I have found a source of income that could guarantee my financial independence from the money I get from writing and from my work in television.

I am pleased to announce that, having filled our house with it and given as much of it to our children as they'll take, I've finally sold a piece of furniture which I made with my own hands.

This woodworking gem of mine went for $225. It is a small walnut coffee table, the cantilevered design of which is too complex and uninteresting to describe.

My friend Nick Gallo, a retired Newark cop, entrepreneur, tennis player, and handyman, opened a small arts and crafts shop in our little town in upstate New York this summer and it was Nick who agreed to take two pieces of my furniture, on consignment, for sale as an art (or craft) in his shop.

I realize that I should give the business aspects of my cabinetwork some attention now to determine whether or not I can abandon my writing career altogether and support my dependents on my woodwork. Actually, our four kids all have good jobs now so I don't have dependents. I have a dependent and she's a very independent dependent.

My dependent will have to cut back sharply, I can tell you, on new shoes, concert tickets, and trinkets to hang from her neck or pin to her clothes, if I go into the woodworking business full time. I have been trying to estimate the profit on this table I've sold and how long it would take me to make enough money to retire at the rate the money rolled in from this one sale.

I estimate it took me one hundred hours of work, including days of sanding. The minimum wage is $4.25 an hour, but because I'm a skilled artisan I'll allow myself five dollars an hour, $.75 more than the minimum hourly wage, for my work. Five times one hundred is five hundred dollars.

The top of the table is an interesting free-form walnut flitch, 34 inches long, 18 inches wide in places, two and a quarter inches thick, for which I paid $85 at a lumberyard that specializes in unique wood. The base was cut from some planks of heavy walnut I made from a tree I bought from a farmer for fifty dollars more than fifteen years ago.

Add to that total of $135 for wood, maybe twenty-five cents for glue, two dollars' worth of tung oil finish, the cost of a few other items, five dollars for some small ebony dovetails I cut to put in one section of the top (Am I losing you?) to keep a split there from widening. Without counting the cost of the electricity for running my power tools, I estimate I spent more than $700 in labor and materials to produce the table.

The tools in my shop include a big Powermatic table saw, a fifteen-inch-thickness planer, a band saw with a four-inch blade with which I can make boards out of logs, a drill press, a shaper, and several dozen small tools and a wide array of hand tools. I'd estimate the cost of the tools I've bought over the years . . . a chisel here, a power tool there . . . as upwards of $50,000 and I'll be wanting to amortize the cost of those now that I'm in the business of selling what I make.

In addition to these production costs which I have to deduct from the $225, I forgot to tell you that I don't get the whole $225. My deal with Nick is that he keeps one third of every sale. My net income, then, was not $225 but $150.

I'm not much of a businessman but even I know that if a table costs me $700 to make and I sell it for $150, I'm going to have to make an awful lot of them to get rich.

As a businessman, I suppose I should think of getting an accountant. I wouldn't need a full-time bookkeeper . . . certainly not until I sell another piece of furniture. Perhaps I could find someone who'd just come in for a few hours in the afternoon. Or maybe my dependent could handle the books for me. That way, I could deduct her as a business expense.

GLOSSARY FOR BOOK REVIEWERS

Book reviewers are, by nature, cruel people and that's the way it ought to be. No one wants to read good reviews all the time. The best reviews to read are the worst reviews. The only bad review I hate to read is a review of a book I've written. It's difficult for any writer not to take some perverse pleasure from a bad review of someone else's book.

What follows are some examples of what I'd like to read, and what I hope I don't read, in my reviews.

I hope reviewers feel free to say my book is "compelling," "engrossing" or "gripping." I certainly hope someone will say my book is one of those, even though it isn't any of them. We're not talking truth here, we're talking jacket blurbs.

If you want to lay it on a little, you might even go for "deeply compelling," "totally engrossing," or "powerfully gripping." "Powerful" alone is very popular these days with reviewers, as are the ever-useful "brilliant," "superb," "throbbing," and of course, "must reading." "Bristles with suspense" or "richly rewarding" would be acceptable. I'm not ready to have my book called "a good read."

"Enthralling" doesn't strike me as a word I'd like to see describe my book, either. I've seen the pictures on the covers of paperbacks that are called "enthralling" and the woman always wears a low-cut dress. She's being held, usually from behind so you can see her from the front, by a man who looks like Clark Gable in *Gone With the Wind*. The illustrators all seem to be my age.

I wish some reviewer would say my book has more depth, breadth, height and weight than it actually has. For example, someone might say, "Mr. Rooney's work [I'd like them to call it 'a work' sometimes instead of just a book] is being compared to Marcus Wistichtesen, Grace Framboise, and the legendary Count Raoul de Pouilly Lagoussant."

When a writer's book is compared to someone else's, it's more impressive if readers of the review have never heard of the authors he's being compared to. It lends class to the reference.

Another phrase I've always dreamed of having used about one of my books appeared in a review of a book about Paul Robeson in *The New York Times*. The phrase is "at once." To me, "at once" suggests a literary work of deep significance.

"The story," the reviewer of the Robeson biography wrote, "is, at once, an American triumph and an American tragedy."

How I'd love to read that my new book is "at once" two things . . . any two.

"Rooney's new work is, at once, hilarious and deeply disturbing." Or "Mr. Rooney has turned out a work that is, at once, amusing and significant."

There are so many good words that might be used in a review of my book that I hesitate to suggest them. I know, though, that a reviewer is often under the pressure of a deadline, so let me just offer a few to reviewers who might be reading this and are in a hurry.

"Memorable," "hilarious," "shocking," "erotic," "enormously witty," "highly evocative," "moving," "sinewy," "poignant," "essential reading," "inspiring," "one of the most important books of this or any other year."

There are, on the other hand, some phrases that I'd hope no reviewer, especially one in a hurry, would use on anything I've written. For example, a word that has no merit whatsoever and reveals a foundering reviewer hard up for something to say is the word "indeed."

"Indeed," I see here in a book section review, "the author draws a dichotomy between being Arab and being modern." I'm not too keen on "dichotomy" either.

But you reviewers will do what you have to do, I know that, and if, indeed, an "indeed" creeps into your review, I'll understand.

Yours, Andry Oooney

What's the most number of times you've ever signed your name at one sitting? Four, maybe? When you bought your house?

The President signs bills with all the important people standing around looking over his shoulder. He interrupts his signature a dozen times and picks up another pen so that he can give one to each of his guests. The President, whoever he is, spends a lot of time signing things.

A while ago a small company that issues special leatherbound editions of other publishers' books on good, heavy paper, asked me if I'd autograph ten thousand copies of a book I had coming out that year. They said they'd pay me a dollar for every autograph.

Well, ten thousand dollars isn't peanuts, but ten thousand copies? Can you imagine signing your name ten thousand times? Even a President would wince.

I laughed and said no.

They persisted. Would I consider signing one thousand copies?

Well, a writer isn't immune to the pleasure of seeing his work printed on fine, heavy paper and then bound in leather, not to mention what seemed like an easy thousand dollars, so I agreed to sign one thousand copies. How I regret ever having said I'd do it.

I was relieved when one large, heavy box arrived containing three smaller boxes, three inches deep, each with 350 single-sheet pages. They had sent me just the page my signature was going on before it was bound into the book.

The printed words on the pages read "THE LEATHER-BOUND FIRST EDITION IS PERSONALLY SIGNED BY ANDREW A. ROONEY." My name was to be signed under that.

The first day I sat down to autograph a sheaf of about one hundred pages, I had a big decision to make. How should I sign my name? I am known as Andy Rooney, but I dislike it. My name is Andrew A. Rooney. It might not seem so to you, but Andrew A. takes several seconds longer to write than Andy, so I opted for Andy. The signed books are due today and I hope they don't tell me they have to be signed with my full name.

I've never had a small job I disliked so much. Every couple of days for several weeks now, I've stopped what I was doing, picked up a handful of pages out of one of the boxes, and started writing my name . . . AndyRooneyAndyRooneyAndyRooneyAndryOooney RandyNooney . . . whoops, throw those two out.

You wouldn't believe how easy it is to make a mistake writing your own name when you write it one hundred times. If you aren't thinking about what you're doing, you can misspell your own name or at least so badly garble the looks of one of the letters in it that you can't use it. Fortunately, they gave me about fifty extra blank pages because I destroyed something like five out of every one hundred I signed.

When I began, I estimated with a stopwatch that I could sign about six a minute, but this turned out to be a foolish estimate. I didn't take into consideration that half the time, after I signed one, I couldn't get the pages apart easily. I'd stop, put my pen down, and make sure I wasn't putting two sheets stuck together in the "done" box.

The company sent along two boxes of ballpoint pens with blue ink for me to use. They said that I should not use a fine black pen because people don't believe the signature is real if it's written with a fine, black pen. They think it's some kind of printed duplication.

I always use a broad, felt-tipped pen with blue ink when I write anything by hand, which isn't often, and that's what I used for the autographs.

One thing's for sure. I don't think anyone who buys one of the books is going to suspect that the signatures were not done by hand. They might suspect I asked my nine-year-old grandson to write them for me, but there's no doubt they're handwritten.

UNLOCKING THE
LOCKER ROOM

Men's locker rooms are not mentioned in the Constitution or any of its Amendments. The Founding Fathers apparently failed to protect naked male athletes from women journalists.

Every once in a while I'm on the wrong side of an issue and I know it, but I can't help myself. I stick to my guns even if they aren't loaded. I'm ambivalent about letting women reporters in the men's locker room. I admit it would be unfair to let male reporters in and keep females out. Life and locker rooms are unfair.

Men's locker rooms are good places. I've known four in my life and each one has been special to me. I loved the comradeship and the whole ritual of what went on in them. I loved being dog-tired, pulling off my sweaty uniform, the hot shower, the talk of the game and the plans for the night.

The demand by women reporters that they be admitted to men's locker rooms after games has been an issue for a long while, but it came to a head several years ago when a woman sports reporter for the *Boston Herald* went in the men's locker room and was verbally abused by some crude jerks on the New England Patriots' football team. At about the same time, Denise Tom, an experienced reporter for *USA Today,* was denied access to the Cincinnati Bengals' locker room by Sam Wyche, their coach. Sam Wyche has acted like a jerk sometimes, too, but I liked what he said after commissioner Paul Tagliabue fined him thirty thousand dollars for barring the woman.

"It was easier for the Commissioner to fine me than for him to find a solution to the problem," Wyche said.

That's true, and they still haven't found a solution.

As much as I think women should be admitted, I have to confess that what I think isn't what I feel. There are things about it that make me uneasy.

Over the years, reporters and athletes have recognized that it is to their mutual benefit to have locker room interviews. Athletes who are paid millions because their names have been popularized by newspapers and television owe journalists more than journalists owe them. Athletes should be available for comment. It's part of what they're paid for and women reporters should be there. But not in the men's locker room. And if they do let them in the locker room, women shouldn't be surprised or shocked if there are naked men there.

One of the good things about a men's locker room is that nudity is nothing. Absolutely nothing. It's not something a man thinks about when he's showering or dressing in a roomful of guys.

If you've ever been in one of those European spas, you know how casually the women attendants walk among naked men. Nakedness seems perfectly natural until someone makes something of it.

By the time a woman gets herself in the position of being a sports reporter for a newspaper, you have to assume she isn't seeing anything in a locker room that she hasn't seen before—even if it's only at the movies. I don't think you can ask the guys to start hiding behind towels or changing the way they use their locker room. It's too good a place.

Men and women, strangers to each other, crowd together in movie theaters all across the country and watch, elbow to elbow, not only nudity, but the most explicit sex acts on the big screen. None of the women sports reporters are under seventeen, and if the athletes just go about their business of getting undressed, showering, and then getting dressed, there's really no reason why it should be any different for a woman to be in there than for a man.

Maybe the women can think of themselves as nurses for a few minutes.

Next week I'm going to search the Constitution again to see if it says anything about men in *women's* locker rooms. If I don't find anything, I'll see if I can get a press pass to a locker room the next time Steffi, Gabriela, Monica and Martina are in town.

CROWD NOISE

Anyone who likes golf on television would enjoy watching the grass grow on the greens. Tennis, the other country club sport, is, on the other hand, a good game to watch on television.

The one thing these two sports share in common is the silence demanded by the players. Will someone please tell me why a golfer can't hit a ball when someone is talking? Will someone explain why Jimmy Connors or John McEnroe can scream obscenities at the chair umpire while those who paid to watch have to remain silent and stone still?

I went out to the U.S. Open Tennis Tournament one night and the matches are played as if it was a piano concert in Carnegie Hall. Fans with tickets and seats are not admitted to the stadium while a set is in progress. They may have to wait twenty minutes to get in if they aren't in their seats when play begins.

Are tennis players really that sensitive? If they are, they ought to get over it. Can you imagine a baseball player coming to bat in Oakland, Chicago, Boston or New York and demanding complete silence from the fans before he'd condescend to try to hit a ball? Does hitting a baseball take less concentration than hitting a golf ball or tennis ball?

Crowd noise is part of the game at a professional sports event and both tennis and golf would be more interesting if they let the fans yell. I go to New York Giants home games and it wouldn't be half as much fun if the games were played in silence. The cheers and hoots from the crowd are part of it.

The most annoying sounds on earth are often the small ones. A dripping faucet in the middle of the night, or the slight sound of something creaking in the living room when you're in bed—those sounds are as loud in your ears as the blast of a cannon.

A person's relatively small voice is often too loud a noise because of its annoying quality. Benjamin Disraeli said, "There is no index of character so sure as the voice."

Watching television, I often get sick and tired of someone's voice and none more than the sound of my own. To be irritating, a voice doesn't have to be yelling at a tennis game.

We change our clothes every day mostly because we get tired of what we look like if we don't, and it would be nice if it were possible for all of us to change the sounds we make when we speak, for the same reason.

Most people don't know what they sound like. I know what I sound like because I'm in the unfortunate position of having my voice recorded frequently and when I listen to it being played back, I cringe.

It isn't only the actual sound of a voice that gets tiresome, either. Each of us acquires mannerisms in our speech that we repeat every time we open our mouths. The other day, when I was saying hello to someone I don't know very well, I heard a tone in my own voice that I find objectionable when my sister uses it. I don't know where my sister and I got the same inflection, but it was like the flash of recognition you get when you see in a child of yours the look of a distant relative.

The sound of a voice would seem to be largely an accident of birth. People with big mouths and a lot of teeth up front usually have good, big voices. You don't see many great singers with small mouths. Just as certainly as the Rockettes have good legs, Metropolitan Opera singers have big mouths.

And speaking of the opera, I wish the audience booed bad opera singers and actors in the theater as freely as they cheer them with applause and bravos—the way we cheer and boo our Giants quarterback.

Rudolf Bing, once the manager of the Metropolitan Opera, eloquently disagreed about boos and hisses.

"Expressions of disapproval are on a level of vulgarity that cannot be tolerated," he said. "The way to express disapproval is not to applaud."

My feeling is that not applauding isn't loud enough for a bad performance you've paid a lot to see.

FRANK SINATRA, BOY AND MAN

There was a small Italian bakery on Mott Street in New York City called Parisi's. Joe Parisi made his bread in two ovens on the back wall of his basement and I liked it so much that I'd often drive downtown to buy three or four loaves even though it meant an extra half hour getting home. I didn't know whether anyone else liked Joe Parisi's bread or not but I found out in a most interesting way.

Twenty-five years ago, I flew to Palm Springs with Walter Cronkite and Don Hewitt, the producer, to write an hour special about Frank Sinatra on the occasion of his fiftieth birthday. I got thinking about the experience on his seventy-fifth.

We made a mess of Frank's house by rearranging the furniture and laying wires for lights all over the place, but he opened the house to us and was a gracious host.

The second day we were there he invited several of us to sit down and have lunch with him. The meal was prepared by an employee of Frank's who seemed to do everything for him—keep the house, take care of his clothes, and cook his meals.

We were having a good time talking and Frank passed a basket of crusty bread my way. I took a piece, looked at it suspiciously, took a bite and sat back, astonished.

"You okay?" he said.

"Where did you get this?" I asked. "I know this. This is Joe Parisi bread. He makes it in his basement on Mott Street two thousand miles from here."

"We have it flown in every week," Frank said. "Great bread."

I've been soft on Frank ever since that day I discovered he had such good taste in bread. Now, twenty-five years later, there's no one I like to hear sing a song as much as I like to hear Sinatra.

When I was young, I was cool toward him and his music and much put off by the crowds of young girls who made fools of themselves in his audience. To me, Sinatra was an awkward, gawky-looking jerk without much of a voice and no charm at all. Those fans my age were indistinguishable from the young people who, generations later, fawned over Elvis Presley.

Sinatra has made about thirty-five movies and even won an Oscar for his performance in *From Here to Eternity,* but everything he does besides singing is a sideline. He's great to see in person but it isn't necessary and that accounts for the phenomenal success of his records.

We went to a recording session of his while we were doing that show and I was surprised at how serious a musician he is. During the session, Sinatra got dickering with the orchestra leader about whether the note should be an F-sharp or an F-natural. I had always assumed the words just fell from his mouth in a random assortment of notes.

It's not just his voice or his knowledge of music that makes Sinatra sound so good, either. People who understand music hear sounds from Sinatra that no one else makes. And it all happened to him, you know it did, as he sings.

It's apparent to anyone listening to Sinatra that he enjoys his work. A performer's pleasure in his own performance is communicated to his audience and no one enjoys himself when he's singing more than Frank Sinatra.

The rap on Sinatra has always been his personal life. You can complain about the life he's lived, but he has an appealing enthusiasm for it that's part of his charm.

There are strange things going on in our brains that cannot be measured by numbers or described in words. It's impossible to say why a poem is good, or why a piece of music, a novel, or a movie is great. You can't apply reason in judging a picture painted by Picasso and come up with an answer that explains its greatness.

No amount of thinking about it can produce an answer to why so many people enjoy listening to Frank Sinatra. Genius is unfathomable . . . but whatever it is, Frank has it.

YES, SIR

Each one of us needs to be rewarded from time to time with something other than money. The cheapest thing, and the one that serves the purpose best, is praise. I'd swap a couple of hundred dollars for a casual and sincere compliment any day.

Companies know about the need to praise their employees. Instead of a raise, they often print pictures of "THE EMPLOYEE OF THE MONTH" in their newsletters.

I've been to a hundred company banquets at which various employees were given plaques, certificates, trophies, silver bowls and gold watches to honor their accomplishments. I don't want to be too persistently cynical, but the presentations are usually designed to do more good for the company than for the employees.

The Europeans, and especially the British, have a way of praising their citizens that we don't have in this country. They knight them. Being knighted is the highest honor you can get in Great Britain.

The British take being knighted very seriously. For instance, once someone is knighted, the British really call that person "Sir" or "Dame" forever after. Laurence Olivier became "Sir Laurence" in England . . . which seemed sort of silly in America.

There are about 3,350 living knights in Great Britain now, and 208 Dames. I was thinking about who'd get knighted if we did it. Being called "Sir" or "Dame" would take a special person. You wouldn't knight someone just because they were good at something. They ought to have a special, knightable quality—like class.

If you're talking about actors, certainly Jimmy Stewart would be called "Sir Jimmy" by now. After her long career and her last performance in *Driving Miss Daisy*, Jessica Tandy would have been knighted and become "Dame Jessica" . . . or should it be "Lady Tandy"? I'm not sure.

Frank Sinatra wouldn't make it, although he does seem to have a way of getting himself in with the right people. Frank's friend Ronald Reagan got an honorary knighthood in 1989. That was probably more Margaret Thatcher's doing than the Queen's. To his credit, I think Mr. Reagan was a little embarrassed about it even though it was only honorary. I wouldn't be surprised if Nancy needles him with "Sir Ronald" once in a while around the house.

The normal procedures for someone who's knighted is for the person to kneel before the Queen while she touches the back of the person twice with the flat blade of a sword. I don't know what that does for them, but that's the ceremony. Considering that we share a common language, we sure are different from the British in many ways.

The highest order of knighthood in Great Britain is The Order of the Garter, but Great Britain isn't the only European country that knights people with different orders. Spain has The Order of the Golden Fleece; Denmark, The Order of the Elephant; Belgium, the Order of Leopold; Italy, the Order of Annunziata; and in France, the equivalent is The Legion of Honor.

All the people knighted in these countries wear different little insignia, pendants and lapel buttons. It's not unlike what our military officers do with rows and rows of medals.

Listen, if it makes people feel special because they got a little praise, why not? Getting knighted sure beats being chosen EMPLOYEE OF THE MONTH in the company newsletter.

TIME FOR SOME NEW HEROES

It's strange, isn't it, that we are so hungry for heroes? Norman Schwarzkopf filled in for several months but now we need another.

We're critical and suspicious of people—or I am, anyway—but we want good guys in our lives. We enjoy thinking someone is perfect. We don't want our hero to be human. We want a pure, unadulterated idol. Whether the hero is a movie star, a religious icon, or a character in a novel, we don't want anyone with human faults. We don't want politicians who are part good, part bad. We don't want sports heroes who are merely good. We want Babe Ruth and Joe Montana.

Our hunger for heroes accounts for why so many people accepted Ronald Reagan as one. He was one in a sense that George Bush is not. Reagan was easier to see as a hero. He had the outward appearance of a hero. He was tall, broad-shouldered, good-looking, quick with a funny remark, and, we like to think, very American-looking. We thought that . . . even though not one in a million Americans looks as good.

We seem to need someone we can endow with virtues we don't have, someone who's better at everything than we are. Our admiration for the person gives us the pleasure of association, too. We think we are a little like anyone we admire. It probably accounts for Jesus Christ. We're lucky so many people chose a person as good as Jesus to make a hero of.

I've heard old friends idolize one of their parents who has died, forgetting that I knew both the parent and my friend's relationship to that parent. In real life, the parent had usually been thought of as less perfect and the relationship between them had been less than idyllic.

Our hunger for someone to admire without reservation accounts for this American tendency to make pop heroes out of people who are not heroic at all. Movie and musical heroes are such. In my mother's and father's lifetime, it was Enrico Caruso and Rudolph Valentino. In mine, it was Frank Sinatra, Clark Gable, and John Wayne. In my children's, it was Elvis Presley and the Beatles. I don't even know who the pop heroes are today but you can bet they aren't heroic.

But that's okay. There's nothing wrong with making heroes of people who were not really heroic because, in doing it, we at least form in our own minds a picture of what a hero is.

When I tell stories about my grandfather, I talk about how I once found a small, ingeniously-made wooden object in our attic. When I asked what it was, my mother told me that it was the model her father had made for a furnace grate for which he obtained a U.S. patent. He made a great deal of money from that and other inventions. I tell my children and anyone else who will listen about my grandfather's inventiveness because I hope my linear proximity to him will make people think a little of his genius may have been handed down.

I do not tell people that when turtles got in my grandfather's fish net at the lake, he took the turtles and smashed their hard shells on rocks along the shore so that they would never intrude on his net again. I want my grandfather to be plain genius, not cruel genius.

Often our hero has qualities we don't have and don't even really want. Most classic American heroes, for example, like Abraham Lincoln, weren't much interested in money compared to doing good for the country. Old-fashioned heroes always renounced money. They turned their backs on wordly pleasures in favor of the simple life. We admire them for it even though we may have two cars in our driveway.

I don't know . . . it just seems to me to be longer than usual between heroes.

THE GOOD GUY
IN THE GREY HAT

The ultimate boss I had for most of my working life, William S. Paley, the Chairman of the Board of CBS, died in 1990 at the age of eighty-nine.

For years I tried to decide whether I liked Paley or not and whether he was a good guy or a bad guy. The fact is, he was living proof that there's some of the good guy and some of the bad guy in all of us.

"The ruthless Paley and the thoughtful Paley were always at war," Sally Bedell Smith says in her book about him.

Whatever Bill Paley was, good or bad or both, he was more of everything than most of us.

Over the years, I suppose I met him forty times. Most of those times were just a handshake in a crowd, but ten years ago his secretary—one of his secretaries—called and asked if I'd write a speech for Mr. Paley. I didn't want to write speeches for him, but I was flattered and curious. I was asked to show up at his apartment on Fifth Avenue one morning at nine.

As I got off the elevator, I was immediately in the foyer of his apartment, looking up at a huge picture of a nude boy leading a horse.

I was ushered into the living room and very shortly Mr. Paley came in wearing a silk dressing gown. I had never seen anyone wearing a silk dressing gown anywhere before except in movies or ads in *Esquire* magazine.

We talked briefly about who he was speaking to, how long he was expected to talk, and then I left, waving to the boy and the horse as I got on the elevator. That night, describing the whole thing to Margie, I mentioned the picture.

"It sounds like Picasso's 'Boy Leading a Horse,' " she said.

It was, of course. No wonder I was impressed. It's worth a couple of hundred million. I must have good taste in art.

A week later, I sent Mr. Paley the speech. (Even behind his back, I called him Mr. Paley.) I heard nothing about how the speech went at the event, which I did not attend, for about ten days. Finally, I got another call. Would I please go to Mr. Paley's apartment again the following morning.

I was accompanied this time by a company public relations executive. As we sat down, a butler brought coffee. Mr. Paley almost immediately asked if I would consider taking a full-time job writing speeches for him.

It would be difficult for me to explain how I felt sitting in the living room of the single most powerful man in my life and having to answer that question. My answer sounds brave but I gave it without thinking because I already knew so well what I thought about the subject.

"Thank you, sir," I blurted, "I couldn't do that. A grown writer doesn't write speeches for other people to read."

I continued, lamely, saying how pleased I was that he asked and prattled on about how important he had been in my life.

"Thank you anyway for coming," he said and, even though I really hadn't started drinking my coffee, I realized the audience was over. It was clear that I was supposed to leave.

Out on the street, I noticed the PR man was crimson.

"My God, Andy. You can't do that. You can't tell Mr. Paley you won't write for him."

The public relations man was upset but I don't think Bill Paley gave it another thought. He was the ultimate pragmatist. All he heard was that I didn't want to do it and then he moved on to his next problem. He didn't judge me.

It never seemed to me, in my early years at CBS, as though Paley was responsible for its success, but over the years I got to be more appreciative of Bill Paley. Someone did a great thing when they created CBS News, the way it was at its best. Someone held to high standards that didn't come naturally to this new form of journalism. As everyone else dropped out of the company, and CBS News and Paley continued, I finally realized that Bill Paley must have been the hero I never suspected him of being.

part three

THE BODY HUMAN

But Which Doctor?

We don't know what's good for us and what's killing us. There's too much contradictory information coming from doctors, medical journals, research people, pharmaceutical companies, and the Food and Drug Administration. They ought to get their act together . . . and they ought to get it together together, too.

I got an angry letter from a doctor at Boston College Hospital because of some remarks I made on television about the conflicting claims and warnings we get about things we eat and drink. The doctor accused me of doing a disservice to the public because, he said, I confuse the irresponsible claims or threats made for the health properties of some foods with what he called "established medical practice."

What is "established medical practice"? Doctors don't always seem to know, why should we? I wrote back and, as an example, cited the stories about aspirin. A Harvard research group announced that two aspirin taken every other day reduced the risk of heart attacks in older people.

Being as I am one of them, I started taking two aspirin whenever I thought of it, confident that I had found the elixir of eternal life . . .

Three weeks later, another medical group announced that aspirin taken regularly might increase the risk of cancer of the colon.

I've stopped taking aspirin frequently.

The problem, Doctor, is establishing the fact. Who sez? There *is* no established practice in many areas of medicine, that's the trouble. Which group is right about aspirin? We know high cholesterol is bad for us. Recently I read the suggestion that low cholesterol might be bad, too. What's the story here, Doctor? It's difficult for laymen to know what to believe.

Practicing doctors hate the *Reader's Digest* story about a new medical marvel that will cure some terrible disease. Doctors don't like the newspaper report or the television or radio medical spot because the person handing out the information is a hit-and-run medical expert who read something or attends a press conference held by a pharmaceutical company and pronounces the advent of a panacea, always with a cautionary note, of course. People don't hear cautionary notes when they involve their health. They want to be able to go out and buy the cure as soon as the stores open in the morning.

The reason for the popularity of the media experts, some of whom aren't expert at all, is apparent. Everyone, at one time or another, is desperate for medical information, especially if it's free, and they're looking for the new, magic cure. The person, or someone close, has something and can't find out what's wrong or how to get over it.

The media doctors are inundated with mail. "I read where you said there is a new cure for cancer. Please give me more information."

The chances are the columnist or commentator had said or written that medical science was exploring the possibility that a certain food or drug might have some effect on the growth rate of cancer cells, or something like that.

He almost certainly didn't suggest doctors were anywhere near a break-through on the cause and cure of cancer, but people hear what they hope.

For months after such a story, the poor practicing physician has to explain: "The drug is in the planning stage, it isn't on the market yet, it hasn't been approved by the Food and Drug Administration, and other medical experts don't think the medicine is good at all and may even be dangerous."

The average doctor is too busy with a day-to-day practice to investigate every medicine or procedure that comes along, and most of them aren't worth his time anyway.

The drug companies go to extraordinary lengths to get the attention of doctors with one of their new drugs, and they complain that the FDA is too slow in approving new drugs. The FDA says that since President Reagan slashed its budget years ago, they don't have the staff to work any quicker.

I don't know or care what the details are. People need someone other than the *Reader's Digest,* the TV doctor or the pharmaceutical company pushing a drug for profit to give us the straight story on new cures for our ills. Someone's got to be put in charge of filtering all this medical information and giving us the right information on what we should eat and what we shouldn't and about what medicine is any good and what is not.

Maybe that doctor from Boston who wrote me would take the job.

CAN YOU HAVE YOUR HEART ATTACK NEXT WEEK?

What all of us want when we're sick is the kind of medical attention a President of the United States gets when he's sick.

Presidents often have some health problems while they're in the White House. President Reagan had an operation for colon cancer and you'll recall President Bush had trouble with his heart because it was beating irregularly. And then, of course, there was Mr. Bush's famous upset stomach in Japan. We're all pleased that our Presidents get such good medical attention when they're ill, but we're jealous. We'd like to have it too, in similar circumstances.

The President was running along the paths of his mountain retreat at Camp David when he noticed he was short of breath and felt his heart beating in an unusual way. He stopped and told the Secret Service people running with him. They sprang into action. On their radio telephones they called for the doctor and a helicopter.

Within minutes, the President was flying to Bethesda Naval Hospital with his doctor on board with him.

What would happen under similar circumstances to me? Say I was jogging near my house and realized I had a problem. I'd sit down on the curb, panicked at the thought of a heart attack, and look for help.

Maybe in ten or fifteen minutes, a kind stranger would notice me and stop to ask if I needed help.

"Yeah," I say. "Could you call a doctor and get me to the hospital?"

"Gosh, I don't know, Andy. I have to be at work by nine. My wife took the car this morning. I'd like to help if I could, but . . . well, listen, I'd be glad to put you on a bus. You have any change with you?"

"Thanks anyway," I say. "I'll be okay."

I walk back to the house alone, about to die. I pick up the phone and call the doctor. I get the answering service.

"This is Dr. Moore's office. Dr. Moore is at the hospital this morning. If you'll please leave your name and number, someone will call you later today."

By that time, President Bush has been checked out by four doctors. He has undergone diagnostic exams on three of the most sophisticated new machines known to medical science. His tests are already back from the lab. An office staff of twenty-three at the White House has made all the calls necessary to reorganize his day and assure his friends and family that he is going to be fine.

Meanwhile, I'm home alone with my heart attack. My wife has left the house for work, shopping or some appointment. No one's in my office yet, so I can't get them to call and cancel the important date I had.

My heart is fluttering. Maybe I should scribble a couple of goodbye-I-love-you notes to the world before I pass out. They'll find me on the floor by the telephone.

In Bethesda, President Bush has already had the good news that he's okay. It's nothing life-threatening. He knows that but I wouldn't. He isn't writing any goodbye notes. His wife and grandchildren are in his hospital room, laughing and joking with him. He leans out the window of his hospital room to reporters and shouts funny answers to their questions for the evening news broadcasts. Easy for him. I'm writing my last will and testament. No one knows or cares.

Three hours later, my doctor's office calls. The doctor doesn't call. His office calls. I don't want to talk to his office, I want to talk to the doctor, but that's out of the question.

"What seems to be our problem?" the doctor's office asks, using the medical plural. The doctor's office isn't even a nurse, she's a secretary who does the telephone work there. She's never even driven past a medical school but she's about to diagnose my case.

"I think I'm having a heart attack," I say. "I think I may be in serious trouble. Can I see the doctor?"

"Just a minute, please," the doctor's office says. There's a silence for a few minutes.

"Mr. Rooney? The first opening Dr. Moore has is July 11th at six A.M., but Dr. Moore will be on vacation all of July, so could you call back?"

By late afternoon, I feel better. It was indigestion. The only thing that makes me feel good about all the medical attention I couldn't get is the bill. If I'd been rushed to the hospital by helicopter, with my own doctor, to see three specialists and have all those tests, the bill would have come to just under $134,000 and Medicare would have paid for eleven dollars of it.

If I ever die, though, because I didn't get the kind of medical care the President gets, I'm going to be plenty mad.

RUNNING THE GAUNTLET

I've had two notices from Dr. Chandler in the past six weeks saying I should come in and have my teeth cleaned and checked for rot, and I ignored both of them. Last night I was brushing my teeth and a filling came out. This morning I had to call his office and plead for an immediate appointment. It was a little embarrassing.

When I go in, I suppose he'll say all those things they say:

"We could have avoided this if you'd come in for a checkup." (That's the medical "we," as in "How are WE this morning?")

I'm fully aware of the fact that it's a good idea to have my teeth checked twice a year. The hygienist scrapes the plaque off and does all sorts of things to my teeth that they tell you not to do yourself . . . like use abrasive toothpaste and sharp instruments. How come it's okay for them and not for me?

The real trouble is not dentists, it's that every medical specialist considers his or her specialty more special than anyone else's. The dentist doesn't seem to understand that your eye doctor thinks you ought to have a regular checkup, too. The ophthalmologist doesn't know your friendly family physician or your internist, who also think you ought to come to them regularly to get checked out. The optometrist doesn't even think you ever have to see an ophthalmologist.

I'm sure it's true that if we were each run through a gauntlet of medical experts every morning before we went to work, we might live forever. One doctor would have us do a series of heart-moving exercises as he checked our pulse; another would have us stand twelve inches from a wall and lean against it without moving our feet or bending our legs because this seems to be a cure for a great many lower-body ailments; our oculist would check for glaucoma and hold up an eye chart to make sure our prescription was still okay; our blood pressure would be taken, our cholesterol level checked; we'd provide blood samples for the hematologist, urine samples for the urologist and shadowy pictures for the radiologist. We'd be regularly scoped internally and placed in the casketlike MRI machine so they can look for foreign bodies in our body.

I get a medical checkup when I feel I need a good scare. A good scare is the best thing I get out of going to the doctor. My blood pressure is usually marginally high and my cholesterol level should be lower. I'm overweight. Sometimes, after I've been to the doctor, all my statistics improve for a few weeks. Gradually, usually after I've paid his bill, my blood pressure returns to normal (which is high) and my weight goes back to where it's been for years (too much).

Over the years, doctors have been dividing our bodies up into smaller and smaller sections for their individual attention. I never heard of a periodontist until ten years ago. It still reads like a misprint. Medical specialists have become more special in every field. For example, during my youth, there were "Eye, Ear, Nose and Throat" doctors. Today you wouldn't catch an eye doctor going down as far as your nose to look for anything wrong with that, and an ear doctor wouldn't give you the time of day if you had a sore throat. It's not his table.

That's what the doctor who sends you to someone else is saying. The fact is, though, I have a doctor I trust so much that I'd take his advice on anything pertaining to any part of my body or bloodstream, including my teeth—about which he presumably knows very little. He has passed me on to some other medical specialist a couple of times in the past, but he does it, I believe, as a matter of medical ethics, not because he doesn't understand my problem as well as the doctor he refers me to.

AWAKE IN THE NIGHT

In the middle of last Wednesday night, I was lying awake, thinking all those terrible thoughts that come to your mind in the middle of the night. I'd had an itch in one spot on my back for several months which I decided, lying there, was skin cancer. Not only that, an occasional flashing in the corner of my left eye when I looked out of the side of it got me thinking I must have a brain tumor.

The following morning, I couldn't remember what was wrong with me, but I recall being worried, so I made a doctor's appointment.

I have just returned from being inspected head to toe and all the places in between and am pleased to report that I don't have any of the things I was sure I had in my nocturnal depression.

I like my doctor. After the examination we sat in his office and talked while he asked me a few perfunctory questions and made notes.

"Any trouble swallowing?"

"No. I'd be better off if I had a little trouble."

"Yeah. You could lose a few pounds . . . but you knew that when you came here."

"How do you do all the paperwork?" I asked, nodding toward stacks of report forms behind him.

He shrugged hopelessly. "Maybe we ought to go to the Canadian system," he said. "Canadian doctors are paid a salary and they don't have to do the paperwork."

"Doctors wouldn't like that," I said.

"Look," he said, "the number of Canadian doctors leaving Canada to come here has slowed to a trickle. A lot of them used to come. That says something about whether they like their system or not. Any trouble breathing?"

"No. Not unless I'm trying to run uphill."

"Unusual number of respiratory problems, colds, flu?" he asked, his pencil poised, in a voice that suggested he knew the answer was no.

"No," I said. "I used to. There are only three people in my office now. That helps. I don't meet as many people to catch colds from."

"Airplanes," he said. "They're the problem. I have a theory. These strange respiratory bugs result from the air travel that people are doing. Someone gets on a plane in Bangkok with one strain of a bug and the plane stops in London and picks up passengers with another strain of bug. People on the plane all breathing the same air. You want a flu shot? Probably a good idea. Some people think they cause the flu but they don't."

I didn't answer but I didn't want one.

"All these viruses change. The AIDS virus is changing," he said. "Wait until it changes so it can be transmitted when someone coughs. Any chest pain at all when you exercise?"

"None. Wouldn't I get a warning if I was going to have a heart attack?"

"Not necessarily. About one in four don't. It accounts for the jogger they find by the side of the road. It's been five years since you had a colonoscopy. We better do that soon."

"Oh, Jeez," I said. "I thought I read something bad about that. Just this week."

"Where'd you read that?" he said quickly and defensively.

"I don't know," I said. "The *Times?*"

"Hasn't been in the *Times.* The first thing I do every morning is read the paper. I wouldn't come in here without reading the paper. Patients come in, they've read about some new treatment and they want to know how come I don't know about it. I don't move before I read the medical news in the paper."

"You're talking to a reporter, you know. I may make something out of this."

"You want a story?" he asked. "When my first wife died, she wanted to be cremated and have her ashes cast over Long Island Sound. The children and I went out on the Sound and I scattered the ashes and then I got thinking . . . she had a lot of gold fillings. There was no gold in those ashes. Where does all the gold go . . . you want a story."

I left, my worry about skin cancer and brain tumor gone. Now I have other things to worry about when I wake up in the middle of the night.

ROLLING INTO THE FUTURE

The chances are that in the next five years you'll use MRI, one of the greatest advances in medicine in this century, even if you've never heard of it. I hadn't until recently.

The initials stand for magnetic resonance imaging. The process is making old-fashioned, dangerous X rays obsolete. MRI is non-intrusive and harmless to the body. It's state-of-the-art medicine.

Ever since a tennis game last June, my right knee has been clicking whenever I climb stairs. Something's going on in there I don't like so I went to an orthopedic surgeon, hoping he'd go in and eliminate my problem with arthroscopic surgery.

The orthopedist told me it would be better if he knew what the problem was first and said I ought to undergo what he said was "a somewhat unpleasant experience, MRI."

"Are you at all claustrophobic?" he asked.

Well, I don't approve of such idiotic mental aberrations as phobias, but I am claustrophobic. I can't even stand having the blankets tucked in at the end of the bed.

"You'll be all right," the doctor said, but I knew by the way he said it that I wouldn't be.

Before I went in for the MRI scan, I read about the procedure and knew that you are put into a container with a strong magnetic field. Radio waves are directed at your body and stir up the atoms. The waves bounce differently off the atoms of each part and a computer in another room makes a composite picture.

When I walked into the reception room of the MRI office, a young woman behind the desk asked me to sit down. "We'll be right with you," she said. "We have a young boy in MRI now. He should be about finished." I alternately sat, stood and paced back and forth nervously.

A young woman came out of the back room in tears. Her seven-year-old son was in the MRI unit because doctors suspected he had a malignant tumor in his intestines. I felt selfish for having wished, before I knew why the boy was in there, that they'd hurry up and get the kid out so they could do my knee.

Finally I was told to take off everything but my underwear and put on a hospital wrap. I was ushered back into the MRI room. The unit looked like a casket for a basketball player.

The technician told me to get up on the table and lie down. When I was settled, he rolled the table into the MRI unit and closed the door. We spoke through an intercom.

"I'm not sure I can take this," I said, fighting my claustrophobia. I feared I'd lose control and thrash out against the walls of my trap.

It was light inside this technological tomb and the happy thought crossed my mind that there wouldn't be any light in the one I end up in. The interior was a dense, light yellow plastic. My shoulders touched the sides and there were perhaps six inches between my forehead and the arched ceiling. My eye itched and by bringing my arm up tight to my chest, I was able to get between the ceiling and my body to scratch the itch. That was the best time I had in there.

Turning over was out of the question and you're supposed to lie still. I lay there, fighting off claustrophobia. The loud clacking sound made by the machine was a welcome distraction.

They had said it would take forty minutes, but I was inside the machine for one hour and ten minutes. That was for one knee. The whole body takes longer.

The process is expensive because it takes so long that they can handle only a dozen or so patients a day. The machine costs two million dollars to install and the technicians and the doctors who read the pictures have to be paid.

I'm so happy to be out of the machine that my knee doesn't bother me anymore.

THE BEST ADVICE

I fell yesterday. Flat. I walked into a heavy electrical cord I had stupidly strung six inches off the floor in my shop and went down like a tree in the forest cut by a lumberjack when it interrupted the movement of my legs. The difference between me and a tree was that I hit the concrete floor instead of a cushy bed of leaves.

I landed on my left knee and both hands as if I'd been doing a push-up. I stayed on the floor a few minutes, assessing the damage. Serious? I remember wondering. I quickly decided that although I hurt a lot, I wasn't hurt. My knee is swollen today but it's just a bang. There's nothing wrong with the hinge. Both hands and wrists are sore and discolored but I'm going to live. It reminded me of how the heels of my hands hurt when I was a kid and fell off my bicycle or fell on the sidewalk roller-skating.

The worst part of my wounds was going to a party last night where I had to shake hands with twenty-five people. I chose to kiss a lot of women I didn't know that well so I wouldn't have to shake their hands.

I'm always surprised at how seldom everything's perfect with any of us. You have a cold, you break a fingernail or you wonder if some small blemish on your body is serious. You wouldn't dream of mentioning it to anyone because it's probably nothing . . . but it's always something. Maybe it's only a pair of shoes that make one toe hurt.

Each of us needs a doctor we can ask small questions. We don't need a complete checkup. I have an office next to Dr. Bob Arnot, who does medical stories for the *CBS Morning News*. He can't walk down the hall without someone asking him for free advice.

We had dinner with an old friend last week who retired as a doctor. He still gets lots of calls asking for advice. There's a market for it. It might be a new field of medicine. There'd be specialists who did nothing but answer silly medical questions.

You'd be able to go to a doctor's office and say, "What is this anyway, Doctor?" If he thought you should go see a doctor about it, he'd tell you.

It should be cheap, maybe ten dollars for five minutes, and it could be done in person or on the phone. Last night my wrists and one knee hurt when I was going to bed. I'd like to have asked a doctor if putting ice on swollen parts does any good nine hours after the incident that caused them to puff up.

One reason some people are always getting banged up is you can't live your whole life being careful not to get hurt. There's just so careful you can be and still get anything done. It was established in our family many years ago that saying "Be careful" to someone doesn't help. Whenever the kids were going someplace, Margie always said to them, "Be careful."

I never told the kids to be careful and I know that there was absolutely no difference in what happened to them when they left home after being told to be careful and when they left home without being told to be careful. People either are careful or they are not. Being told to be has no influence on the care they exercise. I could have been told to be careful ten times at breakfast yesterday and I'd still have tripped over that damn cord.

One reason telling a person to be careful doesn't help is that little accidents like mine occur at unlikely times in unlikely places. When someone gets up on a ladder around the house or when they're going for a long drive in bad weather, someone always tells them to be careful. It's foolish. If you're climbing a ladder or taking a dangerous trip, you already ARE being careful. Almost no one climbs a ladder without considering the possibility he might fall, so a cautionary word from someone on the ground is not only unnecessary, it's irritating.

Ten dollars' worth of advice from a good doctor after you fell would be a lot more helpful than being told to be careful.

HAZARDOUS TO YOUR HEALTH

Last week, I was dressing in front of my locker after a tennis game and chatting with a fellow dressing a few lockers away. I'd talked to him before but it had never been anything more than pleasantries. "Cold out," "warm out," that sort of thing, so I was surprised when he said, "Where do you stand on cigarette smoking?"

I mean, where does any intelligent man stand on cigarette smoking? He's against it. Cigarette smoking has never been much of an issue with me. I never had to give it up because I never smoked, but I'm aware of how hard it is to kick the habit and I'm sympathetic to anyone who smokes and can't quit. In spite of that, I have the non-smoker's smug feeling that anyone who smokes cigarettes has a character flaw.

I was wary of what my locker-room friend was up to. Something told me he was a smoker, although I'd never seen him with a cigarette.

"I don't know," I said in answer to his question. "You can't pass a law making smoking illegal, but I think anyone who smokes is making a mistake." That seemed neutral. I didn't want an argument, I just wanted to dress and leave.

"I'd like to show you some statistics," he said, going to his locker and bringing out a manila envelope with a sheaf of papers in it.

"How come the Japanese smoke more than Americans, but the Japanese life expectancy is seventy-nine years and ours is only seventy-five?" he asked.

I bent over and pulled on my socks.

"Why is that?" he said, pressing for an answer.

"Gee, I dunno," I said. I really didn't want to argue with this guy about whether or not cigarettes are bad for you. I suppose I could be wrong, but the evidence seems incontrovertible, even though I don't know enough to answer his Japanese life-expectancy question. Maybe eating raw fish and smoking cigarettes keeps the Japanese thin and makes up, statistically, in a lack of heart attacks for the years others lose by dying of lung cancer. But I decided not to say that.

When people want to believe something, there isn't much you can do about it. If people believe George Bush is the worst President the United States ever had, you can't persuade them otherwise, any more than you can change the minds of the people who think George Bush is the best President the country ever had.

I have problems of my own without arguing with a smoker over giving up cigarettes. What I ought to give up is food. Food is addictive and I'm hooked on it.

A while back, I was watching a commercial with some of my favorite football coaches. They said they'd lost weight drinking something called Slim Fast and, although I'm not often much taken by testimonials that are paid for, I bought a can of the stuff. I mixed the powdered substance—that's all I can call it because I don't know what it is—with skim milk, blended it and drank it. It wasn't bad.

About the fourth time I drank Slim Fast, I got reading the brochure that came with it. All special-diet stuff gives you the same advice. In addition to the warnings, they list a schedule of meals to be eaten along with their product. This one said you should have at least one "sensible, nutritious, low-fat meal" per day.

Listen, if I could bring myself to eat a sensible, nutritious, low-fat meal each day, would I need Slim Fast? I've seen dozens of diet foods, and in addition to the product they sell you, they usually recommend a breakfast consisting of half a slice of dry toast and black coffee. For lunch you get a third of a cup of lo-cal yogurt, and for dinner you have an ounce and a half of parsley sprinkled with lemon juice and a tablespoon of buttermilk for dessert.

What I thought, as I left the locker room, was that maybe I ought to take up cigarette smoking and raw fish.

HOW I ALMOST
LOST TWO POUNDS

Are you tired of being overweight? Does it make you mad at yourself because you're unable to control the amount of food you eat? If that's true, this is for you. I am going to give you one man's personal story of how he conquered obesity and brought his weight down from a high of 226 pounds to just a little more than 224 in six months—and without denying himself any of the good things in life.

I remember clearly how it happened. It was a crisp, clear January morning. I had overindulged at Thanksgiving, Christmas, New Year's and all the weekdays in between. I stepped on the scale that morning and couldn't believe my eyes as the balance bar teetered for a moment and then settled clearly on the figure 226.

This was not a 226 enhanced by pajamas, slippers or a wet towel. I was starkers.

It was that moment that was to bring such a great change in my life.

Slowly and thoughtfully, I stepped off the scale. I knew I had to act. "I am an intelligent person," I thought, giving myself a break. "How did I let this happen?"

I used to be 185 pounds. I was still 185 pounds when I was discharged from the Army. And then, gradually it started happening . . . 187, 191, 197, 206, 218, 221 and then finally! That dread January morning, 226 pounds.

My pants were tight in the waist and tail. My shirts were snug around the neck, tight across the chest. Even my shoes felt shorter because, with the added weight, my feet expanded.

I dressed slowly that morning and walked down the stairs to breakfast.

"Coffee," I thought to myself. "That's all I'll have. One cup of black coffee."

In the kitchen, Margie had fixed grapefruit and had sliced the good bread we like. The jam was on the table next to the butter.

"I should have told her I wasn't going to have breakfast anymore," I said to myself. "Too late now," I thought. "She's gone to all this trouble. No sends jeopardizing our marriage over a few pounds. Just this one last time I'll eat breakfast."

I put the bread in the toaster and acted as if nothing had happened. I don't think she realized at the time that I was starting a radical new diet that would transform me into the man she used to know.

At the office, I was unusually quiet that day.

"You okay, Andy?" someone asked.

None of us likes to burden our friends with our problems so I said nothing. They knew I was troubled, but I don't think they dreamed, in their wildest imaginations, that I was 226 pounds.

Because I had made a lunch date with an old friend weeks before, I went to a small French restaurant near the office for lunch. The waiter brought the menus and a basket of French bread.

We chatted and my friend took a crusty piece of the bread and buttered it. Not wanting to call attention to the weight-losing crusade I had so recently embarked on, I, too, took a piece of bread. I was careful not to put a lot of butter on it and I don't think my friend noticed that anything was up.

"Dessert?" he said as we sat there talking after lunch.

"Not for me," I said, with a final tone in my voice that he could hardly ignore. He ordered an apple tart with vanilla ice cream.

"Half of this?" he asked, and before I could say no, he reached for my plate and divided his dessert.

Not wanting to reject this generous gesture, I ate it.

So began the first day of the strict regimen I have been following for six months now. I'm pleased to be able to say that this morning I weighed just barely over 224 pounds.

Don't tell me it's not possible to lose weight if you put your mind to it and have a little willpower.

A BAD APPLE IN THE FAMILY

Our grandson, Justin, seemed like a perfectly normal little boy at first. He was bright, cute, athletic and generally behaved the way a young boy does, good and bad.

Then, as he visited us time and again, we began to notice some strange behavior on his part. He was unlike anyone else we'd ever known in the family and we became worried. Justin didn't like ice cream.

It wasn't only that Justin didn't like ice cream, either. He had other strange eating habits.

It first came to my attention one day several summers ago, when he was five. He had been with me up in my shop, where I was making a small coffee table of walnut. Justin was puttering away by my side on a little project of his own, nailing two pieces of wood together, crossways, in what he called an airplane, when suddenly he said, "I'm thirsty."

It was a hot day and I was thirsty myself, so we walked from the shop down to the house and into the kitchen. I opened the refrigerator door and surveyed the shelves for soft drinks. There was plenty of ginger ale and Coke because we had a houseful and we had stocked up. You like to please grandchildren when they visit, in the hope that they'll look forward to coming again. You don't want them crying and stomping their feet when their father and mother tell them they're going to their grandparents'.

"Coke?" I asked Justin. "Ginger ale? We have root beer. Would you like some root beer?" I wanted to please him.

"Do you have apple juice?" Justin asked.

We did have apple juice because his mother, our daughter Martha, knowing Justin better than we did, had brought several bottles. I poured Justin a cold glass of apple juice.

"Can I have more?" he asked.

"Apple juice?" I thought. Certainly his mother wouldn't mind if he had a second glass of apple juice.

"Sure," I said, and poured him more.

"Want anything to eat?" I asked, thinking of the cookies in the cupboard.

It was the time of year when things grow in our area and there was a big bowl of fruit on the kitchen table. It overflowed with pears, grapes, three apples and several peaches.

"Can I have a peach?" Justin asked.

"How about a cookie?" I said, thinking more of my inclinations than his.

"I'd like a peach," he said.

"Of course," I said, and Justin took a ripe peach and ate it with obvious relish.

"Okay," I said, "let's go back to the shop."

"Can I have an apple?" Justin asked.

A grandfather does not deny a five-year-old grandson, working with him in his shop, an apple if he asks for one—even if he has just had a peach.

"Sure," I said. Justin took an apple and bit into it.

It's always been like that with Justin. I don't know what's wrong with him or what can be done to correct this strange behavior. He always eats what's good for him. There's an aberrant gene loose somewhere there. While the rest of us in the family were having ice cream and cake for dessert on special occasions, Justin would ask if there were any grapes. All he ever wanted was more fruit. Chocolate sauce on ice cream didn't tempt him at all.

It got so I hated to have Justin around at mealtimes because he was always eating the right thing. It made me uncomfortable. It must be how smokers feel.

Justin must have drunk several barrels of apple juice in his young life. He must have eaten bushels of apples. We don't know how he got that way, he simply had a taste for healthy food that wasn't fattening.

I hope that by the time Justin gets to college this condition will have cleared up. If it hasn't, I may have to start a crusade and raise money for a foundation on behalf of children who are born without an appetite for ice cream.

DESIRE UNDER THE MAPLES

Why is it, I often wonder at lunch on Saturdays, that I have a desire to eat more than I need? Whether I'm having peanut butter on toasted rye bread or leftover rice mixed with something else I've found in the refrigerator, I eat more of it than I need to keep my body going the rest of the afternoon. At dinner, I stoke up again, egged on by a meal that has been attractively and appetizingly prepared, as though I have to be coaxed to eat.

It seems as though one serious and constant defect in the human character is desire. We have more desire for almost everything than we need. People have more desire for sex than the world needs to overpopulate it. It's as if we were maple trees where only one in ten million seeds germinates. We have this great desire to make more money than we need to live comfortably. We can't stay away from the stores where we buy clothes, tools, home furnishings and gadgets. We have this great desire to buy and acquire more possessions than we need or can use. What is it with all this desire?

As if it weren't bad enough that we have it, there's this mammoth industry in America, the advertising business, whose only work is to increase our desire for a wide range of things we might never have thought of wanting if the advertising business hadn't pointed out to us that we ought to have them.

Many religions teach that real holiness comes from denying desire. Monks and nuns and priests promise their god not to acquire worldly goods, not to have sex, and not to want money. Nirvana for Buddhists is when they've reached the point through prayer where they don't desire anything. For most people who aren't nuns, priests or Buddhists, there's something seriously wrong when they don't want anything. Desire is what keeps them going. It's just that we could do with less of it.

All kinds of admirable acts by ordinary people involve suppressing desire. Bravery is one of them. When someone runs into a burning house to rescue a child, the person is denying his own desire to live. When someone goes on a diet, he or she is denying the desire to eat and the dieter is admired by all of us. So, how come we have all this desire we don't need in the first place? Are we, as some people think, being put to the test? Why do we have to be tested?

All this occurred to me last Saturday when I took my lunch into the living room to eat, watch a little basketball and take a nap. I decided, after I'd finished what was on my plate, that more would taste good, so I went back out to the kitchen and got more. When I finished that, I wasn't what you'd call really hungry, but it occurred to me that a couple of cookies would taste good so I went back and got some cookies. I knew I was only eating because I desired the good taste, not because I needed food.

After lunch I decided it would be pleasant to lie down on the couch and take my nap. I'd had almost seven hours' sleep during the night, which is plenty for me, but I had this desire to lie down and doze off. There were a lot of jobs around the house I should have been doing instead of dozing, but I ignored them and submitted to my desire to doze. Why did I want more sleep than I needed?

I've spent too much time on my desire to acquire new friends and too little time being with old friends. I have great old friends I haven't seen in three months and twenty years. Why do I desire to make a single new friend until I've renewed my acquaintance with my old ones?

Maybe what we need from the medical profession is an anti-desire pill.

If we had a desire for food, money, sex, sleep or a thousand other things, we could take this pill and kill the desire. If they ever invent the anti-desire pill, I'm going to take one next time I sit down in front of the television set with my lunch on Saturday.

YOU ARE WHAT YOU COOK

Handwriting experts claim they can analyze people's character by studying the way they put words on paper. I've never had any doubt that it's possible but, the fact is, you can tell a lot about anyone by the way that person does anything.

We are all so consistently the way we are that it's depressing. We can't get away from our own character. No matter what I'm doing, I do some of it well and some of it poorly and it always reveals basic things about me—for better and for worse.

I drive a lot when I'm on vacation and I cook a lot, too. I can't help noticing that I cook the way I drive. I don't look at a map when I'm going somewhere and I don't read a recipe when I'm getting dinner. I get lost a lot and ruin a few meals.

You can tell just as much about someone's character and personality from the way they cook as you can tell from their handwriting. A psychiatrist puts patients on a couch and gets them to talk to reveal themselves. The doctor could just as well put them in the kitchen and tell them to cook.

The cooks who follow recipes reveal their nature in other matters. They are careful drivers and when they're flying, they get to the airport more than an hour early. Even then, they're nervous about being late.

As someone who hardly ever looks at a recipe or a cookbook, I don't like it when someone who does, cooks better than I do. I don't like it when it turns out the person was right getting to the airport early and I miss the plane. But I don't change. I'm stuck with myself.

We spend so much time doing it that getting meals should be more fun than Americans are making it these days. The worst thing about so-called "convenience" foods is that they've taken the fun out of cooking. We might as well eat vitamin pills with fiber in them for bulk. Good cooking isn't easy but it's not much more trouble than bad cooking and a lot more interesting.

People cook out in the backyard over grills at this time of year. I can't get over how many people use gas grills. The point of cooking out is to get some of the smoky wood flavor in meat or fish. If you're going to cook over gas, why not do it in the kitchen?

There are things I see in supermarkets that make me laugh. Or cry. I see people on limited budgets, often grossly overweight, buying expensive frozen waffles. You put them in a toaster. If they want waffles, why in the world don't they make them? Stores are pushing instant tea and canned iced tea. Canned iced tea is the ultimately ridiculous convenience food. How lazy can a cook get? Next thing you know, they'll find a way to sell frozen boiling water. All you'd have to do is heat it.

I pass the frozen pizza bin. Yeast is easy and fun to work with, but Americans have almost given up baking their own bread. I bought some pizza pans with hundreds of tiny holes in their bottoms recently and I'm on a homemade pizza kick. The pans are a help in getting a good, crisp crust. I like my pizza so that I can pick up a pie-shaped piece in my hand and not have it bend.

Everything homemade costs a third as much and tastes ten times as good. Homegrown tomatoes are ripe in our area now and they're great with mayonnaise on toast for lunch. Mayonnaise is fun to make. It's one of those magic things. You put a little lemon juice or vinegar in a blender with an egg yolk and then start dribbling in some oil. Pretty soon the whole mess begins to thicken and you have mayo. You can add mustard or garlic and salt as you like.

I don't clean up when I've finished making something in my shop and when I leave the kitchen, it's a mess. When I write with a pencil on a piece of paper, it looks exactly like my shop floor and the kitchen sink.

I DON'T NEED THEM—
EXCEPT TO SEE WITH

There was nothing good on the radio driving to work this morning and my mind wandered until I got thinking about glasses. What made me think of them was that I couldn't see the tiny station-changing buttons on the radio without putting the glasses on.

I've always blamed the first ophthalmologist I went to for any trouble I have with my eyes now. Mind you, I don't have a lot of trouble, but ever since I first went to the eye doctor thirty years ago, my eyesight has steadily deteriorated. Today, I can't read a telephone book without my glasses on.

About ten years ago, Margie said I ought to have my glasses checked because I couldn't find something in the refrigerator. Nothing was bothering me but I'd never had my original prescription changed so I went to an optometrist this time. Sure enough, he gave me stronger glasses. I think it's apparent that if I hadn't started wearing glasses, I'd never have needed them.

I know for sure that glasses are habit forming. Every once in a while, I find myself wearing them when I don't need them. I hate myself for that. It's my opinion we should all fight wearing glasses for as long as we can and then we should resist stepping up our prescription for as long as possible. If you can still make out a telephone book with your old glasses, keep them. Just as soon as you get stronger glasses, your eyes get used to them and want more. Just a theory, mind you, and one I realize that specialists who know what they're talking about don't agree with.

—I lose four or five pairs of sunglasses a year, but I very seldom lose my regular reading glasses.

—You can tell some people wear glasses even when they don't have them on. Every once in a while, President Bush speaks without his glasses on and he looks funny. You can tell something's missing. He's obviously a man who wears glasses who doesn't have his glasses on.

—My grandmother was very graceful with glasses. She used a lorgnette hung around her neck with a gold chain.

—I throw away those carrying cases the optometrists give you with their names on them. My father carried glasses in a stiff, black case lined with velvet. It snapped shut with a definite clap.

—Optometrists must be in business with the people who make fine print. Warning labels are a good example. The advertisements telling you the good things about a product are in letters an inch high. The warning about what the stuff does to you if you aren't careful is in little itsy-bitsy type, but you know you should read it.

—The worst glasses must have been the ones with no rim but with a little gold clasp that gripped the bridge of your nose. People who wore them were permanently scarred by little indentations on either side of their nose. Both President Roosevelts wore them. That's why they were called pince-nez (pinched nose).

—I like my glasses. I only wear them for reading or writing, but I think of them as a friend. When I go on a trip, I always take an extra pair. I put them in one of the shoes I pack to keep them from being broken.

—The glasses people wear usually fit their character. Horn-rimmed-type people wear horn-rimmed glasses. Glitzy, diamond-studded people wear glitzy, diamond-studded glasses.

—Contact lenses make a lot of sense, but I'm chicken. I can't bear the thought of intentionally putting my finger in my eye.

—Finding your glasses after you've misplaced them is such a pleasure that it's almost worth the trouble of losing them.

—Of everyone forty-five and older, 90 percent wear glasses.

—If you have to read small print and don't have your glasses with you, you can make a little magnifier out of your hand. Cup your hand into a loose fist, leaving an open tunnel through your palm with a tiny opening at the far end. Put your eye up against your thumb and forefinger, get close, and you can usually read the small print.

THE EARS DON'T HAVE IT

I'd like to consider the ear for a moment.

I use the word ear to refer solely to the sound-catching appendage attached to each side of the head, more or less on a line with the eyes.

As a biological term, the word ear has three parts. The outer ear, the middle ear, and the inner ear. The middle and inner are the more important ears, but I am not qualified to comment on any ear but the outer, and that only from casual observation. I have casually observed a great many ears, my own among them.

Without wanting to be in any way disrespectful to anyone who had anything to do with the creation of ears, and with ears looking the way they do, I would like to say that it seems to me ears might have been improved on considerably in appearance if more thought had been given to their design in the beginning. Even an oyster shell, to use just one example, would serve more or less the same purpose as the ear and, at the same time, be better-looking.

There are few body parts that are less attractive than the ear. You don't hear someone saying of a Miss America contestant, for example, "Doesn't she have pretty ears?" or "Man! Get a load of that pair of ears!"

As a result of the ears' appearance, a person's hair is often arranged to, at least partially conceal them.

One of the reasons haircuts are so expensive is because of where the ears are placed. If it weren't for the necessity of having a barber avoid running into a customer's ears with his shears, and at the same time partially conceal them, haircuts might easily cost half what they do. For a barber, ears are like two bushes on the front lawn when you're mowing the grass.

Because ears are so devoid of beauty, it seems strange that women attract attention to them by punching holes in their lobes and hanging ornaments from them. While woman in Western society hang jewels from their ears, they wouldn't be caught dead hanging something from their noses, as is the custom in some African countries. It is difficult for this impartial observer to discern any difference in the appropriateness of hanging jewels from the ear as compared to hanging them from the nose. If anything, hanging them from the ears is worse because we have two ears and but one nose.

It has long been thought that the ears were placed where they are on a person's head so that the person could hear a noise on either side or from the front, but this, of course, ignores the fact that it is often important to hear a noise from behind, something our ears are not designed to do. This is but one of many shortcomings of the design and placement of the ear.

If one had to point to the greatest service the ear provides, it would be its convenience as a place to secure glasses in front of the eyes. If our ears were on our forehead or at the side of our eyes, like blinders on a horse, optometrists would be hard-pressed to figure out a place to put the side-pieces of glasses.

Ears were poorly placed in relationship to our necessity to wear clothing that is often pulled on over the head, too. We have all experienced the sensation of having our ears caught in the hole at the top of a sweater where our head goes through. The head itself can be forced through even a quite small aperture but the ears invariably get caught.

As far as clothes for the ear itself goes, the situation is no better. Ears are among the first thing to freeze on people who are outside on a cold day and yet very few of us own earmuffs. If we do own earmuffs, we forget where we put them last time we used them. Most people are reluctant to wear earmuffs because earmuffs are comic-looking even on a serious person. As a matter of fact, one of the comic things about earmuffs is that they are most often worn by serious persons.

If the human body is ever done over, no part of it needs redesign more than the ear.

DOWN ON MY TOES

If ears are a problem, though, toes are one of the most useless, least attractive, most annoying and ridiculous parts of the human anatomy.

Those of us alive today were unlucky to be born into an eon during which the toe is gradually being phased out by that Great Evolutionist in the Sky. The toe, as it now stands, is in the last phase of an evolutionary cycle that began when it was an important part of our body. Once, in prehistoric times, toes enabled people's great-grand-ancestors to hang from trees from either end. By that I mean they could hang from trees as well by the toes on their feet as by the fingers on their hands.

Alas, the toe has stumbled on hard times. Far from being a useful digit, man's toes, and of course woman's, are able to do little but stub and poke holes through the front end of otherwise perfectly good socks. In addition, of course, women can paint the nails on toes red.

It seems likely that in ten thousand years, doctors will be looking back at old copies of *Gray's Anatomy* and marveling at the parts people used to have way back in 1993. (According to my calculations, that will be the year 11,993 in the 120th century.)

I could stand naked before the whole world if I had to . . . just so long as my toes didn't show. I have no use for my toes. They have grown in unlikely ways in recent years and no two of them point in the same direction. My so-called "big" toe is shorter by half an inch than the toe next to it.

If the "big" toe is ridiculous, the "little" toe is pitiful. There is not a handful of little toes in the United States that does not have a corn or a spot on them that's been rubbed until it hurts and develops a protective callus. This callus on a toe may help keep it from hurting, but it doesn't improve the looks of something that already doesn't look good. It certainly accounts for why going barefoot is almost unknown, except at the beach where everyone is so busy looking at everything else people have that they don't notice toes.

One only has to compare the foot with the hand to note how worthless the toes are compared to the fingers. The fingers on a hand can be strong, pretty, graceful, expressive, talented. None of these adjectives applies to anyone's toes, not even the most talented, twinkle-toed ballerina's. The best she can do is stand on them . . . which has always seemed to me to be vastly overrated as either an art or a sport. I'm more impressed by a woman who can stand on her head than I am by one in a tutu who can stand on her toes.

To me, the very phrase "toe dance" is repugnant. It hurts just to think of it.

Toes are what make an otherwise acceptable-looking part of our anatomy, the foot, ugly. Glance down at the shoes of the next person you see. Do they look anything like the shoes you see in a shoe store window or in an advertisement for shoes? They do not, because the toes of the person wearing the shoes have pushed them all out of shape. Shoemakers have never learned to deal with toes. They've done okay with heels but they don't know how to make shoes that fit toes.

How can we expect shoemakers to make shoes that fit feet at their front ends where their toes are, when no two people's toes are the same? I don't even know why the police go to all the trouble of getting those silly whorls from our fingerprints to identify us when toes would be a much easier way to differentiate one person from another.

I first became aware of a negative feeling I had about toes as a private in the Army in Fort Bragg, North Carolina. We were asked . . . "asked" is not exactly the word . . . to make a twenty-five-mile march with full packs. By the end of ten miles I was aware of my toes. I knew, without looking, that they were rubbed raw. At the fifteen-mile mark, I couldn't think of anything but my toes. By the time we reached our destination, I hated my toes as much as I hated Sgt. Fischuk, whose idea the twenty-five-mile march was in the first place.

PERFUMES

The Indians concocted curry as a way of preparing meat because they didn't have refrigeration. The hot curry masked the taste of the meat which was no longer what it should have been.

You'll pardon me for thinking so, but it has always seemed to me that perfume was invented to perform the same job for people. I'd prefer that they took a bath and left it at that.

For the past ten years I've been amazed at the emphasis the department stores put on perfume. In many big city stores, there are people standing at the door, waiting to hit you with an atomizer spray of the stuff. Obviously, there's easy money in perfume. If you can sell a one-ounce bottle of something that costs a few dollars to make for $100, the profit piles up.

It's hard to believe women use all the perfume I see being sold in stores.

We've had half a dozen little bottles of perfume around our house for longer than we've had those boxes of Band-Aids in the medicine cabinet. And now they're pushing perfume for men!

I don't like perfume because the closer a person smells like nothing at all, the better the person smells to me. Just as soon as an odor develops or is added to the human body, it doesn't smell as good as it did before. This includes, for my taste, the most expensive perfume ever concocted. There's nothing more objectionable, when you're eating in a restaurant, than to have some woman sweep by who doused herself with perfume before she left home. I prefer cigarette smoke to perfume. They ought to have no-perfuming sections in restaurants.

Smell is the least understood of our five senses—the others being sight, touch, hearing and taste. We know what taste we mean when we say "salty" and we know what sound we're talking about when we say "loud." When we touch something and say it's "smooth," everyone understands the sensation. If the traffic light is "red," we all know what color it is. We have nothing comparable to any of these words to explain a smell.

Every word we use to describe a smell is borrowed from somewhere else. There's no group of abstract words we use to classify odors. We may say "That smells good," or "That really stinks," but smells have very few names they can call their own.

I've read about perfume experts who are called "noses." They mix various essences together to get different smells to put in bottles to sell for too much money. I don't doubt that there are people whose olfactory senses are more highly developed than mine, but when they start telling me what effect a certain perfume will have on me, they've gone too far. They may think it will make me amorous when, in fact, it makes me sick to my stomach. The idea of being around a woman who smells like Cher because she uses Cher's brand of perfume doesn't interest me.

No one can deny some smells are pleasant and others are unpleasant. Scientists don't seem to understand why that is. Neither do they really know why some things smell good to certain people and terrible to others. Cheese is a good example of something that smells good to some people and bad to others.

Good food and fresh flowers are probably the best smells. I remember reading about a restaurant that always had onions cooking on the stove in a big frying pan, even though the restaurant wasn't serving onions that day, just because they smelled so good to the customers.

You associate good food with something that smells good, but some of the best foods don't have much smell. You wouldn't say ice cream smells as good as a cooking hamburger, for instance, but in its own way, the ice cream tastes as good.

If they come up with a perfume that smells like fresh-baked bread, I may put a dab behind my ear myself.

AN HONEST SMELL

Manufacturers of all kinds of products insist on making them smell like something they aren't.

The honest smell of anything is part of its character and to disguise it, eliminate it, or overpower it with some other smell is a mistake. Covering a natural smell with perfume is like painting something that's dirty instead of washing it. It's still dirty.

Almost nothing smells bad until something's wrong with it. Fresh fish, for instance, smell like the ocean.

This thought often occurs to me when I'm helping with the dishes. We use one of those detergents in a plastic bottle and it washes the dishes but it's offensive because it smells of cheap perfume and I don't even like expensive perfume. What would the detergent smell like if they didn't put any perfume at all in it? Would it really smell that bad?

The label listing the ingredients says the detergent is made of a lot of different stuff that's hard to pronounce and "aesthetic agents." That's the one you have to watch. "Aesthetic agents" means perfume. And maybe a little blue dye.

The cakes and cookies that come from the big commercial bakeries are poor because they smell of some imitation flavor that has a heavy, false odor. You can smell a fake cake a mile away. I don't know why fake ingredients, like imitation vanilla, are cheaper than the real thing. You'd think that anything they have to make would cost more than something that is grown.

I find the deodorant and sanitizing sprays used in public restrooms offensive. They shouldn't call them "deodorants." They should call them "odorants." All those added smells do is hide the fact that the place isn't kept clean.

Some things that smell okay one place, smell out of place in another. When I was in college, I worked in a paper mill one summer. Part of the process of turning wood pulp into the mash that produces a sheet of paper is the use of the chemical sulfite. Anyone who has ever lived near a paper mill knows the pervasive odor it produces. I'd passed the mill many times before I worked there and always found it offensive. While I worked there, right over the vats from which the heavy odor emanated, I got used to it. I even sort of liked it. I knew what it was and what it was doing and I didn't mind it.

It's interesting that the leftovers from the carefully selected food we prepare our meals from becomes instantly offensive when we dump the leftovers together and call it "garbage." It's all good stuff, but collectively it's garbage and it smells bad.

Stuff for your hair is always too smelly. Like most people, I find my hair hard to control after it's washed. I hate putting anything on my hair, but I've tried several things over the years and my major objection to anything that controls it, is the smell of the stuff. Hair spray for men is a relatively recent thing and it works pretty well. I can see why women have been using it for years, but it's all so heavily perfumed that I can't stand being around myself when I use it.

Why do they put perfume in men's hair spray? On the shelves in the stores that sell it, the labels often say "Unscented" but they all smell so I let my hair fly.

There was once an attractive young woman named, say, Linda, I used to see around the halls of CBS. She appeared on a local television news broadcast and you could tell when Linda was coming without looking because she coated her dyed-yellow hair with so much hair spray that no hair on her head would have moved in a hurricane and the perfume from it stayed with her like a cloud.

"Did you hear about Linda?" someone asked one day.

"No, what happened?"

"She fell and broke her hair."

p a r t   f o u r

─── ▪ ▪ ▪ ───

POCKET CHANGE

AN ALL-AMERICAN DRIVE

In 1966 I sold a magazine article for $3,500. It was what people used to call "found money," because I was already making a living, so I splurged with it. I bought a sports car, the aging American boy's dream. The car was a Sunbeam Tiger and it cost just about the whole amount, $3,500, and it was some hot little car.

Twenty-six years later, my little Tiger, painted British Racing Green, with its huge 289-cubic-inch Mustang engine, will still blow past almost anything else on the road, although I don't drive it that way. You couldn't buy it from me for $50,000, because there's nothing I could get for $50,000 that I'd enjoy so much.

I don't drive it more than ninety days out of the year because I put it up during the winter, not wanting to subject it to the deleterious effects of ice and salt on the roads.

An enterprising group at my college, Colgate University, organized a reunion last summer of everyone who had ever played football there. I can take or leave most reunions, but this one sounded like fun and Hamilton, New York, is only a few hours from our country home. I set out early one morning to drive the 120 miles in my top-down Tiger.

I haven't felt so free-as-a-breeze as I felt on that drive in a long time. I had no obligations to anyone. It didn't matter what time I got there so I couldn't be late, and I didn't have to do anything when I arrived except eat, drink, and enjoy seeing old friends.

I went with Robert Frost and chose the road less traveled. I took the small, winding, blacktop country roads for most of the trip.

There are a lot of people with things to sell on our roadsides these days. I suppose I passed fifty garage sales, lawn sales or tag sales. We've all bought more than we need or can use over the years and we're looking for a way to unload them on unsuspecting passersby who think, as we did when we bought them, that they're treasures.

There doesn't seem to be much difference between a garage sale, a lawn sale and a tag sale. I passed one sign that said:

TODAY! LAWN SALE IN GARAGE IN BACK

A great many people must have bought new lawnmowers this year because I passed at least fifteen secondhand mowers with FOR SALE signs on them. Even though it was a summer day, there were electric and gas-driven snow-removal machines, too. We had so little snow the previous winter that a lot of people obviously decided those machines weren't worth the space they were taking up in their garage.

There were places that had signs out front saying ANTIQUES, but it didn't look to me as though they had anything very old in them. Most of what they were selling could have been in a tag sale. Half a dozen of the so-called antique stores had wagon wheels out front to lend authenticity to their claim of having antiques inside. I went in a few but I didn't buy anything. Most of what they were selling for antiques would have been called junk if I'd had it in the back of my garage or in the basement.

The towns and villages I drove through were not wealthy, but every one had at least two churches and some as many as four. They had just built a new church in Winfield but I couldn't see what denomination it was. I don't think it's important. Most of the churchgoers in town probably believe pretty much the same thing no matter which church they go to. The difference between a Baptist and a Methodist or a Presbyterian and a Catholic in America's small towns is more social than philosophical.

It's too bad religions can't get together and share a building. They'd have better churches that way. That's how the great cathedrals of Europe were built. Everyone in town pitched in. Americans like their individual little churches, though, no matter how plain they are and there's a case to be made for preferring one to a Gothic cathedral.

It was Founders' Day in Sharon Springs. The fire trucks were assembling at one end of town for a parade with odds and ends of uniformed people. As I drove slowly through town, I passed perhaps thirty people seated at intervals on folding chairs, along the main street, waiting for the parade to troop by. I didn't stay to watch, but it looked to me as though there were going to be more people in the parade than on the sidelines watching it.

I passed several hospitals and entertained fleeting sad thoughts about pain, unknown to me, behind their windows. I thought how much better a time I was having than the patients inside. I thought how strange it was that we could be so close and yet so remote in spirit from one another.

Several communities had kiosks set up as you entered town, with signs saying: TOURIST INFORMATION. It has been my experience that the booths that offer tourist information are usually closed.

I was having a wonderful time enjoying America from the cockpit of my Tiger. It all looked like a cover on an old *Saturday Evening Post.* I suppose someone else, driving in the other direction, looked at this old guy in his green sports car and fitted me in as part of the Norman Rockwell look, too.

I don't remember what the article was about that earned me $3,500. But the times I've had with the Tiger have been worth far, far more.

OUT OF POCKET

The more money people have, the less of it they carry with them when they leave the house.

Opposite of that is what I used to do when I worked in a paper mill one summer while I was in college. I'd collect my paycheck on Friday, cash it and put the money in my pockets until it was all gone. My pockets were usually empty by Wednesday.

In Minneapolis last winter, I was reminded of those Wednesdays. I was staying in a hotel fifteen miles out of town. The press facilities for reporters covering the Super Bowl were at the Hyatt downtown, much nearer to the Metrodome than my hotel. The buses were leaving my hotel for the game earlier than I wanted to go, so I drove my rented car downtown and parked it in the Hyatt garage.

On the way to the pressroom, I passed a newsstand, so I picked up a paper, went to the cashier and fished around in my pocket for money. Nothing. I had come out without a penny in my pocket. I put the paper back and stood thinking about what to do.

I didn't have time to drive all the way back to my hotel in heavy, game-day traffic. I had a bus pass to the Metrodome, so I decided I could get through the day without money.

At the Metrodome I found my seat early and walked out back to get an ice cream bar.

"Which do you want?" the Häagen Dazs man asked as he dug down in his case.

"Dark chocolate with . . . no, hold it," I said. "I guess I'll wait until later." I had suddenly remembered my financial condition.

On the way back to my seat, I met an old friend, Marya McLaughlin, for many years a CBS News correspondent in Washington. She was with the great Eugene McCarthy, longtime senator from Minnesota.

"Say, Marya," I said while the senator was talking to several fans of his, "I left the hotel without a nickel."

"What do you want?" she asked.

"Five is plenty," I said. "I just want a Coke." I thought a Coke sounded better than ice cream.

She gave me five dollars.

After the game, having bought an ice cream bar and a Coke, I left and returned to the Hyatt with fifty cents. I wrote for an hour and then went upstairs to a good restaurant there to reward myself with a drink at the bar and dinner.

I checked my coat and went to the crowded bar. As the bartender looked toward me for an order, it hit me again. I only had fifty cents. I glanced toward the coat room. Fifty cents wouldn't even get me my coat back.

"Holy mackerel!" I thought. "And my car. It's been in the garage all day. That's going to run me plenty."

"Hey, Andy," a friendly face at the bar called to me, "can I buy you a drink?"

"Boy, can you ever," I called back.

I talked for ten minutes with the drink-buyer, which I felt was the least I owed him, and then went to the restaurant a few yards away and started walking between tables, hoping desperately to see someone I knew.

"Hey, Andy," I heard again. I turned and it was Bob Anderson, one of my dearest old friends in the whole world.

Well, maybe not one of my dearest. To tell you the truth, I don't know Bob well at all, but he's a capable producer at CBS and at that moment he looked like my best old friend in the world. I sat with Bob and three friends of his who had broadcast the Super Bowl back home for a French football audience.

We talked for ten minutes before I finally came out with it.

"Say, Bob," I said to my dearest old friend Bob whom I hardly knew.

Bob gave me twenty dollars. I left, retrieved my coat for a dollar, and got my car out of the garage for $8.50. Back at my hotel, I found my money by the telephone in my room where I'd left it. I ate dinner in the dining room and went to bed.

The experience cured me of thinking you're rich if you go out without any money in your pocket.

WEALTHY IS BETTER THAN RICH

For years I've been listening to everyone talk about taxes and the rich. Almost everyone, even the rich, say they want to tax the rich more. Television anchormen who make several million dollars a year make it clear that they are in favor of soaking the rich. I don't understand this, but there are a lot of things I don't understand about television anchormen.

When you think of it, this anchorman attitude—and I include such women anchormen as Diane Sawyer—is one of the nicest, most unselfish biases anchormen have. It lends credibility to their other biased views.

I was with the crowd on this tax thing for several weeks. "Why shouldn't the rich pay more?" I said to myself. "Bush is favoring his rich, Republican, Yale, Texas oil pals. Why should the middle class pay more and the rich pay less? Raise taxes on the rich and lower taxes on the poor and the middle class." That was my position.

That was my position, anyway, until the other day when I heard that the rich are people who make $100,000 a year. It was at that very moment that I began to turn against the idea of soaking the rich. It was then that I began to doubt that the rich should pay more, not less, taxes. What made me change my mind was, I realized that, even though I'm not a friend of George Bush's, I was one of the rich they were talking about taxing.

There are several words being used in this tax talk to describe people with a lot of money. "Rich" is the crudest and bluntest of them. "Wealthy" is a more discreet word and sounds like older, family money, not something the person got by participating in some stock fraud or banking scam. Wealthy people are also known as "well-to-do."

My attitude now, after realizing I am rich, is that we rich people are the ones who make the economy go. It's our money that greases the wheels of the free enterprise system. You'd have to be some kind of Communist to advocate raising taxes on us poor, uptrodden rich.

I firmly believe that the more you lower taxes on us rich, the better off the poor and the middle class will be. Like President Bush, I'm only thinking of the good of our country and of the poor and the middle class. Lowering taxes on the rich will actually help the poor and so I'm in favor of lowering away on my taxes.

You may wonder how it was that I decided I'm one of the rich people they talk about. Well, there are ways you can tell. I've been poor in my life so I know that being rich and being poor is different. How can I tell? Let me count the ways:

—I buy 89 octane gas, not the cheaper 87 octane. The 87 octane is for poor people and the cars of the poor. The 93 and 94 octane gas, on the other hand, is for the very rich.

—When we eat out at an expensive restaurant, I often have a shrimp cocktail. This is a sign of money because a shrimp cocktail with five or six little shrimp and some lettuce can run you four or five bucks before you even order your main course.

—I don't play with old tennis balls.

—I don't save plastic bags.

—When my socks get holes in them, I throw them out.

—I harden my arteries with real butter, not margarine, and when I make a salad, I throw away a lot more of the outer leaves than I did when I was poor or middle class.

—I do not use coupons at the supermarket because, as a rich person, my time is worth more than the thirty-seven cents I'd save by spending several hours collecting coupons.

—If I turn the light on in a room and then leave for a couple of hours, I don't bother to turn the light out.

That's how I know I'm rich and that's why I'm in favor of higher taxes for the poor and middle class and lower taxes for the rich who have made America what it is today—unfortunately.

More Savings Than Loans

Americans used to routinely put some of their weekly pay in a savings account. Now they depend for their future on their company's pension plan, Social Security and luck. None of these are as safe as we used to think they were and we don't trust savings banks, either.

I love the idea of saving anything, but all the things I enjoy saving are as hard to know where to put as money.

I am, at the moment of writing, in a workroom in the basement of my house. It's separated by a door from my shop where my tools are. Without moving, I can reach the tall, four-drawer file cabinet which I haven't used in years because it's full of stuff I've saved. I just pulled out one drawer and looked at one of about twenty fat folders. My 1961 income-tax return with all the receipts that went with it is in there.

You might think it would be easy for me to throw it away. The IRS is never going to question me about taxes I paid thirty years ago, but the folder is a gold mine of memories for a writer. Everything I look at in here reminds me of something that would otherwise be lost forever in the far recesses of my brain. Maybe I can use it . . . you know, my memories or something. I'll save it.

Here's a receipt for a Ford station wagon I bought that year for $3,764.13. It says "ten passenger," but I don't think it held that many unless they were kids. We probably had ten kids in it, too, the day we picked up a lot of Brian's friends for a birthday party. What a day. I remember that. But I might not have if I hadn't saved the receipt for the Ford.

There are twenty-three legal-size cardboard boxes piled on top of each other or stashed away under something else down here. They're filled with magazine articles I've written, articles about me, television scripts, original book manuscripts, old pictures, programs for banquets I've gone to with the names of everyone there. I save names.

Up on one of the bookshelves I've attached to the walls down here, I see two graceful old wine bottles, empty now but still pleasant to look at. I've kept them.

Those empty coffee cans over there look terrible, though. Nothing aesthetic about them. I ought to save them out of sight. Of course, I'm running out of places that are out of sight.

I wish I had a better place to save these elastic bands, too. Maybe I could put them around the coffee cans and save them that way.

There's a difference between saving and collecting. Some things, like pennies, collect while you aren't watching. I don't save pencils, they collect on me. I want one by the phone or on the table next to my chair in the living room, but they collect upstairs on my dresser where I never use one.

My shop is in the same condition. I've saved. I cannot bring myself to throw away a nice piece of wood, no matter how small it is. Last week, I cut a circle out of a piece of nine-inches-square mahogany. I am left with a totally useless scrap of mahogany with a big hole in it. When I go, someone's going to find it among my possessions because I can't throw away such a nice piece of a tree that grew so long and so beautifully.

One drawer in my shop has a collection of special small-machinery parts and nuts and bolts. They all go to something. I must have taken a machine apart at some point and no longer remember what the parts are for . . . but

I save them. I don't dare throw them out for fear I'll find what they belong to the next day.

People who don't save things fail to understand that the future usefulness of the item saved is not the important thing. If I take pleasure in saving something, I don't care whether I ever need it or want it again. The fun was in having it, saving it . . . and I wish I could say the same thing about money. Saving it simply isn't enough fun.

PANNING THE CAR FOR GOLD

Each of us, at one time or another, dreams of striking it rich by accident. It happened to me last Sunday.

It was 52 degrees when we finished breakfast—not really warm, but the sun was hitting our driveway so I drew two pails of water, threw in the sponge, and went out to wash my car. The hose isn't turned on yet because I didn't know for sure we wouldn't get any more freezing weather.

I moved quickly, because I wanted to finish before anyone else in the family came out and asked me to wash hers, too. She does that.

As I was about done with the exterior, I looked at the floor in front of the driver's seat. There was caked mud, fragments of leaves, an elastic band, two little white paper receipts from the grocery store and other bits of debris. I decided to go in the house and get the vacuum cleaner. It was this simple decision that produced my windfall and made me a wealthy person beyond Ed McMahon's wildest promise.

Under the two front seats, down behind the cushions between the seat and the doors, I found enough money for a down payment on a new car . . . if they'll take $1.78 for it.

Besides the cash, I found one glove, a small radio I'd taken to a Giants game last fall, and the spare key to the ignition which had been missing for three months.

Spurred on by my success, I went after the glove compartment. In the glove compartment I found my emergency eyeglasses, a credit card I reported stolen six months ago, and several road maps so old that I got them way back in the days when gas stations gave them away free. In the back of the glove compartment, there were three paper clips, a comb, and an additional eighty-four cents in small change.

In the trunk I found the rubber shoes I use for slushy snow, an old peaked cap, two cheap plastic raincoats, several books I bought last summer at a garage sale, a piece of the red glass from the taillight which I broke backing into a telephone pole and a brown envelope with seven Christmas cards in it that I never mailed.

Over the years of my life, I've lost a lot more than I've found. I don't know who finds all the things the rest of us lose. The only person I ever knew who found more than he lost was Charley, the man who used to work as a volunteer up at our local dump.

The dump isn't a dump in the traditional sense, because everything heaved over the railing onto the cement-floored pit below is pushed into a pile by a bulldozer and then scooped into a huge truck by a front-loader and crushed into a compact bundle or burned.

When you back your car up to the railing at the dump, Charley, a big, gruff man about sixty-five, looks over what you have and tells you where to drop it. Old refrigerators and television sets go one place, garbage, leaves and old newspapers go another.

Old couches and chairs are Charley's specialty. He loves to see a worn old easy chair come to the dump, one that has seen thousands of hours of television. He has you set it aside over by his battered pickup truck.

"Never fails me," he told me. "I get couple dollars out of every chair. Sometimes more. Two diamond rings once the same week. Watches. The works. Some things down there I wouldn't even want to tell you."

When the people who bring the chairs leave, Charley takes the cushion out and then cuts the chairs open. He's not sentimental about an old chair. It's down in the soft crevice between the upholstered arm of the chair and the material covering the springs that Charley finds gold.

I hate to think of the cash and worldly goods that are destroyed when old cars are crushed and melted down for scrap and when old easy chairs are dumped with no Charley at the junkyard to check them out before they burn.

From now on, the last thing I'm going to do with an old car before I trade it in, or an old easy chair before I throw it away, is wash it and vacuum the inside . . . with careful attention to the little nooks and crannies under the cushions.

AN UNDEVELOPMENT
PROGRAM

There are quite a few people in the United States who have as much as two billion dollars, according to *Forbes* magazine. That's two thousand million dollars.

That's the kind of money I'd like to get used to having. First, I'd buy some woodworking tools I've always wanted. Then I might get a four-wheel-drive car with a winch on front. I might get myself a small tractor with a backhoe and a front-loader, but then I'd set out to spend most of my money on something important. I'd undevelop a lot of land around us that's been developed.

The first thing I'd do is buy up every other house in the little town we live in and tear them down so that there would be space between houses. In some cases I'd take down two houses to make some good-sized vacant lots. Every town should have some vacant lots.

If anyone had a special affection for a house, I'd leave it, of course, and everyone else I'd pay handsomely for their houses so they could buy better ones—but somewhere else.

There wouldn't be any of those cute playground things like fancy swings or jungle gyms or elaborately painted concrete tunnels on the vacant lots. Kids could start from scratch and do what they wished with the open space.

There wouldn't be any formal baseball fields, although if the kids wanted to bring a few flat stones to use as first, second, third and home, I'd have no objection. I'd be careful not to hurt the trees when I tore down the houses to make vacant lots. A kid who has never climbed trees or built a tree house hasn't had a proper childhood.

We have a river alongside our main street that flows into a sound leading to the ocean. In the summer the little harbor is filled with colorful boats at anchor, although you can't see them because stores and commercial buildings have been built between the street and the river so you look at the fronts of those. The backs of the stores look at the river. Anyway, I will buy every building on the river side of the street and, with the exception of a few old buildings with special character, demolish them. The ugly brick drugstore, the liquor store, the grocery store, the deli, the dentist's office are not nearly so good to look at as the little harbor would be if you could see it from the street. I like the businessmen but not their buildings.

Once I finish my vacant lot program and open up the riverfront, I'm going on to something that may be even more ambitious. I'm going to tear up miles and miles of big roads and make more small, narrow, winding roads. We have some now and they give our town its character.

Over on Route 1, the major commercial road that runs through a lot of neighboring towns, real estate operators have built dozens of shopping malls. I'm going to tear down half the shopping malls anywhere near us. I'm going to offer the land, at very attractive prices, to some of these Midwestern farmers who are having such a hard time. I'm going to set these farmers up in business not too far from where we live and, instead of shopping malls, in summer and fall we're going to have rows and rows of fresh vegetables growing where the aisles of the stores used to be.

We used to have some swampy wetlands in town but they've been mostly drained and there are rows of houses where the frogs used to be. I'd spend a few million making swamps out of that land again. It would be fun to see how long it took the frogs to find it.

Unimprovement is what most American small towns need the most. Real estate developments ought to be left to the cities. Just as soon as the cities start moving in on the suburbs, it ruins the cities that the businesses move out of and ruins the suburbs they move into.

If I had any of my two billion dollars left after I'd put the town back the way it was when we got there, I'd pay to have all the power lines buried. I notice the water main and the sewer lines don't go through the trees.

GOODBYE, OLD PAL

It's too sad to talk about, but I'm going to talk about it anyway. If I'd had a gun, the humane thing to do would have been to shoot it. I didn't have a gun so I turned it over to a stranger. I hate to think what he's going to do with it.

After fourteen years, during which it gave me dependable service, I traded in my 1977 Ford Country Squire with 141,327 miles on it. "Traded in" is not exactly the phrase, though. When I asked the dealer how much he'd give me for it on a trade, he took one look and said, "I'll tell you what I'll do for you. I'll take it off your hands and won't charge you anything."

I have to admit it was no cream puff. It had seen more action than most M1 tanks.

Last week I dropped a quarter to the floor, and realized the car wasn't in tiptop condition when the quarter dropped through a gaping hole in the floor to the street.

The front seat rocked back when you sat in it because the bolts that held it to the floor didn't have much of a floor left to hold on to anymore.

When the car was three years old, I had it undercoated. I still have the guarantee they gave me against rust "for as long as you own the car." It had rusted out in a lot of places but I didn't have the heart to take it in and demand my money back. Even so, companies ought to be more careful about those as-long-as-you-own-it promises. "Lifetime" guarantees ought to make it sure whether the lifetime they're talking about is yours or its, too.

The old car was yellow and brown, the brown being that fake wood they decorate station wagons with. Over the years, some of the stripping came loose, and for a time I'd go in and have it replaced, but I gave up on trim years ago and the car didn't look good where the trim was missing along the sides.

There were no hubcaps, either. The original ones were lost, and every time I got secondhand replacements they'd fly off when I was going fast on a major highway. They'd roll along with me for ten or fifteen yards and then turn off and bounce into the ditch.

There's no question about it, the car didn't look good, but the engine was still great and, until I got worrying about the rear end dropping out and the brakes failing in Tom Wolfe territory, I stuck with it.

People were often surprised to see me driving it.

"Hey, Andy!" they'd yell. "You can do better than that!"

One night last winter we went to dinner at a fancy restaurant with valet parking. It was a terrible night, with slushy snow, and I hated to take our good car out of the garage with salt on the road, so we used the station wagon. When I pulled up to the restaurant, I thought the kid parking cars was going to call the headwaiter inside to warn him there was a guy coming in who might not be able to pay the check.

I was never much for turning a car in while it still ran well, and the old wagon's enthusiasm for humming along, eating up the miles, was undiminished. The hood didn't close tight, the back door lock was broken, the knob kept coming off the window handle by the driver, and the window washer–squirter hadn't worked in seven years but the car always got me where I was going.

The hinge on the glove compartment door jammed a while back so I had taken the whole glove compartment box out of the car. There was no place to keep papers so I put them in the well in back. That was a good space under the floor toward the tailgate door. I emptied out the well before I abandoned the car and found some treasures. One paper was the odometer guarantee the dealer gave me when I bought the car new. There were two miles on the car, according to the certificate, so I only actually drove it 141,325 miles.

The booklet that came with the car called simply "FORD 1977" was unopened. I leafed through that.

"Ford welcomes you," it starts, "to the growing group of discerning people who own and drive Ford-built vehicles." I wish I'd known that all the years I drove the car. It would have been a comfort to me to know that I was welcome and discerning.

The neighbors are going to be pleased that I've given up on it, I know that. I leave the house at six-ten every morning in the winter and the car would start up quickly but it would always stall twice before it caught permanently. Always. They must have lain there in bed morning after morning, waiting for the start, the stall, the restart, the stall, the restart.

It was a sad time for me when I pulled away in my new four-wheel-drive car, leaving that dependable old baby behind.

"Goodbye, old Pal," I mumbled. "We all have to go sometime."

THE NEW CAR RITUAL

Having abandoned my trusty fourteen-year-old station wagon, I needed a replacement. I wasn't long in pursuit of one before I realized that the relationship between car salesman and customer hasn't changed. I mean, this is war.

In the first place, like rugs in a Turkish market, there is no fixed price for a new car. It's negotiable. The buyer is at a disadvantage because he doesn't know how much leeway the dealer has or how desperate he is to get rid of the car. We do all know that anyone who pays the amount listed on the paper stuck to the side window is crazy. We also know that if the dealer gives you a $1,500 "rebate," he gets it from you before he gives it back to you.

I had decided I wanted one of those boxy, four-wheel-drive cars referred to sometimes as "sports-utility vehicles." They're also called "off-road vehicles," although if they go off the road it isn't usually on purpose. We live on a hill and drive a lot in snow, so I thought the four-wheel-drive would be practical and fun.

Most car manufacturers make one of these cars·and I went into ten lots or showrooms. I hate it when the salesman is all over me, but on the other hand, I walked out of one place because the only salesman around was on the phone for ten minutes, talking to his wife about what to bring home for dinner.

Being a car salesman is a terrible job. I dislike and mistrust them but I feel sorry for them, too. If all dealers agreed not to have car salesmen, we'd all pay less for our cars and it would have little effect on car sales in general.

The first 4 x 4 I looked at had a sticker price of $26,995. I told the salesman that isn't what I had in mind to pay for a second car.

"All I want," I told the salesman, "is an engine, four wheels, a windshield wiper, a radio, a heater and an air conditioner."

The basic cars had the same engine as the expensive spread but they had less chrome, you had to wind down the windows and lock the doors individually, the steering wheel was nonadjustable and the cloth seats were manually, not mechanically, adjustable.

Even at my age I still have strength enough to wind down a window and I'm not interested in color-coordinated trim, racing hubcaps or hot and cold running water.

The salesman took me to a car with a sticker price of something like $21,500. I still balked.

"Come into my office, We'll see what we can do," he said.

It was the old come-into-my-office-we'll-see-what-we-can-do ploy. He hit a few buttons on his adding machine, wrote a number on a slip of paper, and slipped it across the desk to me as though it were a secret he didn't want the rest of the world to hear. I don't know why he didn't simply tell me the price, but that seems to be part of the car salesman's technique.

The number read "$15,300." It was basically the same car I'd seen with the sticker price of $26,995. It WAS the car with the sticker price of $21,995.

Now, why wasn't that the price on the sheet of paper stuck to the car's window? Why does selling a car have to be such a con game?

I've already put 430 miles on the car in a week. They tell you to keep the speed down to 55 mph for the first 500 miles and I never had a new car that I didn't worry about having driven 56mph during that period. You forget how slow 55mph is on a highway. People blew their horns and gave me dirty looks as they passed, for blocking traffic.

The car seems good except for a few little things. I've caught my little finger in the door handle where it springs back to a closed position, three times. Twice it drew blood and I got drops of blood on a new summer jacket. How can a major car company put out a car with a handle in which you could catch your finger even if you're dumb?

The salesman didn't mention it might happen.

BROUGHT TO YOU BY...

I was sitting in a steady downpour at a football game, enjoying the action from the cozy privacy of my hooded slicker, when the referee blew his whistle and interrupted the action.

The instant the whistle blew, television went to a McDonald's commercial. I know because when I go to a game, I carry a small radio or television set with me. I like it because the announcers often see things I miss.

With no information coming into my ear, I looked up at the scoreboard to review the situation on the field, but they had taken down the game statistics—the down, distance to go for a first down, and yardline the ball was on. In place of those vital statistics was an ad. There were a thousand little lights spelling out HESS GASOLINE.

The scoreboard was flanked by a huge BUD LIGHT sign on one side, a MARLBORO CIGARETTE sign on top, and the name of a New Jersey bank on the other side. On the scoreboard itself there was a smaller sign, lit in red, saying PANASONIC.

Above the top row of seats in the stadium, there were billboards pushing cigarettes, gas, bread, banks, beer and Bell Telephone.

As I listened, read and watched this commercial phantasmagoria bombarding all my senses, there was a sudden blast from the stadium loudspeaker system, advising everyone that WNEW, a local New York radio station, would be giving away $1,130. To get the details of the contest, so we'd have a chance of winning, we were to listen to their morning disc jockey, Ted Brown.

In addition to all this, there were frequent promotional announcements over the stadium loudspeaker, intruding themselves into my thoughts about the game.

With all that advertising, I didn't know whether to smoke a cigarette, get gas, have a sandwich, move my bank account, make a phone call, drink a beer, buy a Big Mac, get a new car, or have a nervous breakdown.

The man next to me had bought a program for three dollars and offered to let me look at it. I found nothing in it except some hot air about the teams and players designed to separate one sheaf of advertisements from the next. Even the names and numbers of the players, which is all any fan wants, were out of date.

Is all this advertising what I pay twenty-six dollars a ticket for? Do I put out a total of $260 to travel thirty miles to each of ten Giants home games for the privilege of being advertised at?

If people are watching a football game at home on television, at least they're getting the game free. They should expect to come up with some kind of *quid pro quo,* but if fans pay to get into the game they should be immune from advertising. It's bad enough that officials on the field regularly stop the game to allow time for television commercials.

Americans have been brainwashed by advertisers. They've taught us to expect it everywhere and that's where we get it. We're lucky they haven't bought the ceilings over our beds for billboards so they can sell us something when we're lying on our backs. There's no place we can go and be free from advertising.

How do car dealers get away with putting advertising on the license plate holder or rear bumper of every new car they sell? Anyone who pays $17,000 for a car shouldn't have to be a rolling commercial for the dealer.

In many big cities, the ads on the buses and taxicabs make them look like the back pages of a bad magazine.

At the movies, the lights dim, the curtain parts and everyone expects the movie to start. What they get is a series of long teases for the theater's next movie. "Coming attractions" are as familiar in a theater as popcorn. There are even tacky movie houses that use the time before the picture starts for slide-projected ads for local businesses.

We pay to get in to see these?

When I park my car at the railroad station to take the train into the city, I often return to find several fliers advertising a local car wash or taxi service under my windshield wiper. When we were kids and played games, it didn't matter what game, there was always one place where you were safe and couldn't be tagged. That's what I want. Someplace I can go where I can't get tagged with an advertisement.

A $171.50 ROOM AT THE INN

The folder, prominently displayed in a plastic holder on top of the television set in my room at the Washington Marriott Hotel, said: WILL YOU LET ME KNOW?

It turned out that Bill Marriott, president and chairman of the board of Marriott Hotels, whose picture is in the folder just above his signature, wanted to know what I thought of my room . . . his room, actually.

There were fifteen questions I was to answer, some with as many as twelve parts. The completed form was to be mailed to "Mr. J. W. Marriott, Jr." I guess that's "Bill."

I decided not to fill out the questionnaire because if I had sat down to answer all those questions, I'd have had to stay another night.

Instead, I wrote a letter:

"Dear Bill,

Let me say at the outset that, for a big chain, your hotels have been a cut above the average.

You won't be surprised that my first comment is about the price, though. My room was $171.50 a night. It was just a room, not a suite or anything.

Isn't $155 plus $16.50 tax a lot for one person in a hotel room?

I had breakfast in the room and was pleased that I could get it at six-thirty A.M. It's always hard to decide how much to tip the room service waiter and you solved that problem for me by adding a 17 percent 'service charge.' You were a little generous with my money, I thought.

The small glass of 'natural fresh orange juice' was $2.95, the English muffin was $2.25 and included two little containers of jam. The price for two cups of coffee was $3.25. Total, including tax and the compulsory tip, $10.68.

Hotels have got to find a better way of squeezing orange juice. It always has too much of the bitter oil from the rind in it. It ruined what was otherwise good, fresh juice.

The muffin was okay, the jam that came with it, only fair. Good butter came with the muffin in a dish with ice, although someone in the kitchen had already buttered the two halves of the muffin, a questionable practice.

The coffee came in an insulated pot and was good, but I want to tell you, Bill, I thought $3.25 was a lot for two cups of coffee.

The funny thing about the coffee is that on every floor you have free coffee set up near the elevator for people who just want to grab a cup and run.

I want to be honest with you, I only ordered the $3.25 coffee delivered to my room once. Next time, I'm going to tiptoe down the hall and get it free.

Your showers are good but why in a bathtub? Obviously, bathtubs are legal menaces in a hotel room, and then you have all that trouble with people not putting the shower curtain inside the tub, so the water runs down into the ceiling of the floor below.

The bath towels are great. My criterion for a good towel is one I can wrap around my waist easily. Yours go around, even my waist, twice.

There were two good little bars of soap, one for the sink and one for the tub, but I used one for both and took the other one with me. That okay by you? Not stealing, is it? For $171.50, I thought you could afford it.

There were several in-house movies available on the television set, two of them dirty. I was tempted to look at one, but the notice says they're charged automatically to the bill. I was afraid, if I turned to one of them, some big flashing light would go on down at the desk saying ATTENTION! ATTENTION! ANDY ROONEY IS WATCHING A DIRTY MOVIE!

That's about it, Bill. I got your little card on my pillow every night, along with the chocolate candy, saying HAVE A NICE EVENING.

I don't think those cards have any effect on what kind of an evening I have, Bill, and if eliminating them would reduce the price of the room, even a little bit, I'd be for cutting them out.

Sincerely,
Andy Rooney"

MY MAILBOX
RUNNETH OVER

The red sticker on the cover of the catalog read: "THIS MAY BE YOUR LAST CATALOG!"

And, in smaller print, "Our latest computer report shows you haven't ordered in a while. Place an order now and you'll continue to receive every issue of our catalog!"

Is this a threat or a promise?

I would be happy to pay a modest amount if I could be assured of never again getting a catalog that I didn't ask for. My mailbox runneth over. Not one in ten pieces of mail is anything I want to look at, and I'm not including bills. When it comes to catalogs, not one in fifty has anything I want to order.

Last year, I suppose we got an average of twenty-five catalogs a week in the mail. That's 1,300 catalogs and I ordered one thing from one of them. Two, actually. I ordered one pair of shoes from a place that specializes in wide shoes. The other 1,299 catalogues, with postage, represent several thousand dollars—wasted on me.

It's not always possible to tell how you got on a catalog list, but there are several things that do it:
—Having a hobby.
—Having a baby.
—Winning the lottery.
—Being old.
—Buying a house.
—Giving to a charity.
—Using a credit card.
—Being listed in the telephone book.
—Giving your name and address to a store when you buy something.

There ought to be a law compelling any company that sends out unsolicited catalogs or advertising material to include a stamped, self-addressed return postcard. It would say simply: *Remove my name and address from your mailing list or be fined $100 for every piece of literature you send me after two weeks from the date of this notice!*

The catalogs we get most of are in three categories. The clothes catalogs are mostly Margie's and they got her name off the charge cards she has with those stores. She also gets a lot of seed catalogs. Many of the catalogs that come for me are from woodworking tool companies. Seed and tool catalogs I don't mind.

There's a similarity in the literature of many of the catalogs. The catalog I get from a company that sells wide shoes, for example, may have the same catalog writer that another company uses to try to sell me woodworking tools.

Some of their favorite phrases are:
"Once you've used our . . ."
"Ordinary [blanks] are made from [blank] but our [blanks] are designed specially for us and made by old world craftsmen from the finest [blank] money can buy."
"Try our [blank] once and you'll never use another [blank] again."
Banks, credit card companies and insurance agents abuse the mails.

Yesterday I got an official-looking letter from a large New York bank. On the envelope it said, "IMPORTANT! PERSONAL!" (They always use a lot of exclamation points. Nothing that claims it's important and has a lot of exclamation points in it is ever important at all.)

IF you get a letter from a bank, you should be able to trust the bank not to con you. Some of what you get from banks is important and there shouldn't be any confusion about what is and what isn't. Anything from a bank that doesn't pertain to your account, should be clearly labeled on the envelope "SALES PITCH!"

Then we could throw out that stuff from the bank with the catalogs without worrying about it.

I object to the devaluation of the importance of our mail. Mail is special when it's personal and when it's serious business. It ought not to be diluted with junk that diminishes the satisfaction we all get from our mail.

DYING TO GIVE
TO A WORTHY CAUSE

This is your last chance to give this year!

Over the last few weeks of every year, most of us are flooded by requests for money from good causes, fair causes and causes which I suspect are fraudulent money-raising schemes by clever direct-mail operators. They all make giving to them sound like the chance of a lifetime. The good causes are seriously hurt by the scams because we get suspicious of all of them.

I give my share but giving isn't as satisfactory as it should be. Too often, I don't know where my money goes or who it goes to. I can understand why there are recurring stories about the very rich person who finds a unique and satisfying way to be charitable other than by contributing to one of the major charity organizations. (I liked the man who went to a predominantly black high school in New York and promised to pay for a college education for every one of the kids who stuck at it and graduated. A lot of them graduated and he got his satisfaction firsthand.)

The reason for our dissatisfaction is clear. If every one of us could be certain that the money we give actually went to the people who need it, there'd be more than enough money to provide a merry Christmas and a happy New Year for every poor person and every good cause in America.

Too often, the people who need it the most don't get it at all. If they get any, it's very little. Charity has become big business. The people who raise money for good causes often have a good thing going for themselves. There's nothing dishonest about professional fund-raisers, and yet all of us are turned off by the idea that the people raising money for the poor are taking 25 percent, or in some cases more, off the top for themselves. It may be right, but it doesn't seem right.

They like to say "it costs money to raise money," but some of the tricks they use turn me off. One day just before Christmas, a package was delivered to our home by priority mail. It was from a reputable-sounding charity with a big name in Los Angeles. It contained six colored crayons, some art paper and various other items I never looked at.

I was supposed to draw something with the crayons and return it to them. I'm not clear what they were going to do with what I was to send back.

Is this any way for a reputable charity to raise money? It hardly seems so to me.

I also got a package with two yo-yos in it that had something to do with fund-raising for a children's hospital. It did not get my attention.

A veterans' organization sends me a roll of stickers every year. Each sticker has my name and address along with a picture of the American flag. They're to be used on envelopes and I'm supposed to keep the stickers and send back a donation. It's hard to throw away your name printed one hundred times next to the American flag, but that's what I do because I know nothing about the organization. I do know that not every organization that proclaims itself "veteran" or uses the American flag as a logo is worthy.

What we all need is a readily available rating chart for all charity organizations. It would tell us how much each one of them raises and how much of what they raise goes to the charity and how much goes to "administrative costs." There are some groups doing this, and their findings should be printed in every local paper as a guide.

By law, a fund-raising organization ought to be compelled to state, on every piece of literature that goes out, how much of what they take in goes to the charity and how much goes to pay for the cost of raising the money.

The college I attended went to great lengths in a letter to make dying seem like an attractive proposition to me. I can actually save money if I do the right thing by the school in advance of that event. It sounds so good I can hardly wait.

THANKS, CHIEF

It's difficult to express my gratitude to the New England Chiefs of Police Association, and Chief Richard Abele of Norwich, Connecticut, and Chief Joseph Pascarella of East Haven, Connecticut in particular. They have written me a letter on the association's behalf.

In the letter, they offer me the opportunity to have a wallet card from the New England Chiefs of Police Association, a decal for the window of my car identifying me with the Police Chiefs' Association, and a certificate of appreciation from them. In addition, they say, my name will be listed in their annual publication. I swell with pride at the very thought.

All this is available to me, according to their letter, for only twenty-five dollars. What a bargain! I've paid more than that in New York for a parking ticket.

I've seen Cadillacs with these police association decals on their windows and I've always envied the people who have them. They often have license plates that spell their name, too. I've thought they were jerks but I envied them. I too wanted a decal on my windshield identifying me as a friend of police chiefs everywhere . . . but especially the ones hiding in the bushes alongside the roads I drive.

Chief Abele is only Fifth Vice President of the Chiefs' Association. Chief Pascarella is Secretary, so I think I'll write him a letter.

"Dear Chief [I'd write],

Before I send my check to the New England Chiefs of Police Association, I'd like to have some guidelines as to what the twenty-five dollars entitles me to that an ordinary citizen, who doesn't cough it up, won't get.

I assume I can expect some pretty friendly treatments from your men, can't I? Your men *are* in on this, aren't they?

I drive around New England a lot, Chief, and I want to be honest with you. On major highways, I've been known to hit 70mph. Will my decal get me a wink from an officer up to 70? How high does the friendly treatment go from officers who have read my name in your annual publication and see the decal on my windshield?

How does the wallet card work? I don't know exactly how to say this to you, Chief, but . . . do I just present the card alone to the arresting officer or should there be, well, you know . . . a little something tucked in there with it?

My question is this, Chief Pascarella. What do I need in addition to the decal to get me off scot-free if I get a ticket for parking in a No Parking zone in your town?

Your letter says that all you Police Chiefs are 'fighting for good law enforcement.' Well, by golly, Chief, I'm with you one hundred percent there. You sound like my kind of a policeman, because that's what I'm for too, and if twenty-five dollars to your organization will put us over the top and make New England a safe place for women and children, not to mention a place where I can drive over the speed limit and not get arrested, I'm on your side. More power to you. This is crime-fighting at its best.

Up until you offered me this opportunity to have one, Chief, I've always thought there was something sneaky going on between cops and the people who have those decals. I thought sending a check to a police benevolent organization was a small payoff for protection. Little did I know that the people who send checks to you are merely supporting the high ideals of your organization which, of course, are too numerous to mention in your letter.

One further question, Chief Pascarella. I have two old New York City parking tickets I never paid. How good a friend of the New England Chiefs of Police is the New York Chief of Police? Under the right circumstances, Chief, I can be a very generous donor to worthwhile organizations like yours.

We are all indebted to chiefs like you who are upholding the high standards of police everywhere. Look for my check in the mail. My windshield and wallet can hardly wait for your stamp of approval.

Sincerely,
Andy Rooney"

p a r t   f i v e

...

THE EVERYDAY

BORN TO LOSE

I'm a world class loser.

There are very few people better at losing things than I am.

Last night, as I was getting into bed, I thought to myself, "Maybe losing stuff would make an essay." So I scribbled some notes about it on a piece of paper, turned out the lights, and went to sleep.

I cannot find the piece of paper I wrote the notes on about losing things. I got down on my hands and knees and looked under the bed. Nothing. It's not mixed in with the sheets. It's not in my pajama pocket and it isn't on my dresser. I'll find it a week from now.

Over the years, I've lost thousands of things. One reason I lose so much is that I have so much. I am an acquirer of things, a possessor. Once I get something, I keep it . . . unless I lose it, of course. It's hard to find a place to put all of my possessions, so they're just left around. They tend to get lost or, perhaps, covered over by other possessions.

My shoehorn was gone this morning. I had to stand there trying to worm my feet into my shoes without breaking down the backs.

I lose fingernail clippers at a great rate . . . and sunglasses.

If I need a screwdriver, I can only find the one with the Phillips head when I'm dealing with a single-slot screw. And, naturally, vice versa.

Where do all the flashlights I buy go?

Someone gave me a beautiful fountain pen for Christmas. I can't find it. I don't use it; I just don't want to lose it.

At this very moment I cannot find my driver's license. I'm driving 150 miles upstate tomorrow and it's illegal to drive without a license, but I'm going to make the trip anyway.

"I really do have a license," I'll explain to the policeman if I'm arrested for speeding. "I just can't find it."

This goes over big with policemen. I know because I've tried it before.

I have regular places where I look for things I can't find. They're never in those places. We have dozens of little drawers in tables and chests around the house, and I always look in those for things I can't find. Nothing. I've looked in those drawers ten thousand times and have yet to find a single missing item in them. I don't know why I persist in looking there.

In the office, Jane is good at finding things but she often doesn't realize I've lost what she finds, so she doesn't tell me she has it. The items are just the same as lost as far as I'm concerned.

Several years ago, I got a small lump of money for one of my books, so I decided to invest in the stock market. Someone knowledgeable about money told me to buy Exxon. I bought Exxon. It did very well, but after the unpleasantness in Alaska, I was embarrassed to be an Exxon stockholder and decided to sell my shares. If I ever ran for office, some reporter would discover that I owned a small amount of Exxon stock and ruin my chances for election by revealing it.

I'd sell the stock in a minute if I could find the stock certificates. The man who sold the stock to me said there was a process I could go through to recover my stock without the certificates. It would cost me about one percent of the stock's value. This fellow sent me a letter describing how to go about recovering my investment but I can't find his letter.

The value of an item doesn't seem to have anything to do with my ability to lose it. For example, I lose a lot of things of very little value in the refrigerator. Last Saturday, I wanted lunch and remembered I'd put some leftover rice in the refrigerator. I could not find it and everyone else swears they didn't eat it.

Things are even easier to lose in the freezer than in the main part of the refrigerator. If our refrigerator could be preserved for scientists of the year 3000, they'd find a treasure trove of gustatory Americana in there that I've lost.

My idea of heaven would be to die and awaken in a place that has all my lost things.

Too Many Things

Today, in a calm, cool, introspective sort of way, I am looking at the problem of things. We are all inundated with them. Even homeless people on the streets of big cities have things they don't want to part with. They don't look like any good to me, but no one else's things ever do. I wouldn't give you a nickel for anyone else's things. But I wouldn't part with mine for anything.

I have no place to put all the things I have and if I start to put one thing someplace, there are already a lot of other things there so I have to put it someplace else—or pile it on top of the things already there. This is especially true of paper things.

In searching for a way to blame someone other than myself, I have concluded that some of the space problems come about when we acquire too many tools and gadgets that have only one, limited purpose. A good example is the counters in our kitchen. They're littered with one-purpose items. Sometimes it's hard to find space to slice an onion because of all the kitchen tools we have that do just one job.

Examples of bulky tools we seldom ask to perform are the electric orange juicer, the electric can opener and the big, space-taking cake-mixing machine. We don't make cakes. The orange juicer replaced the simple juicer we used to have. We'd cut an orange in two and press each half down on the thing that sticks up and twist until the juice was out of it. Then we'd put the little orange juicer back in a drawer. It didn't have to be plugged in and it didn't clutter up the counter. Oranges are too expensive to squeeze now anyway.

The electric can opener sits there day after day, week after week, waiting for us to open a new can of coffee. That's about all we use it for. It replaced that simple, hand-operated can opener no bigger than a screwdriver that was kept in a drawer with twenty other tools. It had a bottle opener on it, too.

The knife is the opposite of the specialty tool. A good knife takes up very little room and does a thousand things. If you're making a bacon, lettuce and tomato sandwich, which I did today, you can slit open the package of bacon, slice the tomato, cut the lettuce and slather on the mayonnaise with the same knife. You can also cut a piece of string with it, open your mail, cut out the sections of a grapefruit or threaten to stab a robber with a knife . . . although you'd probably be better off if you didn't.

We got into trouble with kitchen space in America when the word "appliance" became popular. My dictionary says, "Appliance, an instrument or device designed for a particular use."

The proliferation of things in a kitchen came about with this kind of specialization. Where we once had one thing, like a spoon, which did ten jobs, we now have ten appliances, each of which does only one.

A toaster is an exception because you use it often enough to make it worth the space it takes.

As though the electrical appliance we buy for one purpose doesn't occupy enough space of its own, the manufacturer usually advises us to keep the packing box it came in, in case we have to return it for repair. Thanks a lot, Mr. Manufacturer. And where would you suggest we keep the box it came in? On the kitchen counter?

It isn't only kitchen tools that are specialized. Upstairs, in the bedroom, my closet and dresser drawers are filled to overflowing with items I use infrequently or never. My tuxedo hangs there, taking up space month after month, waiting for New Year's Eve.

Where do you put the hose and lawnmower in the winter and the snow shovel and the down jacket in the summer? If we put the lawnmower in the garage when it snows, there's no room for both cars. We have two cars, one for one purpose, the other for another. Their trunks are filled with things.

THE SPACE WASTE

More things ought to be the same size.

We all like individuality. We like being different and it's a good thing in people, but when it comes to the objects we're trying to deal with in our lives, it would be easier if they came in standard sizes.

Look, for instance, at the shelves in your kitchen where you keep cereal, sugar, salt, flour, rice, baking powder, oil, vinegar, and a hundred other frequently used items. Every container is a different size and shape. You don't want a can of baking powder as big as a bag of flour, but even two boxes of cereal are seldom the same size. What results is a lot of wasted space!

Everything in our lives is hard to put away, pack, store, park, stack, ship, or keep in the garage or the basement because it's an odd shape. Nothing fits in order with other items.

Anything round is a waste of space. In a box of twelve or twenty-four round cans or bottles, 15 percent of the space is wasted because of that funny-shaped empty place between four cans where they can't come together. (I made that up. Maybe it's 25 percent.)

The square, wax-covered, paper milk carton is a practical size and shape because it uses all its space well. It's tall enough so it uses the air space around it in the refrigerator but not so tall that you can't get it in under the shelf above it. A jar of mayonnaise is just the opposite. It takes up more than its share of room because it's short, fat and round.

While I concede that you can't ever have a square potato, a square lemon, or a square head of lettuce, there's no reason they couldn't put Coke, coffee and Campbell's soup in square containers.

I often look in the so-called medicine cabinet in our bathroom. It's filled with wasted space. (I say "so-called" because there's no medicine in there except for a bottle of aspirin.) A new tube of toothpaste lies on its side, taking up a third of one shelf because you can't stand it on end or put anything on top of it. A tube of toothpaste is a terrible shape and it keeps changing as you use it.

The little can of Band-Aids is not at all like the shape of the bottle of mouthwash or a razor I use when my electric one doesn't work.

I'll bet that if someone who knows how to measure volume was to make a survey of the actual number of square feet and square inches in a clothes closet, a kitchen cabinet, a dresser drawer, or the trunk of a car, and compare these figures with the actual number of square feet and inches used, it would turn out that more than half the space is empty and wasted.

We have five suitcases in a closet in our house. None is the same size and, while they're all rectangular, you can't put one on top of the other in the closet because they don't fit on top of each other. It makes suitcases hard to store when you aren't using them—which is most of the time.

Books on our bookshelves are in a wide variety of heights and thicknesses. I think of a book as average when it's about eight and a half inches tall and an inch and a half to an inch and three-quarters thick. Most of our bookshelves are nine inches tall, but we have as many as one hundred books that are more than ten inches tall and won't fit in the nine-inch shelves.

The publishing companies might think of getting together and agreeing to three standard-size books so we could plan our bookshelves.

I'm particularly aware of the disparity or complete absence of uniformity in things when I take the mail out of our mailbox. The post office people even put out stamps in a wide range of sizes. What purpose does this serve? Who wants to lick a big stamp?

The one thing in all our lives that's the worst shape, the least convenient, the most ridiculous-looking and the most difficult to fit into clothes, chairs, or the back seats of cars . . . is the human body.

WHAT CHAIR SIZE ARE YOU?

Since prehistoric days, when our ancient ancestors rolled rocks into their caves to sit on in front of their television sets, mankind has been in search of the perfect chair.

Not only has modern man failed to find the perfect chair, but most of the chairs people sit on are uncomfortable. Manufacturers make them as though we were all the same size and shape, and we're not. It's as important for a person to have a chair that fits as it is for that person to have shoes that fit, and yet we seldom think of fit when we buy a chair. We have a hat size, a shirt size, or a glove size, but we don't know our chair size.

"One size fits all" is a dumb phrase, whether you're talking about clothes or chairs. One size doesn't fit anybody and that's how chairs are made, for everybody.

As an amateur woodworker, I've made some chairs and they're very difficult to construct. You can measure everything and design the chair so you think it's going to be comfortable, but until you actually sit down and try it, you don't really know how it's going to feel. By that time, it's too late to make adjustments. You've got the chair all glued together. You can cut a little off the legs and see if that helps, and maybe even cut a little more off the front legs than the back legs to change the angle, but you can't alter the basic contour of the chair.

I seldom make the same thing twice so if I do come up with a comfortable chair, I don't mass-produce it. I've never made more than three of anything the same.

The chair I spend most time in has shaped my life as much as I've shaped the chair. I may be less of a person than I otherwise might be, because the chair I sit in for hours every day is too relaxed. It's not a go-get-'em chair that I can sit in and be alert to move quickly in any direction to take advantage of opportunities. Both it and me are laid back. Once I settle into my chair, I don't get out of it except for a darn good reason. It's a big effort to get to my feet from the position I'm sitting in. I don't know how I ever lived through the early years of television before hand-held channel-switchers, when you had to get up and go to the buttons on the set across the room.

For the past thirty-five years I've been sitting in my green leather chair in our living room and the basic problem is, it's too big for me. If the chair were shoes, they'd be size twelve, and my feet are size eight and a half. If I sit way back in the chair, the seat is so long that my legs can't bend at the knees. Because of the shape of the chair, I sit slumped down in it with my legs resting on a shaped footstool I made for that purpose. This is comfortable but it's easier to fall asleep than to do something purposeful, like read, when I'm in the chair.

As a result of this position that I assume for several hours every evening, I've fallen asleep during some of the best television shows on the air. I've seen ten or fifteen minutes of more half-hour and hour shows than I could count.

After all these years, my chair has become a kind of slum. It was made of good leather and I like the green color, but it has cracked and worn now in several places and the natural brown color of the hide shows through.

I know what I should do with my chair, but it would be almost as hard as taking an old, sick dog to the veterinarian's for the last time. I can't bring myself to pile the chair in the back of the wagon and take it to the dump. Not after all the hours of comfort it's given me.

"Why don't you take it to Goodwill or the Salvation Army?" I'm often asked.

Poor people have pride like everyone else and no self-respecting poor person would accept my old chair as a gift in the condition it's in.

My chair has, I'm afraid, assumed much of my shape and abandoned some of its own. It's the way a pair of shoes conforms to the shape of your foot, and they end up looking so little like shoes and so much like your feet that you have to throw them away. A stranger could look at me and then look at my chair and know we belong to each other. It's as distinctively mine as my fingerprints.

Perhaps the best chairs being made in the world these days are being put into expensive cars. The driver's seat and the passenger's seat can be adjusted to almost anyone's dimensions at the press of a couple of buttons. A few companies are making contour chairs you can lie back in and adjust in your living room, but why aren't they making anything like the best car seats for our living room chairs?

KEYS

There have been two keys in a small drawer on top of my dresser for ten years now. I don't know what they're for and I don't dare throw them away. Who knows? They may be important.

I carry in my pocket, except when I forget and leave it home, a key ring with seven keys on it. Three of them are a mystery to me, but I don't put a key on the ring for no reason, so obviously those keys open important places in my life. But where?

The one thing I know none of those keys open is the front door of our house. The front door is always locked because no one but an occasional stranger ever comes in that way. It's a good, big, wide door and it's sturdy and safe, but, as far as I know, there is no key to it. This problem is further complicated by the fact that the doorbell doesn't work. Over the years an awful lot of Jehovah's Witnesses must have spent a lot of time out there, pushing that dead button and waiting for one of us to come to the door. By now, our friends know the bell doesn't work so they either come in through the kitchen door or knock real loud at the front door. We'd give them a key to it if we had one.

A lot of people seem pleased with themselves for having big key rings but I'm unimpressed. No one important carries twenty-five keys. No one should have to carry more than five keys, and I'm a little embarrassed for having seven myself . . . even if I don't know what three of them open. I suspect that when anyone has a huge key ring, they couldn't tell you what half the keys are for.

The automobile manufacturers, for all they've done wrong, have done a good job with car keys. We all know what one looks like and we know that the one with the square top is for the ignition and the one with the round or oval top opens the doors and the trunk. This is standard in the industry and it's very handy. Even in the dark you know which key fits the ignition.

Car keys aren't as important as people think they are, of course. Millions of cars are stolen every year and almost all of them are cars that were locked by their owners. Not having a key to a locked car doesn't seem to slow down a car thief by more than thirty seconds. I've always wanted to have my car fixed so I could press a button and start it without a key. No car thief would ever suspect it could be started that easily.

It's strange that combination locks aren't more popular. I have one on my locker in the dressing room where I play tennis and it's convenient. The average combination lock has three numbers you have to dial, forward and backward, and that's unnecessary and silly. My lock has forty marks for numbers on it. I go to four, then back around past four to seventeen, and then directly to twenty-nine. Why couldn't they make a combination lock with just two numbers?

If someone started trying to open my lock to steal some soggy tennis clothes and an old racket, the mathematical probability of their hitting those three numbers would be 64,000 to one. If the combination to my lock could be opened by turning to just two of the forty numbers, the mathematical possibility of guessing it right would still be 1,600 to one. That would take a thief a long time. I'd certainly come along and catch him before he got it open.

It's too bad we have to have locks at all. It's impossible to guess but not many people would steal if there were no such thing as a locked door. It's that one person in a thousand, or maybe even ten thousand, who makes locks and keys a big business. I hate locking a door for that reason. It's as if I suspected everyone in our neighborhood of being a thief. It isn't good for the soul to go around being suspicious all day.

I hate locks and I hate keys, and I'm glad I got thinking about this, because right now I'm going upstairs and throw those two keys on top of my dresser in the wastebasket, and then I'm going to take my key ring apart and throw away the three keys I can't identify.

A HARD NIGHT'S SLEEP

I'm not happy with the bed I sleep in. Actually, I like the *bed* okay. It's the mattress I don't like because it's too hard.

People who like hard mattresses act as if they were more virtuous than those of us who like a soft mattress. I want a mattress I can sink into. When two people share a bed and one likes it hard and the other likes it soft, there's a problem. There's a market for a mattress that's divided down the middle, hard on one side and soft on the other.

A mattress is a difficult thing to buy because you don't know whether it's what you want until you've slept on it for a while and, by that time, it's too late to take it back if you don't like it.

We've been sleeping on this mattress for eight years now. I wanted to make sure I didn't like it before I spoke up. I'm sure now. Lying in bed, sleepless last night, I decided I had to come forth.

I don't know what to do. It was an expensive mattress because it was especially made for the big sleigh bed. The bed is several inches wider than a standard king size and there's something about the corners of the mattress down at the bottom of the bed that had to be made with little cutouts in them.

This is no laughing matter. It's a serious problem and there's no one to go to with it. I can't throw the mattress out and yet it seems wrong to keep something on which I'm uncomfortable for six or seven hours a night seven nights a week. If I was a prisoner being asked to reveal secrets and they tortured me by making me sleep on the bed every night until I confessed, I'd break down and tell all. Anything to get off the bed. I fall asleep in my chair in front of the television set many nights and I think it's fear of going to bed that makes me do it. I suffer from mattress-dread.

I've read articles about hard mattresses being best for a person's back but I don't believe it. Why would a hard mattress be good for your back? A mattress that resists conforming to your shape is bound to be less comfortable than one that takes on every bump and bone in your body.

I sleep on my side, changing sides half a dozen times during the night. I'm not certain what it is that makes me decide in my sleep to turn over. Even in this comatose state, my brain seems to get the message from the pins-and-needles feeling that my arm is asleep, and it signals my muscles that they'd better do something about it before the limb turns gangrenous from lack of blood to it.

When an arm goes to sleep, it's the mattress's fault. There are a limited number of places to put your arm when you're sleeping on your side, and it often gets caught under something heavy. If the mattress was more forgiving, there wouldn't be so much resistance and this wouldn't happen.

I don't know how the caveman and cavewoman ever got to sleep. How can you fall asleep on a rock? You can say they got used to it but you never get used to an uncomfortable bed. It's probably why cavemen are extinct. They couldn't stand living any longer without a good night's sleep.

The relative firmness of a mattress is only one of several differences that people sharing a bed can have. I, for instance, am perfectly happy getting into bed at night but I don't like to feel trapped there. I don't want to be wrapped like a mummy with the sheets and blankets tucked in tightly at the sides and at the bottom. The first thing I do when I climb in is kick the covers out from under the mattress at the foot of the bed where they've been tucked.

My dictionary says a mattress is "a casing filled with a resilient material placed on the floor or bedstead to make sleeping more comfortable." The mattress on which I spend something like six hours, two hundred nights a year—for a total of fifty twenty-four-hour days—does not meet that standard.

It makes sleeping uncomfortable and I'm tired of it.

WASTEBASKETS

One of the singers on the Arthur Godfrey television show of years ago was an earthy and effervescent young woman named Janette Davis. Janette came bubbling into the studio one morning with stories about having been to a party at the home of the great lyricist, Cole Porter.

"I couldn't go," Janette said, overcome with laughter. "He had a gold-plated toilet seat in the bathroom and I couldn't go."

There are certain things in our lives we all use which should not have much attention called to themselves. It is for this reason that a gold-plated toilet seat is inappropriate and why Janette felt constrained.

The same rule applies, perhaps in a lesser sort of way, to wastebaskets. Wastebaskets play an increasingly important part in our lives, as the proliferation of paper threatens to bury us before we can throw it out, but a wastebasket is a strictly utilitarian object. Any attempt to make it a work of art is an unnatural act.

Why, then, have floral designs on wastebaskets become so popular? Who decides to put a hunting scene on a wastebasket? The wastebasket should be the least conspicuous item in the room and yet any department store you visit has space devoted to the sale of hand-decorated wastebaskets that do everything but glow in the dark.

It's clear to me what a wastebasket should be. The ones I remember best must have been in a school I went to or perhaps the same model was in several schools. They were made of some light metal, painted dark green. They stood about eighteen inches high. The top was round and about a foot in diameter. The basket was tapered so the bottom was perhaps ten inches in diameter.

The opening was just the right size. It was big enough to give you a chance of hitting it when you balled up a piece of paper and tossed it from ten feet away but small enough to be inobtrusive. It held a day's supply of the classroom debris of about twenty-five wasteful students and no one ever thought much about it. That's the way a wastebasket should be—inconspicuous.

A wastebasket, in addition to being unadorned, should be round. No one needs a funny-shaped wastebasket. For one thing, an irregular shape is too easy to miss.

The wastebaskets I dislike even more than ones with flowers painted on them are those made of Lucite or clear plastic. A wastebasket should be opaque. It's bad enough to have to look down at its contents from the top without having to look at all the junk in it from anywhere in the room as though it were a goldfish bowl.

There's no question we need more wastebaskets. We need a wastebasket in every room where formerly two or three around the house were ample, but we don't need smaller, cuter, designer wastebaskets.

Wastebaskets are frequently a gift store item now and gift stores are usually small and cute with small, cute owners so they sell small, cute wastebaskets. They may be hand-painted by some local artist who, fifty years ago, would have been busy with useful work making patchwork quilts or hand-embroidered handkerchiefs.

The small wicker wastebasket beside my chair in the living room isn't nearly big enough for the junk mail, the fliers and the catalogs that come every day. If there were space in our living room, I ought to have a compost heap next to my chair. I wouldn't mind if I had an opening there for a chute that led to a trash container in the basement. It's a good thing we don't have to throw the junk on television in our wastebasket.

I'm surprised that, as far as I know, no one I know has invented a disposable wastebasket. It need not be ugly but it could be made of the same kind of paper we throw in it. Instead of doing the dirty and tedious job of emptying the wastebasket, with those inevitably unpleasant bits of debris stuck to its bottom, we could just toss the whole thing.

A good wastebasket is a very satisfying piece of equipment but that's all it is, equipment. It is not a work of art and no amount of artistry applied to one will make it a work of art.

As many as a hundred times a day I enjoy the small pleasure of discarding something . . . getting rid of it . . . putting it out of my life. There are few minor sensations more satisfying than dropping something you no longer want into a wastebasket and I resent anyone minimizing my pleasure by making the wastebasket look like something other than what it is.

THE IDEAL SHOWER

Next to a good bed, a good shower is the most important thing in the house. I don't know any simple pleasure that exceeds that of taking a nice warm shower on a cold day, or a refreshing, cool shower on a hot day. Let me tell you what a good shower is in case you don't have one: A shower is a square or rectangular area at least forty-eight inches long and thirty-six inches wide with a water-spraying device overhead.

You might think the bigger the shower the better, but that's not true. A shower should be cozy. When you're in the shower you want the feeling that you're in a little room all your own. It should be tight and well built, tiled from floor to ceiling so that you have confidence nothing is leaking out onto the bathroom floor, or down into the ceiling of the room below it.

A good shower is not in a bathtub. A shower in a bathtub is a make-shift arrangement. Getting in and out of one is dangerous and ruins the whole healthy feeling you should have when you leave a shower. I know bathtubs with showers overhead that never have a bath taken in them. Once the youngest person in the family passes the age of seven, the tubs should be torn out and discarded . . . made into planters, maybe.

Our downstairs bathroom has had a tub with a shower in it for all the forty-one years we've lived in the house, and except for Gifford, our great white English bulldog, no one has taken a bath in that tub since Brian left the fourth grade. The best improvement we ever made to our house was tearing out the bathtub in the main upstairs bathroom and putting in a tile shower with a glass door.

A shower should have a place to put soap where it's out of the line of fire of the nozzle squirting water at you. If the soap is where it gets hit by the spray, it's always soggy and the soap dish should be moved at any additional cost. The builder who put it there should be sued for mal-practice.

A great many people go through their whole lives taking a shower every morning under unsatisfactory conditions. You hear of people moving to Seattle or Dallas because of a new job, but a bad shower is a better reason to move than a new job is. I urge everyone with a bad tub shower, ringed with curtains, to have a proper shower installed, or move. Anyone who buys an automatic garage-door opener before getting a good shower has his or her priorities in disarray. Anyone who puts in a dishwasher before getting a good personwasher, doesn't know how to live.

The shower should shoot a heavy stream of water at your body, not a faint spray. The nozzle should be easily adjustable so that you can have water all the way from a wide spray to a dense, hoselike hit. Water should be available in a variety of temperatures from too hot to too cold.

A shower should have a door, not a curtain. You should be able to close the door with some assurance that no matter what you do in there, no spray is going to end up in a pool on the bathroom floor. The shower should have a hook just outside its door so that you can reach for your towel and dry off a little before you step out onto the bath mat. A shower should have an adjusting device that is not too smart. No one wants a shower whose controls are smarter than he is so he doesn't know in advance whether he's going to get hit with a lot of hot water or a drizzle of ice water. Controls should not only be easy but the lettering on them indicating HOT, COLD, ON, OFF ought to be big enough so that a person who needs glasses to read with can read them without glasses. If I was to build a new house, I'd start with a good shower and put the rest of the place up around it.

THE INCREDIBLE
SHRINKING ROLL

Once again, I'd like to talk about something I'd rather not talk about—toilet paper.

Is it we who are getting ripped off?

Is it my imagination, or are there far fewer sheets in a roll than there used to be?

In our house, it's always been a trick to leave enough paper on the roll so you don't have to change it, but not enough so the next person in the bathroom can get away without putting on a new roll. In the past few years, everyone has had a lot more practice changing rolls because the necessity for doing it comes up more often.

Not only are there fewer sheets in a roll than there used to be, but in some brands each individual sheet is smaller. I've often noticed that the roll fits in the holder with more room to spare at the ends than there used to be.

It isn't only toilet paper, it's all paper products. With the magic of modern technology, they've found a way to roll up a smaller number of paper towels to take up twice as much space. There's a genius at work in the paper products industry, and it's costing us a fortune in air. It would be interesting to sit in on a board of directors meeting at one of these companies that makes rolls of paper.

"Ed, can we hear from you? Any ideas for increasing profits?"

"Well, chief, I've been thinking. Our toilet tissue roll measures four and three-eighths inches wide. I've been doing some figuring. If we reduced that to four and a quarter inches, it would be a three-percent savings in paper. I mean, who's gonna notice?"

"Good thinking, Ed. I wonder why we never thought of that before."

"What do you think, Charley?"

"Actually, we did think of that before, boss. We reduced the size of the roll in 1971, 1974, 1982, twice in 1986, and again in 1988."

"Mmm. Any complaints?"

"Not a one. People don't like to complain about toilet paper being too small."

"Good. Let's go with the smaller roll. They'll have to buy the stuff more often, and we can get more rolls in a box when we ship 'em."

If I have one regret about my life, it's that I never saved one of the original boxes of Kleenex. If I had it to do over, I'd save one of everything I ever bought in my life so I could compare the size, price and quality with what they're selling as the same thing now. Every ten years, for instance, I'd get out the old box of paper handkerchiefs, the roll of paper towels and toilet paper, and compare them with the new ones. I just know that every one of them is smaller than it used to be but I can't prove it. I don't have one, and there's no museum of toilet paper where you can go to see what one of the original rolls looked like.

The rolls of paper towels are a disgrace. I'm an all-American boy when it comes to paper towels. I use a lot of them. It's a waste, but that's the way I was brought up, to waste things. A roll of paper towels used to be firm when you grasped it. Now, there's so little paper in some of the rolls and so much air that your thumb and forefinger almost meet if you squeeze the roll. It feels more like a loaf of mushy white bread than a roll of towels.

The paper companies even have the audacity to advertise their loose rolls as a virtue. They point out how "soft" their paper towels are. It isn't the paper towels that are so soft. It's the package that's soft because the towels are so loosely rolled.

IF IT'S BROKE,
YOU CAN'T FIX IT

A lot of my things are broken.

The light in the upstairs hall isn't working. The bulb blew three weeks ago and when I started to take it out and replace it, I twisted the glass part of the bulb out of its socket. Now the socket is stuck in the fixture. It seems like too small a job to be worth calling an electrician at forty-five dollars an hour, but if I try to fix it myself, I'm never sure which switch in the fuse box in the basement controls which part of the house. I hate to throw the main switch because that means I have to go around the whole house resetting everything when I put the power back on.

We bought something called a Defiance refrigerator because they made one that exactly fit the space we had available. The refrigerator runs almost constantly. When we asked about it, the dealer said, "Yeah, they do that."

The automatic icemaker stopped working several months ago. The repairman has come twice, but it still doesn't work. There's a limit to how much time you can spend waiting for a repairman to come. I guess we'll go back to ice trays.

Someone backed into the side of my car in a parking lot. There's a dent and some scratches on the panel under the window on the driver's side. It isn't very noticeable to anyone but me. I notice it every time I get in the car and it bothers me, but not enough to pay a couple of hundred dollars to get it fixed. You can't do anything but change the oil in a car now without having it cost a couple of hundred dollars.

If car dealers wanted to double their business, they'd arrange to have cars dented in parking lots. There's nothing that gets you thinking about a new car more than a dent on your old one.

The backspace key on the old Underwood that I keep next to my computer isn't working. People who know how to fix old typewriters are dying out fast.

I paid $220 to have a telephone connection, known in the business as a "modem," put in the computer I use at home. When I brought it back from the repair shop, it didn't work. I called them and they told me it was a problem with the software I was using, not with the modem they installed. I called the fellow who set up my software program and he said it was their problem, not his. That's another $220 down the drain.

And, speaking of drains, the toilet downstairs keeps running after you flush it. You have to jiggle the handle. I took the top off the tank but I never know how that stuff works in there.

The belt on my big sander keeps running off the wheels, no matter how many times I adjust it. It's a pain in the neck to take anything back to the hardware store and have them send it to the manufacturer. Almost no one fixes anything like that. What usually happens is, the piece of equipment sits around for a year or so, and finally I give up and buy a new one.

That's what I finally did with the cordless phone I bought a year ago. We had one just like it up in the country that worked great, so I bought another for home. It was never any good. There was always static on the line and the volume was so weak that you couldn't hear what anyone was saying. I lost or misplaced the guarantee, which is usual for me. After almost a year of feeling terrible every time I looked at the cordless phone, I threw it away and bought a new one. The only satisfaction I got was revenge. I bought another brand.

Then there are dozens of minor possessions that aren't right. The flashlight I keep in the big drawer in the kitchen has a loose connection. It goes on sometimes but it doesn't go on others and, sometimes when it does go on, it goes off again. I've always had a lot of trouble with flashlights.

It has been clear to me for many years that what the world needs is fewer salespeople and more repairmen. I have never met a repairwoman. Maybe that's the solution to the shortage.

SMALL IS BEAUTIFUL?

Every time I think about buying something expensive, I read where they're coming out with a new model pretty soon, so I don't buy whatever it is.

Usually what I read is that they're making it smaller, lighter, more powerful and, sometimes, cheaper. Why would I buy the old model when I can wait a month or two and get the new version?

Over the years, this new-model phenomenon has saved me a lot of money because I hardly ever buy that either. Sometimes I never even see it on the market and I forget to buy it. If I do see it in stores, it is often the same day that I've read still another story about an even smaller, lighter, more powerful model that will be out within the year. It will make the current new model old-fashioned.

Today, I was reading about a new memory chip that will enable manu-facturers to produce a computer so small that it can be carried in a man's pocket but which will have the same power as a big, desktop computer. It will, the story says, "fit in the palm of a man's hand."

Over the years, I've read hundreds of stories about products that will "fit in the palm of a man's hand." The story never says it will fit in the palm of a woman's hand. The interesting thing to me, as a writer, about this new computer story is that it said the letters on the keyboard would be too small to be hit with a person's fingers. Anyone writing on it would have to hit the keys with a small stylus that will come with the computer.

I know I'll be losing that stylus, but still it was great news to me because I'm a hunt-and-peck typist. This most modern of all computer technologies means that, for the first time, I will be put on an equal footing with touch typists whose flashing fingers have, for all these years, been able to hit the right keys without looking.

As a three-fingered typist, I'm fast but I have to look at the keys I'm trying to hit. Now the touch typists will have to hunt-and-peck with the stylus the way I do with my fingers. It's sweet revenge for all the years I've felt inferior to them. Maybe I'll write a hunt-and-peck manual. I've thought of some titles:

How to Hunt and Peck
Hunting and Pecking Made Easy
Hunting and Pecking for Fun and Profit

I may buy one of these miniature computers, stylus and all. I'm hope-lessly addicted to little things. I have a small, thin radio the size of a credit card that I put in my shirt pocket when I go to a football game. I buy miniature flashlights, miniature television sets, tiny tape recorders. When I see a miniature jackknife with a lot of miniature blades, I buy that. I own a Minox camera, known as "the spy camera that fits in the palm of a man's hand." I have a very small 8mm movie camera. In the trunk of my car I even have a miniature spare tire.

One of the first small things I recall buying was a Swiss-made Hermes typewriter. Most correspondents used them during World War II because they were light and reasonably good to write on. I still have mine, although I haven't written on it in twenty years. That's one good thing about miniature anythings: when they become outdated and you can't bring yourself to throw them away, they don't take up much space in the back of a closet or in the basement.

I'm not sure what our strange fascination with small things is. I'm hooked on them even though I don't recall ever buying the miniature version of anything that worked as well as the cumbersome, regular-size model. When I travel, I pack all my little things and take them with me. If they were the big old models, I couldn't get them all in my suitcase.

Keep in mind, I don't use these things when I travel, I just take them with me in case I need them. They're so small and convenient.

A MAN MAKES THE CLOTHES

Every once in a while, you get a piece of clothing that fits well, feels right, and looks good on you. In between, you get twenty that don't do any of those things. I can count on the fingers of one hand the pieces of clothing I've bought over the years that were just right. That's the same hand that gloves never fit.

Sometimes it's hard to know why you like a shirt or a jacket and, for a woman, I'm sure it's the same with a dress or a skirt. I bought a pair of khaki pants in Maine from L. L. Bean five years ago and they're a little tattered now but they're still my second all-time favorite piece of clothing. My favorite was a pair of flannel pajamas I had when I was eight which, much to my annoyance, my mother threw out when I was nine. I called L. L. Bean to order several more pairs of those khaki pants and, wouldn't you know, they no longer have them. That figures. One of the characteristics of a favorite piece of clothing is that it can't be replaced. It doesn't matter that you look for the identical thing in the same store. Either they don't have it or the second one is not as good.

A lot of sizes don't make sense. It always strikes me as a waste that good men's pants are made with so much extra cloth. If you go into a men's clothing store and try on the pants, they're always made with enough material in the legs for someone seven feet tall. For anyone less than that, the pants have to be cut off and the brand-new material thrown away. It's the same with skirts. They have to be made for tall women and short women and with hemlines varying from the ankle to halfway up the thigh.

You get to know the size of various parts of your body that have to be hung with cloth, but your size never bears much relationship to what's on the label. Men's sport shirts come in small, medium, large and X-tra large. You have to translate that. Small is tiny, medium is small, large is medium, and X-tra large is large. It's like eggs in the supermarket.

Socks are a joke. The label says something like "Fits sizes 8 to 11." I've never known what 8 or 11 stands for in sock sizes—it can't be inches—but whatever size your foot is, the chances are your socks don't fit. They're either too tight in the toes or you've got a flap left over up front.

It's hard to say what happens to old favorites that hang in your closet for a while. Clothes you once liked seem to change. I have clothes that I haven't worn in ten years, but I remember how much I used to like them, so I save them. The fact is, though, they don't usually look good when I try them on. I'm unaware of the changes taking place in my shape from year to year, but my clothes know.

Ronald Reagan used to keep a lot of his old clothes when he was in the White House. Even when Nancy wore a new dress, he'd wear an old suit. He had one that was funny-looking with a reddish tint to it but I admired him for going back to it all the time. He must have felt comfortable in it even when the questions he was being asked at press conferences made him uncomfortable. He wore shirts with collars several sizes too big, too. Someone must have told him they were more flattering to the neck when you get older. I'm in favor of men's clothes that don't call much attention to themselves. We aren't birds that need bright plumage.

I admire good dressers but I'm not one of them and I can't say it bothers me much. I buy good clothes but when I put them on, they lose whatever character of their own they had and assume mine. To put it as nicely as I can, I'm a slob. I mean to dress well but I fail.

If I had my choice, I'd have L. L. Bean send me ten pairs of those pants they no longer make and never wear any pants but those.

OUT OF FASHION

Stores sell more clothes in the spring than any other time of year. The newspapers are filled with new fashions. I think of fashion as being for women, but a lot of ads are for men. The special sections include just enough articles so they'll have some filler in between the ads.

Advertisers must know what they're doing, but I'd be surprised if many men look at an ad for a new suit and say to themselves, "I'd look good in that. The color is interesting and I like the new cut. I think I'll buy one of those."

I don't know any men who throw away clothes before they're worn out because they've gone out of style. I have several dozen neckties that are too narrow that I no longer wear but that's the only concession I make to fashion. I keep the ties because I know the time will come when narrow ties are the fashion again. The rest of my clothes I just wear, year after year, oblivious to whether they're in fashion or out of it.

Women are crueler throwing out old clothes than men are. Most of the clothes that come into the secondhand shops are dresses, skirts and women's suits. A man tends to wear his clothes until they're gone . . . and then he goes back to the same store and buys another suit just like the one he's worn out.

The only clothes I shove to the back of my closet or give to Goodwill are things that no longer fit me.

The models in the clothes ads for men always look perfect. Where do they get these guys? The ones wearing suits have several inches of hand-kerchief sticking out of their breast pocket. I never see a man with a handkerchief sticking out of his pocket unless it's the President appearing on television. The models have never sat down either, or their suits wouldn't look like that.

Even the President doesn't wear a handkerchief in his breast pocket when he's not going to be on television. Does the American public really care whether their President has a handkerchief in his pocket or not?

A lot of men in ads wear suspenders. Suspenders, like handkerchiefs, are used mostly for looks. They're a prop to make a man look macho. The number of men who actually wear suspenders except to have their pictures taken in them is fewer than the number of men who smoke pipes. Suspend-ers are worn for show 99 percent of the time and for holding up pants one percent. This is an informal survey I have taken, just by looking around. The men who wear suspenders to hold their pants up are fewer than the number of women who wear pantyhose for warmth.

One article I read by a woman who must be a men's fashion expert, said that a new jacket designed by Giorgio Armani "is long, lean and liberating. Its loose fit and nonaggressive spirit have left their mark on men's fashion this year."

Well, sir, you could have fooled me because I didn't even know a mark had been left on men's clothing this year. I was completely unaware of the nonaggressive spirit in the two pairs of underwear and the raincoat I bought.

I think they have a harder time making fashion out of men's clothes than women's. Edging toward nakedness always makes women's fashion shows interesting and daring. The skirts get shorter, the bathing suits skimpier, the décolletage décolletagier.

What can you do that's comparable with men's clothes that's as comparably interesting? As a result, men are left with suspenders and handker-chiefs.

Looking at a big, special, men's fashion advertising supplement maga-zine, folded into a Sunday edition of *The New York Times,* I realized I'm going to be out of style again. And as if the clothes weren't enough to date mine, there are ads for men's perfume—when perfume is sold to a man, it's called cologne—and I don't wear perfume. I'll stand out in a crowd because I'll be the only one who doesn't smell.

Everyone will stare at me as though I were a freak.

SHADING THE TRUTH

The fashion section of my Sunday paper reported that women will be wearing their hair short this summer and will also be wearing old-fashioned sunglasses.

Who makes these announcements? Who knows what women will be wearing this summer or next fall? Who knows how short they'll have their hair cut?

Do women read that they'll be wearing old-fashioned sunglasses and then go out and buy them, or do women go out and buy them before the paper reports that's what they'll be wearing? It's a mystery to me.

Of course, there's one more possibility and it may be the most likely: Manufacturers of old-fashioned sunglasses start the rumor that women will be wearing old-fashioned sunglasses this summer. That's the American way.

I'm not even sure what old-fashioned sunglasses are. Mine never have a chance to get old-fashioned because I lose them or break them long before they're out of date.

It always annoys me, though, when something practical like sunglasses is taken over by the fashion industry. If it's something we all need, the fashion industry should keep its hands off. No one wants a designer tooth-brush because it looks great. Sunglasses are not basically decoration and shouldn't be treated like Christmas tree ornaments.

Dark glasses—or sunglasses—are a great invention. Slipping on a pair when you're out in the glare of a hot sun is wonderfully comforting, almost like stepping into the shade, and I dislike the cute ones or the ones with bangles, beads and rhinestone glitz stuck to them.

It's amusing in the summer to walk by a swimming pool or along a beach or lakefront and note how many of the attractive women are displaying almost all of themselves in their brief bathing suits but are hiding behind dark glasses. If you can't see a person's eyes, they're hiding.

People in dark glasses are inscrutable. You can't tell anything about their character. They're anonymous faces behind two blank circles. The wearer of dark glasses can stare at anything, unobserved. He or she can look you up and down and you never know you're being watched because you can't see which direction the person's eyes are pointing.

What our eyes look like, what they do in conversation, is important to a lot of decisions we make about people. We decide they are open and honest, shifty and not to be trusted, friendly or unfriendly, just by looking into their eyes. It is very unsatisfactory to talk to someone wearing sunglasses and it strikes me as strange that women, who will wear bikinis that conceal less of them than a man's necktie would, hide their true identity behind dark glasses, even when the sun is behind clouds. I suspect that wearing dark glasses gives women who are wearing next to nothing else a sense that they are clothed.

Sunglasses give different impressions at different times. Hollywood stars who started wearing them years ago, gave dark glasses an aura of glamour that hangs on today in the advertisements for dark glasses. There's the potential for evil though, with anyone wearing dark glasses. I don't trust anyone who wears them when they don't need them.

Years ago I saw a woman walking towards me on Fifth Avenue in New York. She caught my eye because she was wearing a huge pair of decorated dark glasses that covered half her face. The woman would not otherwise have attracted my attention but the glasses called out for people to look at her. It was as though they blinked on and off saying "MOVIE STAR! MOVIE STAR!"

The woman, I realized as she passed, was Marlene Dietrich, hiding from her public. If she hadn't been wearing her sunglasses disguise, no one would have noticed her.

A NECKTIE REVOLT

I am prepared to lead a revolt. My cause is the necktie. I'm against neckties.

For all the years of my adult life, I have submitted meekly to the male

custom of wearing a piece of colored cloth tied around my neck because
I am a coward when it comes to clothes. I wear what everyone else is
wearing for fear of being pointed out and laughed at if I don't.

The phrase "blue-collar worker" used to apply to men who did manual
labor. They were chiefly distinguished at work by their dress. They wore
blue denim shirts and no neckties. The "white-collar worker," on the other
hand, wore a suit, a white shirt, and a tie.

Somewhere about twelve years ago, a strange phenomenon started taking place. Up until that time, the white-collar worker generally had more
prestige attached to his job. He was usually better educated and paid a
higher wage than his blue-collar counterpart.

All that was before plumbers, electricians and Chevrolet mechanics
started charging $65 an hour for their time. Although the office worker is
still more apt to wear a white shirt, he (or she) is no longer necessarily paid
more for what he does and the chief difference now between a man who
is a blue-collar worker and one who is a white-collar worker is not the
collar of their shirts, but the fact that one wears a necktie and the other
doesn't.

The time has come for white-collar office workers to give up this last
vestige of their sartorial superiority and go to work without their neckties.
If I see the slightest movement in this direction, I'll join in. I still don't have
the courage to go it alone.

The reason this crusade against wearing a necktie comes to me at this
time might be interesting to you. Or it might not, of course.

A few days after Christmas last year, I went to Brooks Brothers clothiers
in New York City. For years, Brooks Brothers has set the standard for good
men's clothes in the United States. Their merchandise is dependably first-
rate and their styles are conservative and in good taste. They are consistently
expensive, like anything any good. They appeal to the people who have the
kind of money we all dream of having.

During most of the year, Brooks Brothers' store is church-quiet, with
just a few customers conversing quietly with the salesmen. I am always
impressed with these Brooks Brothers employees because they are so much
better dressed, better educated and more knowledgeable about everything
than I am. I'm fairly certain they couldn't afford to be that well-dressed
unless they get free suits from their employer.

On this occasion shortly after Christmas, Brooks was humming with
activity. It was the kind of day that I imagine the salesmen deplore because
they seem to be above the crass world of commerce. The occasion, of
course, was Brooks Brothers after-Christmas sale.

For the past twenty years, I've been going to Brooks Brothers once a year to buy the five new ties I allow myself. The ties have always been terribly expensive but I've thrown caution to the winds and paid for five of them marked down from perhaps $12 to $9.95. Two years ago, I noticed the $25 ties were marked down to $18. I balked, but bought. Last year, their $35 ties were cut to $27 and I bought just two.

That's it for ties at Brooks Brothers, though. Those two may be my last. This year, I was fingering a tie that appealed to me and when I turned it over, the price tag said $62. Sixty-two dollars? For a necktie? For a piece of clothing that keeps me neither warm nor modest? Surely Brooks Brothers is joking. I think of $62 as the price of a suit with two pairs of pants.

"How much is this sixty-two-dollar tie marked down?" I asked.

"I'm sorry, sir. The ties aren't marked down this year."

That broke it for me. It's all I needed to hear to give me the motivation I needed to start an anti-necktie revolution.

MUSIC FOR A TIN EAR

I t was a small blue box about five inches long and two inches wide. It had been in an old suitcase in the attic for thirty-five years. The box had gold lettering but I recognized what was inside before I read the name "Hohner" on it. It was my old harmonica. (As I recall, we called it a "mouth organ" more often than we called it a harmonica.)

I folded back the top of the box with the snap spring and there it was, nestled in its blue velvet couch as good as the day Uncle Bill gave it to me on my twelfth birthday.

From time to time for several years after I got it, I dreamed of becoming a great harmonica player. I'd spend perhaps ten or fifteen minutes trying to master it and then give up. I even bought a little booklet called *Ten Easy Ways to Harmonica Mastery* but I never learned to play it. I could blow out and suck in and get a noise, but what eluded me was learning the trick of covering some of the holes with my tongue to get the right notes, while blowing air through the others.

This harmonica of mine must have been a pretty good one. I suppose it cost five dollars when it was new. You could always tell when a harmonica was from the ten-cent store because the highest and lowest notes were not true to the scale. Sometimes you couldn't get any sound at all out of the last two slots at either end of a cheap harmonica. This one was good.

Hohner made beautiful instruments and they got more and more complicated as the price went up, with more holes for more notes. I decided at some point, and rightly so—even though I may have decided it in frustration over not being able to play it—that the harmonica was a minor musical instrument. When you hear someone accomplished playing the harmonica, you don't think so much about good music. You think how amazing it is that the person can play it at all. It's more like a vaudeville trick.

It wouldn't be possible to say who the best violinist or pianist of all time was, because there have been so many great ones, but there's no question that one man, Larry Adler, was the best harmonica player there ever was. Larry was an American who was accused of being a Communist by Senator Joe McCarthy in 1950. Nothing was ever proven against him but he moved to London and it just about ruined his career.

Larry attended the prestigious Peabody Conservatory in Baltimore and that led, indirectly, to his taking up the harmonica. One day near the end of the school year, they had their formal recital at the Conservatory. Larry was supposed to play Grieg's Waltz in A Minor on the piano which he was studying, but instead he played an elaborate version of "Yes, We Have No Bananas."

He was thrown out of school.

I hadn't thought about harmonicas since I was a kid until I arrived in the little town of Torgau, on the Elbe River in Germany, with the 2nd Armored Division. It was the day U.S. forces in Europe driving west, met up with the Russian Army driving east.

It was a wild and joyous scene that day, because both the Americans and the Russians knew it meant the German Army was beaten and the war was all but over. What made the meeting even more memorable was the music. Torgau was the site of the Hohner Harmonica factory. The Russian soldiers had burst through the factory doors and found thousands of harmonicas and accordions in storage rooms there.

It seemed to me at the time that every Russian soldier knew how to play an instrument. Several thousand Russian civilians who had been enslaved by the Germans and forced to do menial labor, had followed along behind our army as it advanced toward the Russians coming in the other direction. Among them was a woman with a magnificent soprano voice who had been a Moscow opera star before the war. There was an impromptu concert in the center of Torgau that will always be the major musical memory of my life. Thousands of Russians sang in concert and all those who weren't singing were playing their recently acquired harmonicas and accordions. There has never been such a magnificent musical event to match it.

Harmonicas haven't been very popular now for quite a few years. It's about time for a revival. Our grandchildren are coming for Easter. Maybe I'll buy one for each of them . . . on second thought, maybe I'll give them the harmonicas as they leave. Their parents will be delighted to have music in the car on the drive home.

I hope I can find a Hohner.

PROGRESS DOESN'T MEAN GETTING AHEAD

This is a confession. I am writing on a computer. I admit this with some reluctance because for all my adult life I've written on one of the great machines of any kind ever made, the Underwood No. 5 typewriter.

Alas! My trusty Underwood sits here by my side now, gathering office dust. I use it a few times a week but I've all but abandoned it.

This word-processing computer is a marvel. It's easy to move sentences and paragraphs or even whole pages from one place to another and it's easy to make corrections before I print what I've written.

You'd think then, with this wonderful new tool I'm using, that I'd be a better writer, wouldn't you?

The sad fact is, no machine ever built for anything seems to end up saving time or money, making life better or improving our performance.

There are 123 million cars in the United States. We drive a total of one trillion, four hundred billion miles a year.

Are we happier human beings since the automobile was invented and we can get more places quickly? There's no evidence this is true.

When I was a kid, we drove to a summer place we had on a lake about seventy-five miles from our home. Much of the trip was on small, narrow, dirt roads and it took almost four hours. Once we got to the lake, we stayed for the summer.

They built a six-lane highway twenty-five years ago and the trip takes one hour now. Is our summer vacation better because of the highway? It is not. Our secluded spot on the lake is crowded now, easily accessible to everyone, and we seldom go there anymore.

For many years I carried a big old Hamilton railroad pocket watch that had to be wound every day. It kept good time . . . not great time but good time. Depending on the temperature, it would gain or lose ten seconds a week. Every few weeks, I'd reset it. Now I wear a quartz watch that doesn't vary a second a year. Is my life better organized because I know the exact time? Am I more prompt getting places than when my pocket watch was a little fast or a little slow? I am not.

I don't know why technological progress is so little help. The latest invention always holds such promise but then, ten years later, we look back at what it's done to our lives and seldom are we able to say that the invention has made us happier or more productive.

In that remote cottage on the lake, we lived at night by candlelight and kerosene lamp. Their flickering flames were fascinating to me and I'd often go to bed and stay awake reading by the lamp for hours. Now I have a special reading lamp attached to the headboard of the bed. It casts a bright, easy light to read by. Am I reading more? I climb into bed, turn out the light, and go to sleep now.

We did over the kitchen and have a big, serious two-oven gas range with the added convenience of a built-in microwave in the top oven. Is dinner vastly better at our house than it used to be? Not that I notice.

My mother washed our clothes in a big tub in the cellar on a washboard. She hung the clean laundry on a line in the backyard. She washed the dishes by hand and used a hand-pushed carpet sweeper to clean. We have a modern clothes washer, a dryer, several electric vacuum cleaners, a dishwasher and a smorgasbord of detergents under the sink. Do these modern conveniences mean everything is made instantly spic and span in our house? Don't ask.

Tennis rackets and golf clubs are made of hi-tech materials that cost a fortune. Balls travel faster and farther. Is Ivan Lendl more fun to watch because of his new racket than Bill Tilden was? Is Jack Nicklaus a better golfer because of his clubs than Bobby Jones or Ben Hogan? No way.

There seems to be an inevitability about our lives that no amount of technological progress can improve.

· · ·

STRAIGHTENING OUT THE WORLD

"THE PEOPLE HAVE SPOKEN"

"**T**hey're all a bunch of crooks," right?

It's clear that Americans don't trust their politicians—but politicians are not all a bunch of crooks. A lot of them are public-spirited citizens trying to help keep the world together for the rest of us while we sit around complaining.

I think I know why people don't trust politicians. It's those campaign speeches they make. Campaign speeches almost always make a candidate sound phony and dishonest.

Some politicians sound better when they make their concession speeches late at night after they've lost on Election Day than they do on the campaign trail. There's something about defeat that brings out an honest streak in them.

There are several rules for standard concession speeches. The rules are these:

1) Thank your supporters. (Your supporters hiss and boo, refusing to accept defeat.)

2) Pay your respects to the democratic process and say things like, "The people have spoken."

3) Announce that you've called your opponent and congratulated him. (Your supporters hiss and boo again.)

4) Say that there's a lot to be done in the United States in the difficult days ahead and we'll all have to work together.

5) Put your arm around your wife and say how wonderful she and your family have been. (Your wife stands by, bravely, but with tears in her eyes.)

Losers often quote someone talking about defeat. Lincoln is a favorite. Adlai Stevenson did that best in 1956 after his loss to Dwight Eisenhower. He said he felt like Lincoln when Lincoln lost an election. Lincoln had said that he felt like the boy who stubbed his toe in the dark.

"He was too old to cry," Lincoln said, "but it hurt too much to laugh."

In 1972, when George McGovern lost to Nixon, he quoted Stevenson quoting Lincoln but he reversed the punch line.

"It hurts too much to laugh," the boy said, according to McGovern, "but I'm too old to cry." It's better the other way.

Just once I'd like to hear a candidate say what he really thinks when he loses. It would sound like this:

"Well, that's it, folks. The American people have spoken and, as usual, they don't know what they're talking about. They elected my opponent and they're going to be sorry. It's times like this I wonder about the democratic process and one man, one vote. Some of these people are so dumb they shouldn't be allowed to vote.

"A little while ago, I called this dishonest little dimwit I ran against and I told him he was the sorriest candidate I ever saw.

"Now, my wife here . . . she doesn't care. She looks as if she's crying, but she's laughing with tears in her eyes. She says I can make more money in a real job than I could in politics anyway.

"As for my supporters, a lot of help you were. If you worked so hard, how come I didn't win?

"To tell you the truth, it was a terrible experience and a big waste of my time.

"That's it, folks. Now if you'll all leave me alone, I'm going out and tie one on."

IN DEFENSE OF CONGRESSMEN

Maybe we're being unreasonable when we expect our congressmen to be honest. We're asking too much. What do we expect of ordinary mortals, anyway, perfection?

Sure, some congressmen cheat and steal, but it's because we don't pay them enough. Is a little graft, a few thousand corrupt bucks, too much for us to forgive these underpaid public servants? Why do we make them defend themselves against all these silly charges?

Because we've all heard the statements congressmen accused of misconduct make in their own defense and because there is always talk of more charges against more congressmen, perhaps it would save us all time if the congressmen simply referred to their defense statements by number.

Here are the names and numbers of ten of the most familiar defenses congressmen use:

1. "There is absolutely no truth whatsoever to this rumor." (Often used the day the charges are first made public.)

2. "I look forward to this investigation. I have done nothing to be ashamed of. I'm confident that, when all the facts are revealed, I shall be vindicated."

(That's for a few days later when it becomes obvious the charges are true.)

3. "I was quoted out of context. The media is abusing its First Amendment rights and making a mockery of government in order to sell a few newspapers."

4. "I'll be the first to admit it. I made a mistake. We all make mistakes."

(This is the basic "mea culpa" or "Yes, I did it" defense. The congressman does not point out that, in actual fact, he was not the first to admit he made a mistake. Or that he got rich making the mistake.)

5. "I may have used poor judgment. Is there anyone in this room who hasn't been guilty of using poor judgment once in his lifetime?"

(This "poor judgment" defense is actually a variation on the "mea culpa" defense. It can be used when a congressman is caught investing $100 in a dry oil well and getting a return of $10,000 on his investment although none of the other investors gets anything . . . and it turns out the person who gives him the $10,000 has an interest in a bill before Congress that could make him a few million.)

6. "I resent my wife's honor being impugned and my family being dragged into what is essentially a political attack on me. Is there no limit to the lengths my opponents will go?"

(This is for when someone in the real estate business in the congressman's hometown pays a congressman's wife a salary to get in bed with the congressman.)

7. "Let me just say that I have never knowingly violated the rules of ethics of this body. I would never break any rule of this House that I was aware of. I didn't know stealing was illegal if you were a congressman. I think my record is clear on this."

8. "I want to be frank and honest with you. If I had it to do over again, I wouldn't do it that way. If we all had 20/20 hindsight, we'd do things differently."

(The last resort is the resignation statement, used when it becomes obvious the guy will either be run out of office or indicted.)

9. "I have decided that, in the interest of this great deliberative body

which I love and, without in any way admitting my guilt in these matters, I will not put it through the pain of any further investigation."

10. "I have decided that I will resign in order to spend more time with my family."

THE BACHELOR PRESIDENT

A President of the United States should not have relatives. I'll vote for the first candidate who comes along, man or woman, who isn't married and doesn't have children. Wives and children have never been anything but trouble for a president. (I may make an exception if Jerry Brown is ever a candidate.)

Along with the pledge of allegiance at the swearing-in ceremony, the President should officially renounce his family, divorce his wife and declare himself to be free, alone and independent of entangling alliances for the duration of his term in office. If priests and nuns can do without husbands and wives, why can't Presidents?

In all our U.S. history, there has been only one American President whose wife didn't get a lot of bad publicity with what she did or did not do with the decorations when she moved into the White House. There has been only one President whose kids didn't give him a lot of grief while he was in office. That man was James Buchanan, our fifteenth President. You never heard any scandal involving James Buchanan's wife or children, did you? Of course you didn't and that's because Buchanan was never married and didn't have any children, either. Way to go, Bucky!

President William Harrison had a wife and ten children. We want a guy like this planning for the country? We'd have to put a new wing on the White House.

President Warren Harding had a wife but no children. At least he got it half right.

Even such a paragon among Presidents as Abe Lincoln had family problems. Lincoln's wife, Mary, was publicly criticized for being a big spender.

In 1990, President Bush had to pretend the mess his son, Neil Bush, was in with the Silverado Bank was just a nattering little matter on his mind but we knew it was more than that. I'll bet that, in private, George Bush gave his son hell about his connection with that shady financial deal.

Barbara Bush seems like a nice, motherly kind of woman, but as far as the presidency goes, she's nothing George couldn't do without. For example, she's in favor of a woman's right to have an abortion and he's against it. This is a strain in any family, but when the man is President and the woman is First Lady, it's worse. Can you imagine their conversation when they're alone in the privacy of their own bedroom in the White House?

Relatives were nothing but a problem for Ronald Reagan when he was President. First it was Nancy who got him in trouble by spending all that money redecorating the White House and borrowing expensive clothes from designers on the strength of her selling power as First Lady.

Then it was those rebel sons and daughters President Reagan had. I never knew for sure which of his kids were whose. Reagan acted as though he wasn't sure, himself. Either Mr. Reagan didn't like some of them or they couldn't stand him. Whatever the case, his family situation never looked good to the rest of us.

It didn't help President Reagan that he'd been married before and that his first wife, Jane Wyman, had her own television show. It would have been easier for President Reagan if he'd never been married at all except in the movies.

If a President has never been married and has no children, it cuts down on the number of nasty books someone's going to write about him, too.

President Nixon had a brother who brought him nothing but grief and so did Jimmy Carter. Poor Jimmy was trying to do his best with the terrible Middle East problem and right in the middle of the whole thing his lovable, irresponsible, beer-guzzling brother, Billy, took a job as an advisor to some Arab country, giving them so-called public relations help. Jimmy must have been so pleased.

It's hard enough being President without having to be a husband and a father too. Next time, let's look for a bachelor President.

A LACK OF INTELLIGENCE

What's a nice country like the United States doing in a tawdry, dishonest business like spying?

If they cut the $30 billion Central Intelligence Agency budget by 75 percent tomorrow it wouldn't be a month too soon. "The CIA" is a better way to refer to the agency because it avoids the word "intelligence."

There are a dozen reasons why the United States should not be engaged in the sort of activity the CIA specializes in, but you can reduce those to two:

1. Spying is illegal, immoral and unethical.
2. Spying doesn't work and it's a waste of money.

This would be a good time to get rid of most of what the CIA does because there's a common perception that we're in no imminent danger of attack from anyone. The common perception is important because it would make it easier to drastically cut CIA funds. You couldn't do it years ago when we'd all convinced ourselves the Soviet Union was poised to wipe us out. This was a popular belief which, for its own good, the CIA didn't discourage.

Intelligence agencies of every country work the same way. They convince citizens that they're about to be attacked by another country and, because of the threat, there's a need for all sorts of spy and intelligence activity. When the threat doesn't materialize, the intelligence agency doesn't admit it was wrong. It's smarter than that. It takes credit. It says the enemy didn't attack because it warned us so we built up our defenses. The enemy knew we were prepared so they changed their minds about attacking us.

The faulty intelligence provided us by the CIA about the Soviet Union for forty years, which neglected to inform us it was about to fall apart, cost us thousands of billions of dollars.

A nation's intelligence is wrong as often as it's right. How come we didn't know Saddam Hussein had as much nuclear strength as he did have?

How come we didn't have the information that North Korea was about to attack South Korea in 1950? The Cubans had weapons we didn't know about when we were thinking of going in there in the 1960s. How come we didn't know? Why couldn't our spies locate the hostages in Lebanon for six years?

The course of events in the world has been little changed by anything spies ever came up with. They make good movies and good novels but they aren't good for much else. The legendary Mata Hari of literature was a fabulously brave and beautiful woman. In the books, she is sentenced to death as a spy and, standing in front of a French firing squad, legend has it that she bared her breasts in the hope that the French soldiers would be too distracted to shoot. In actual fact, Mata Hari was a pretty unattractive prostitute who never got much useful information out of anyone.

Spies are, generally speaking, maladjusted social misfits who can't make a living at anything else. The spies of our country and the spies of the enemy are the same people. They're interchangeable. When you hear of defectors, it's almost always spies who defect, not other government officials. Spies defect more often because dishonesty is what they deal in and they get their kicks out of deception.

Intelligence agencies are impervious to the kind of inspection or criticism that other agencies of a democratic government are subjected to. When the CIA is questioned about anything, agency officials have a standard answer: "Sorry. Torture us but we're patriotic Americans. To reveal that information would compromise the security of the United States." They spend half their time not spying but trying to catch other spies.

There's a case to be made for collecting and interpreting information from and about foreign countries. That's why the CIA should be left with 25 percent of its budget but with none of its spies. The novelists of the future should have to go it alone.

STRAIGHTENING OUT
THE WORLD

O ne of my dominant memories of China is the indifference to cruelty to animals in some parts of the country. It's provincial and ugly-American of me to think of a nation with such a great and ancient tradition in that limited way, but that's what happens when you visit a foreign country for a short time. Your impression of it is inaccurate because you see so little.

Chinese farmers routinely strapped their pigs to flatbed carts and sat on them while their donkeys pulled the farmer and his pig to market. I wondered how the pig being sat on felt.

I know pigs are slaughtered and chickens beheaded here, and I suppose it is no consolation to the animals that we hide their demise from public view, but I confess to thinking it's more civilized.

In Kunming, I ordered chicken in a restaurant and as I waited for my meal, I gazed absently out the window onto the back courtyard. A Chinese man with a machete grabbed a chicken by the legs, whacked off its head, and dunked the whole thing into a vat of boiling water before plucking it. I lost my appetite for lunch, having seen it being prepared from the beginning.

Restaurants had tables with a small hole in the center about four inches in diameter. The tables could open and close from the middle. They'd take

a small monkey and close the table around its neck so only its head pro-
truded. The diners cracked open the monkey's skull, poured boiling water
over it, and ate the brains with chopsticks.

Caged dogs were routinely selected by restaurant patrons. They'd point
to one. The dog would be killed and cooked.

I write down these vignettes because I've been haunted by the memory
of not doing anything about what I watched.

"What did you do?" one of my children asked me years ago when I told
them about my memories of China.

I didn't do anything. That's why I can't forget them. I've thought ten
thousand times about what I could have done. How do you change the
attitude of a billion people toward animals? Or was it any of my business?
If I'm so kind to animals, how come I'm not a vegetarian?

Obviously nothing one American said to one Chinese farmer would
have made life or death any better for pigs in China.

What do any of us do when we are faced with an event that is terrible
to behold but beyond our ability to influence? Do we make a gesture or
turn our backs? Turning away seems wrong but can Americans educate the
whole world to the ways of what we think is civilized behavior? And are
we sure ours IS the civilized way? Can we eliminate barbarism, cruelty, war,
hunger and disease everywhere in the world? Should we try? I think not.

I'm torn between amusement and anger that the liberals in America—
and I think of myself as one—who complained about President Bush taking
us into a war against Saddam Hussein, shortly thereafter joined the conservatives by complaining because we didn't continue on into Baghdad and
eliminate Saddam Hussein at the time.

The fact is, there's too much wrong in the world for us to correct and
President Bush was probably as right about stopping Schwarzkopf short of
driving into Baghdad as he was right getting us into the war in the first
place. We did one good thing and the fact that it has often seemed, in
retrospect, as if the Kuwaitis didn't deserve it, is beside the point. Doing the
right thing is independent of the act's beneficence.

Television reports have, in the past, shown us heartbreaking pictures
of starving infants in the arms of their Ethiopian mothers, who were
themselves paper thin. Ethiopians are still starving but our cameras have
moved on.

There is just so much of the world's unhappiness we can take on as our
responsibility. We can't protect all the dogs and pigs and monkeys. We can't
feed all the hungry or free all the oppressed. Nothing the United States does
or doesn't do in Iran, Iraq, Syria, Jordan, Turkey or Israel, is going to have

any ameliorative effect on what happens in the Middle East. It's sad but it's true. We ought to help feed the starving people of the world when we can but there are too many terrible things happening in the world for us to tend to all of them. When we do one thing, we don't do something else. The best we can do is make the one little part of the world we know best as free from hunger, cruelty and dictatorship as we are able.

It isn't fair to ask all of us to worry about everything happening everywhere. There are events that are beyond our ability to control. If we try to solve everyone else's problems everywhere, instead of going about our business and making this at least one good country, we won't accomplish anything for anyone.

REINVENTING CIVILIZATION

If a nuclear war kills 90 percent of all of us and destroys civilization, will there be anyone left who'll know how to put our world back together? How will they start over? Will a new Thomas Edison come along and invent the light bulb again so we can see in the dark?

With the weapons we have, it is certainly possible that someday a minor country with a nut for a leader and the ability to make a nuclear bomb, is going to drop one. The country bombed, the United States for example, will retaliate with a bomb of its own. Poof! There goes most of civilization.

Suppose the only people left alive on earth were those in remote areas. There'd be some Eskimos, a few hundred thousand people in faraway areas of Africa, and some of the natives on remote Pacific Islands might survive the holocaust. There might even be a few hundred West Virginia coal miners who were three hundred feet down when the bomb hit, but the sophisticated civilizations in the crowded urban areas would be gone. All manufacturing facilities would be destroyed. Our books, our papers, and our records would be turned to ashes. You and I would be gone.

Would the people left alive repopulate the earth and rebuild the kind of civilization we have today?

It always irritates me to see some idiot who can't multiply nine times seven, driving a sophisticated car that it has taken engineers one hundred years to perfect. All a driver has to know how to do is press a few buttons, push some pedals with his feet, and turn the wheel in his lap in the direction he wants to go. He doesn't have to know anything about the machine he's driving. Except for the fact that I can't do it myself, it seems to me as though anyone who drives a car ought to know how one works and ought to know a little about how to fix one if it breaks.

Most of us have no idea how the things we use work. We turn on a light, switch on the television set or press the button on a computer and that ends our technical know-how. If it breaks, we don't know how to fix it. We climb in our cars, fasten our seat belts, turn on the ignition and that's all we know about a car.

Would people who had been smart enough to drive cars, use radios, open refrigerator doors, and turn on electric lights, but not smart enough to understand radio waves or electricity, be able to start all over and make those things? It doesn't seem so to me. I wonder if it would take more or fewer years to progress from zero to where we are today than it took us and our ancestors?

How long would it take people to reinvent the telephone or come up with a color television set . . . not to mention the remote-control device that changes channels for us from our chair across the room . . . and, of course, the Bud Light or Diet Coke we drink watching it? Would the natives of the island of Borneo set sail in dugout canoes to find a new world in Hawaii? Would there be new Christopher Columbuses rediscovering the new world? Who'd work out the multiplication tables and how long would it be before there was another Super Bowl?

The people left alive on earth would be isolated. They wouldn't know how to get to other parts of our world. When would the equivalent of the Wright Brothers come along among them and reinvent the airplane so they could fly there? How long after the Wright Brothers would we get a Charles Lindbergh in the postbomb world? Would there be anything to read while they waited? A new Shakespeare? A Hemingway?

The answer probably is "Yes. But in a few hundred thousand years."

If The Bomb is dropped—or maybe I should be saying "when" it is dropped—the people left won't have to start quite as far back as the cavemen did. They'll already have the wheel, and they'll know what electricity does, but they'll need brand-new geniuses like Alexander Graham Bell and the inventor of the toaster oven, to think up ways to use it.

I wonder if they'll start with black and white television and 78rpm records and work up to color TV and compact discs next time around, or will the new civilization have someone smart enough to go direct to color first? Or will there be anyone smart enough to do any of that?

And if civilization did ever get back to the point it's at now, would someone reinvent the nuclear bomb—and would someone else drop it again? It seems likely.

THE LOWERING OF THE LAMP

I t'll take another couple of hundred years but you can see it starting. The world and all the people in it are swirling around and mixing together like paint in a can. Differences are going to disappear.

It's transportation and communication that will do it eventually. Barriers, real and cultural, between countries will slowly break down. If we're lucky, the world will take the best of everything from each country. I think, for instance, that the Japanese will drop their chopsticks in favor of our knives and forks and they'll give up their language for ours because it's a better language than Japanese. Maybe, in exchange, we'll eat more rice and adopt some of their work habits. I hope the world learns to cook like the French and Hollywood learns to act like the British.

With radio and television it's inevitable that, eventually, the world will speak one language. It's too bad in a way, but inevitable.

We'll all have the same newspapers, read the same books, and use the same money. Already it's interesting to see how, just in the last twenty-five years, the food and cooking style of one nation has mingled with the cooking of others.

The food in London and Washington, D.C., is infinitely better than it was twenty-five years ago because each of those cities has had a great influx of good chefs from France, China, Japan and Mexico opening restaurants. Americans are stir-frying now with garlic, ginger and soy sauce.

This mixing of all the people of the world will be better for the poor countries and worse for the rich ones. We're rich, so, in some ways, it'll be worse for us in the United States. We'll all have to be a little poorer in order to make other nations richer.

In the U.S., we're feeling the pressure from Mexico, from Haiti, from South and Central America, Korea, Taiwan and a dozen other countries with vast numbers of people who want to come here . . . and we no longer want them to come.

Each new wave of immigrants is resented by the one immediately preceding it. In New York, Puerto Rican cabdrivers, who ten years ago couldn't speak English and were hated by the drivers with a European background who came after World War II, are complaining themselves now about all the Haitian cabdrivers.

Immigrants usually fill the jobs that pay least because they're willing to take anything to get started. The people who came here twenty years ago resent the newcomers because they'll do the job for less, so they get it. It's paradoxical that this country which was made what it is by immigrants, no longer wants them.

We should send a crew of a thousand workmen out to the base of the Statue of Liberty to chisel off those words that Emma Lazarus wrote so long ago. They no longer bear any relationship to the immigration policy of the United States. We aren't mean or heartless. There is simply no way we can take in everyone who wants to come here. The most liberal, kindhearted Americans among us don't want the wretched refuse of anyone else's teeming shore. We have our own poor, homeless masses.

The problem isn't unique to the United States. Every relatively prosperous nation has it. Half the population of India and Bangladesh would like to come to Great Britain. In France, the city of Marseille is overwhelmed by Algerians and Tunisians.

Germany opened its doors for many years after World War II and the Eastern Europeans flowed in. Now the Turks, for instance, who came there because they were needed, are no longer welcome because they are no longer needed.

Every country erects its own barriers—none higher than ours—but in spite of them, hundreds of thousands of immigrants get in anyway. They come illegally through holes in border fences and through legal loopholes.

The world seems to be becoming one big, unhappy family.

THE WORST OF US

The trouble is . . . and I mean the trouble with almost everything . . . the trouble is that about 10 percent ruin it for everyone.

That's the way it is with plumbers, garage mechanics, businessmen, doctors, lawyers, the homeless, taxpayers, blacks, whites, the rich, the poor, and politicians.

We acquire our prejudices from the worst of the species. We're right about that 10 percent being bad, but we're wrong when we extrapolate and conclude that "politicians are crooks," "businessmen are ruthless," "mechanics are robbers" or "the homeless are bums."

There are thousands of public servants doing good work as government officials in elected offices for less money than they could make in business but, as politicians, they are reviled because of the association we make in our own minds with a handful of politicians who get caught stealing every year.

A great many doctors who are more interested in medicine than money are forced to defend themselves from malpractice lawsuits by paying huge sums to insurance companies. If there were not a handful of careless or incompetent doctors and a handful of lawyers more interested in money than justice, doctors wouldn't need insurance at all. Doctors don't have the right to be inept or careless but they ought to have the right to be wrong sometimes.

Insurance would cost all of us 90 percent less than it does if it weren't for the bad apples who burn down their homes or places of business, report as stolen items that were not stolen, or strike a deal with their collision-repair place.

The average businessman is not a fat, cigar-smoking exploiter of cheap labor. He's a smart and able person who got ahead by working hard.

The tunnels under New York's Park Avenue, where the trains come into Grand Central Terminal, are home to a lot of the city's homeless. As I got off my train one day, I read one of the messages scribbled in chalk on a steel support that holds the street up off the tracks. It said, "THE RICH DIDN'T WORK FOR IT. THEY INHERITED IT." It read as though it were written by a college-age Communist of the 1930s. Most of the rich are rich not because they inherited money but because they worked better and harder. They certainly worked harder than the writer of that silly sign.

The police in half the communities in American don't have a much better reputation than the criminals because of a few dishonest cops who steal and their honest colleagues who know but don't report them.

When I go to a garage to have a car repaired, I'm suspicious. It's easy for a mechanic to con someone who doesn't know a spark plug from his elbow and the two or three times I've been taken by mechanics, have made me suspicious of all of them.

The homeless on the streets that the average big city dweller sees give the homeless a bad name. They aren't the people social agencies mean when referring to "the homeless." The visible homeless are the minority, the social misfits who are, for the most part, homeless by choice. They prefer to live free of any obligation whatsoever to anyone or anything. A home is an obligation they can't handle.

What we too often don't see is the silent, hidden majority of the homeless. They are the unfortunate families who have no place to go. We don't see destitute mothers with three children without food or a home. They're hidden from us.

We all get the impression of an evil world with evil people in it from the news. News is what's different and unusual. The bad people are unusual.

The action of the average citizen going about his business in a responsible way isn't reported because it's too common, too usual.

We get the impression the whole world's going to hell from a few people trying to lead us there.

ON GUARD

New York City has been decorated, in the last ten years, with hundreds of wonderfully attractive fruit stores run by Korean immigrants looking to make their way in their new country. The fruit stands provide cheerful evidence that America is still a land of opportunity for anyone willing to work hard and long hours.

The other evidence the fruit stands provide is not so cheerful. Coming to work every morning, I pass ten of these fruit stores with their colorful pyramids of oranges, grapes, pears, peaches, bunches of bananas and mounds of exotic fruit like mangoes and persimmons.

The stores all look the same. The husband and wife are inside arranging fruit and working the cash register. A younger Korean immigrant, usually one who doesn't speak much English yet, is stationed outside. If the store is on a corner, he stands at the corner so he can see both sides of the display of fruit. His only job is to stand guard against thieves and his presence ruins what is otherwise a pretty picture by reminding us of the pervasiveness of crime in the city. One out of three people at the fruit store has to devote all his time to security. It's about what we all pay for security.

The money and effort the fruit stores have to spend protecting themselves must cost them a substantial part of their daily income. It must also be why one pink grapefruit costs $1.15.

We've never had so much crime in America, major or minor, and it's costing all of us more than we know. The costs are hidden in taxes, insurance, rent, police, locks, fences, iron gates . . . and grapefruit. You don't write a check or charge crime to your credit card, but one way or another, you pay for it whether you're robbed or not.

Crime is contagious and we're having an epidemic. Teen-age muggers and robbers don't give a damn because they hardly ever get caught. If they are caught, they go free. If they do go to prison, they come out tougher and more likely to commit a violent crime than when they went in.

Our police can't handle crime. The courts can't handle it. Our prisons can't handle it. Crime is out of hand in America and prison is no more the answer to crime than charity is the answer to poverty.

In New York a middle-aged man was mugged and robbed on the subway. The man pulled a gun from under his coat and shot one of his assailants dead. It's a sad fact that all New Yorkers cheered. I cheered. Everyone advised the man who did the shooting not to turn himself in. He was a different kind of modern-day Robin Hood who didn't steal from the rich to give to the poor. He killed a mugger.

The dead young man turned out to have had a long police record. There was no reason at all why he shouldn't have been in prison except that the whole system of justice is an overflowing septic tank with no more room in it.

Young people steal because they live in a world where "everybody does it." They are governed more by what their friends think than by the law, and their friends don't think there's anything wrong with stealing.

There were more than two thousand bank robberies in California last year. California leads the league in bank robberies. Frequent as bank robberies are, the bankers involved in the Savings and Loan scam cost Americans one thousand times more than the robbers. The guys with the masks and guns steal petty cash compared to what dishonest bankers and stockbrokers take from the customers.

Michael Milken, one of the greatest thieves the world has ever known, probably wouldn't steal a grape from a fruit stand but he stole billions of dollars on Wall Street. Like the teen-agers, he must have said to himself, "Everybody's doing it. Why shouldn't I?"

What we need is some of those vigilant fruit-store guards on Wall Street.

CRIME ON WHEELS

The two boys were maybe sixteen or seventeen. I don't know whether to call them boys or men. They were tooling down the street, full speed, on their bikes. I say "their" bikes. One of them was on an expensive eight-speed model and the other struggled to keep up on a small bike made for an eight-year-old. I recall thinking, with my warped, prejudiced mind, that I doubted if either could produce a sales slip for those bicycles.

The two seemed to be in an awful hurry if they were just out for a ride, too, but I didn't think much more about it. I went into a small grocery store near the office, looked around, chose a container of blueberry yogurt from the refrigerator, and stood in line briefly to pay for it.

As I came out of the store a few minutes later, I saw two legs sticking out the door of a big, white Mercedes parked at the corner half a block away. They belonged to someone lying across the front seat. It was a strange sight and I stopped to look.

The boy on the small bike was by the car, looking up and down the street. The second bike was on the sidewalk. Obviously it was the second boy who was lying across the front seat of the car.

Suddenly the legs moved, and the body that went with the legs appeared, clutching a rectangular object with wires dangling from it. It was the Mercedes' radio.

I yelled "Hey!" which didn't make any sense, and started to run towards the two. That didn't make any sense either. They were off and gone before I got anywhere near them. And what would I have done if I'd reached them? Did they have guns? They undoubtedly had knives. What would they have done if I'd accosted them, put the radio back and say they were sorry? Or would they have stabbed me?

Trying to recall what I'd seen, like one of those memory tests, I realized what had taken place. When I first saw the two riding so fast, I think they had just broken the window of the Mercedes. Then they'd taken off and they'd ridden around the block, making sure no one was following them. In a few minutes, they'd returned to see if anyone was paying attention to the broken window. No one was—they wouldn't be in New York City— so the one boy removed the radio and the other was the lookout.

When I sat down at my desk later, I felt plain lousy. It was a petty crime but a mean one.

I wish they hadn't been black. Almost all that kind of crime in New York is done by young black men. If I were black I would be in a rage, not angry with the white society that created these racial problems several hundred years ago, but with wanton young blacks who are making it hard for whites to get over their prejudice and impossible for decent black people to get a fair chance.

Violent crime and theft rose more than 3 percent nationwide in 1988. People who live in the West were most apt to be victims, the Justice Department reported recently, while those in the Northeast were least likely to be attacked or have something stolen. If you live in the Northeast, you'd have a hard time believing that.

According to a poll, of every 1,000 people in the four sections of the country during 1988, 126 were victims of crime in the West, 103 in the

Midwest, 99 in the South, and 73 in the Northeast. I think that Northeast poll must have been taken in Northern Maine, Vermont, and New Hampshire, not in New York, Connecticut or Massachusetts.

When they come out with this year's crime statistics, I know one that won't be figured in. I never reported what I'd seen and owners of white Mercedes are ripped off so often, I'm sure that owner never did, either. There's so much crime in some parts of the Northeast and so few cops, many people don't bother.

That's the trouble these days. Crime pays.

My Neighbor, the Stranger

One night the sirens wailed and the lights flashed and the police cars came. The ambulance stopped in front of a house less than a block from ours. One of the neighbors had committed suicide.

That night I lay in bed thinking about the neighborhood. We don't really have one anymore. The days of going next door to borrow a cup of sugar are gone. If you run out of sugar, you drive over to the twenty-four-hour store and buy five pounds.

I did not know this neighbor's name. I would not have recognized her if she had knocked on our door. It seemed wrong to me, lying there that night, that we hadn't known she needed help. I don't know what we could have done, but neighbors should know when someone just down the street is desperate.

A woman from a small town in Connecticut wrote an angry article in *The New York Times* recently about the imminent closing of the local post office. She said, among other things, that a local post office is the one central point in a small town that brings people together.

A daily visit to the post office provides a purpose-filled walk for many people who don't otherwise get out of the house. In addition, those who went to the post office could learn to their sorrow that Mrs. Johnson's cat had one white paw missing and they could scan the evil faces of the ten most wanted.

The Postal Service is trying to operate like the big business it is and sentimentality doesn't enter into the decisions of a big business, so hundreds of post offices in small communities all across the country are being closed.

Everyplace we go, we're having fewer personal contacts. Bank clerks were always nicer people than bankers, and while the conversations were never long, I used to talk with a clerk at my bank named John, at least once a week for twenty-five years.

"People who used to cash checks for twenty dollars are cashing them for one hundred dollars now," he said once, and I stored that away as one of the few genuine pieces of information I had about our economy.

John was replaced four years ago with a machine into which I insert a plastic card. The machine then belches forth twenty-dollar bills at me. It tells me nothing, not even where to get change. There certainly aren't any good movies about bank robbers in Hollywood's future. The bank robbers today don't wear masks, they don't even come into the bank. They do it by juggling numbers in some remote office. It's all part of a widespread social estrangement that's affecting every area of our lives. Bank robbers aren't even meeting bank tellers.

When I was young, part of my education away from school was going to Evans' grocery store. Mr. Evans would get items down off the tall shelves with one of those pincers on a stick, and when I handed him the money my mother had given me with which to pay our bill, he'd tell me a lot of people couldn't pay him because of the Depression. That made me understand the Depression better than anything my fourth-grade teacher said about it.

It was the kind of information you don't get in a supermarket. This morning the only information presented to me at the store was that BABY WITH TWO HEADS IS TWICE AS SMART!

It was the headline on one of those grocery store newspapers and I didn't give it any more credence than I gave the headline on the paper next to it saying that Elizabeth Taylor is pregnant at sixty.

The gas station used to be another source of special information when the attendant, who filled your tank and washed your windshield, made change. He always knew about the accident over on the interstate last night and was ready with other bits of information not available elsewhere.

I hope no one's working on inventing an automatic hair-cutting machine. Some months, about the only news I get that isn't on television is from Manny, my barber.

The decline and closing of local post offices isn't the only way we're losing personal contact with each other. A hundred windows to our neighbors' worlds have closed to us in the past twenty years. We've lost touch with them. We peep in on the artificial lives of people in the television dramas and see less and less of our neighbors who are watching the same show.

We knew the problems Bill Cosby's family had on television and we knew they'd be solved. We don't see the ones next door that are not so easily solved. We don't see the neighbor about to commit suicide.

p a r t   s e v e n

. . .

THE FOLLOWING THINGS ARE TRUE

THE FOLLOWING THINGS
ARE TRUE

A great number of people are unsure of what's true and what isn't. From time to time, in an effort to help those who are confused, I present lists of things that are true. Herewith:

—More movies are too long than too short.

—In spite of any recession, prices always go up. They may not be going up as fast in hard times, but they still go up.

—If Beethoven was played as loud as rock music, I wouldn't like that, either.

—People don't think they really look like pictures of themselves.

—You don't see as many parakeets or canaries in cages as you used to.

—Chinese food isn't as popular as it was twenty years ago. Here, I mean. It's just as popular as ever in China.

—Self-service hasn't made gas any cheaper.

—A gas station attendant always screws the cap back on the tank tighter than I do.

—If there was no crime, local television news broadcasts would have to go out of business.

—Considering how poor they say they are in Russia these days, it's surprising how many of them wear those mink hats.

—Imelda Marcos' popularity in the Philippines is enough to shake your faith in democracy.

—Cough drops aren't much help when you want to stop coughing.

—We're all a little prejudiced about something.

—We make more friends than we have time to keep, but we make more enemies than we have time to fight, so it evens out.

—Believing there are differences in races doesn't make anyone a racist.

—It's surprising how convincingly someone who's guilty can say he didn't do it.

—There's a delicate balance between the pleasure of being with people and the pleasure of being alone.

—Things are at their worst when you can't sleep in the middle of the night.

—A lot of people spend too much time being careful.

—People who say that breakfast is their favorite meal don't enjoy food much.

—Getting up and down off the floor is easier when you're young.

—It doesn't snow as much as it used to and, furthermore, it never did.

—If you have a vague feeling you may have forgotten something, it's absolutely certain that you've forgotten something.

—The handicapped don't use many of the parking spaces set aside for them.

—We all assume we're smarter than when we were younger—but probably not.

—Licking a stamp or an envelope is a disgusting thing to do.

—No matter where you stood, the war in Vietnam was one of the worst episodes in American history.

—You get so used to what everyone looks like in their clothes that you don't think about what anyone looks like naked—and it's a good thing.

—When checking a cookbook, look for the noun, not the adjective. For molasses cookies, don't look for "molasses." Look under "Cookies, molasses."

—We're lucky the Japanese don't speak English.

—Generally speaking, shoes don't fit very well. We just get used to where they hurt.

—Cheerleaders with short skirts and megaphones are out-of-date and have no effect whatsoever on the performance of the team they are exhorting.

—People use coffee tables a lot more to put junk and magazines on than they use them to put coffee on, but the name sticks anyway.

—A dining room table twenty-nine inches high is too tall to eat from comfortably, but that's what most tables are. In some restaurants, the table is too high and the chair is too low.

—All television programs should be broadcast simultaneously on radio.

—Three-quarters of the homeowners in America never use their front door.

—Men's undershirts aren't long enough when you're working around the house Saturday because they pull out at the waist when you bend over.

—I don't drink beer from a bottle and I don't see why anyone ever drinks it from a can. I don't drink a beer very often and cannot imagine drinking two. When I drink a beer, it tastes best if I wet the glass and chill it in the freezer for a few minutes first. Two make me bilious.

—No one in prison for murder is guilty when they tell their story on television. I've never seen a guilty murderer.

—Two-door cars are a pain in the neck and I'm never buying another.

—They ought to play the second half of the Monday Night Football game first so we'd all know how it came out without staying up past midnight.

—It's apparent to me how old I am when I read in the paper that they're handing out condoms to kids in the New York City schools. I didn't know what one was in high school and wouldn't mention the word in mixed company to this day.

—The shades are always down in my office. If it's a beautiful day outside, I don't want to know.

—People who don't remember when you had to choke a car to get it started are lucky.

—When you come up to the checkout counter in the supermarket with a shopping cart full of groceries, the cashier always says, "Will that be all?" or "Is that it?" Does she think you're just leaving the stuff with her while you go get more?

—There is a definite difference between Coca-Cola and Pepsi Cola and one is clearly better than the other. I can't even drink the other.

—They say squid and octopus are catching on in American kitchens, but not in ours.

—Most kids in school like their teachers.

—Not many Americans could fill in a blank map with names of the United States even if it had the outline of the states on it.

—Stores with the cheapest merchandise use cheap bags that often break through at the bottom before you get to the car.

—If it wasn't so annoying, it would be amusing to hear politicians speak less than the truth most of the time.

—I'm fed up with stories every year about whether this is going to be a good or a bad Christmas for stores. There's just so much economic news I want at Christmas. What I want to know is, is it going to be a good year for *us?*

—It's hard to get used to your age no matter what age you are. The trouble is, you're that age for such a short time. Just when you begin to get used to it, you get older.

—When I hear a promotional ad on television for news shows and they tell me about a story they're going to have on tomorrow, I don't watch it. If they knew what the story was yesterday, it's not news, it's history.

—It's easy to start hating someone on a television news broadcast. If the newscaster's mannerisms annoy you, man or woman, you start paying more attention to them than to the news and it ruins the show for you. It accounts for why you hear people say, "I can't stand Peter Jennings. I hate Dan Rather. Tom Brokaw is terrible." Not to mention Andy Rooney, of course.

—Less than half the fresh fruit you buy is any good, but you keep buying it anyway. You're always hoping for that perfect tangerine, that perfect melon, that perfect peach or pear. Most fruit-store fruit rots before it ripens. Melons are the most expensive disappointment. Only one out of ten is any good. Unfortunately, that can be great.

—On vacation I sleep less. I hate to waste it.

—When you pump your own gas at a self-service place, it's hard not to end up with a little gas on your hands. There might be a market for a machine that dispenses little packets containing a piece of wet cloth or paper that you could clean your hands with. I'd pay a nickel but not a quarter. Maybe that's the business we'll go into.

—It's difficult to stop the gas pump on an even amount of money.

—You still see someone paddling a canoe on a lake or river once in a while, but I haven't seen anyone rowing a boat in years. The basic flaw in a rowboat has always been that you can't see where you're getting to.

—There's too much glass in a car on a hot, sunny day. We don't need all that windshield to see out.

—There are a lot of things around the house that aren't any good that I don't throw out.

—I've passed a lot of Christian Science reading rooms in cities around the country, but I've never seen anyone reading in one. I'm not sure whether they're for Christian Scientists or whether they're to attract people from other religions to Christian Science.

—People don't know much about any religion but their own—and a lot of times, they don't know much about that one, either.

—It's hard not to drop at least one sock or a piece of underwear when you're emptying the clothes dryer.

—The weather is almost always something other than normal.

—Hollywood movies are the best art America produces.

—I can't help wondering where all the Russians are today who bugged the hotel rooms of American visitors and spied on everyone who came there just a few years ago.

—The pencil that comes with an expensive pen and pencil set is never satisfactory. You have to be able to sharpen a pencil.

—If the mailman knew what I was going to throw out without opening, he could save both of us a lot of trouble by throwing it away before he delivered it. I'd like to give our mailman power of attorney over the mail.

—The best thing that's bad for you is butter.

—I can name everyone who lived on our block on Partridge Street fifty years ago. Most people don't know the names of all their neighbors today.

—Tying a shoelace is a small but satisfying thing to do.

—The lives of people who plan carefully don't go according to plan any more often than the lives of people who don't plan them at all.

—There are a lot of magazines with one or two articles in them that I want to read but the magazines are too expensive to buy for one or two articles. The time should come when we can each make up our own magazine from a computer index in our home and have every article we want to read from a lot of different magazines.

—Automobile tires are better than they used to be. Paper handkerchiefs like Kleenex, are not.

—If a bottle of wine is really good, you can't afford it.

—There aren't nearly as many shoe repair shops as there used to be because people don't wear out the soles and heels of shoes by walking on them much anymore.

—Learning how to type should be mandatory in grade school.

—When I was in high school, the final score of a basketball game was 38 to 29 or, at the very most, 47 to 36.

—There are some good things on television except when you want to watch. If there are two good things on the same night, they're opposite each other. There are usually some good things on the night you have to go out, too.

—It is comforting for people with illegible handwriting to know that a lot of brilliant people have terrible handwriting.

On the other hand, of course, a lot of dumb people don't write so you can read it, either.

—New clothes always look good in the mirror at the store, but I end up not wearing about half of all the clothes I buy.

—Stores have got to make a greater effort to have prices come out even so we don't get left with so many useless pennies.

—It would be good if there were some way to feed information to the brain intravenously.

—If I could start over, I'd be a much better person.

THE FOLLOWING THINGS
ARE TRUE ABOUT SPORTS

—There's more talk about money on the sports pages than in the business pages of the newspaper.

—Of all the balls we use to play games, the football is the most interesting. It was a crazy idea to play a game with a ball that isn't round, but it's worked out fine. As a matter of fact, the football is a work of genius. You can kick it or throw it as well or maybe even better than a round ball, and its bounce is just unpredictable enough to add an interesting element to the game.

—When I hear about a golf tournament, I still expect Arnold Palmer to win it.

—I saw Muhammad Ali referred to as "the best-known fistic gladiator the world has ever known."

Not by me, he isn't. I'd put two boxers ahead of Ali, both for well-knownness and fighting ability. They are Joe Louis and Jack Dempsey.

Sports heroes from one generation who never compete against each other are hard to compare. Some athletes remain well-known long after their playing days are over and sometimes after anyone is left alive who saw them play. The name Babe Ruth has probably survived the years better than any other sports figure. It's amazing, when you consider that he played before television, that Babe Ruth is still the best-known American sports figure of all time.

—What talent major league baseball managers have escapes me. Football coaches sound like Phi Beta Kappas by comparison. Baseball managers may have some brains, but I've never heard one with an education.

—I'm not clear why the man running a baseball team is called a manager while the one running a football team is called a coach.

—Another difference is in the way they dress. A baseball manager wears a baseball uniform to work. A football coach doesn't wear a football uniform on the sidelines, even though it wouldn't look any sillier.

—The game of baseball may be in trouble in the near future and it won't be simply because of the multimillion-dollar salaries of so many of its players. The biggest problem for baseball's future is, kids aren't playing it as much as they once did. In big cities, they're playing basketball instead.

There aren't any empty lots left, so the city kids are all over at the blacktop behind the school shooting baskets.

A sign of the problem shows in the makeup of major league baseball teams. Fewer than 18 percent of major league baseball players are black. In pro basketball, 72 percent of the players are black.

—When we were kids, we used to cut the cover off old golf balls and unwind the rubber string underneath. Someone spoiled our fun by saying a golf ball might explode if you cut into it, so we stopped playing with them.

—I don't resent the players' salaries being so high. What I resent is the price of a hot dog or a beer at the stadium.

—I'd rather play tennis indoors on a rainy day than outdoors on a sunny day.

—It's a mystery to me why there are no black jockeys.

—I love to watch a football game on television, but it's nowhere near as good as being there. If you're at the game, you watch what you want to watch. At home in front of the TV screen, you watch what someone else chooses to show you.

—Players for the home team ought not be allowed to encourage the crowd to drown out the opposing quarterback's voice when he's trying to call signals.

—It's surprising that so many cities and towns have enough open land left for golf courses. I should think members of most golf clubs would have voted to sell the land to developers. That's what I think of golf club members.

—I was thinking of taking steroids but I wouldn't know what to do with a lot of muscles if I had them.

—Sometimes when I'm watching a game, I hope a team wins so much that you'd think it really mattered.

—Sports announcers usually work in pairs and none of them seem to be clear in their own minds about whether they're talking to each other or to us.

—Some games are better on television than others. It makes a big difference how interesting the waiting time is between the action. There's a lot of time when nothing's going on in both football and baseball, but serious fans enjoy anticipating what their team's going to do next. The waiting time isn't dull.

Hockey is the worst sport on television and there's no waiting time.

That's partly true of basketball too, but there's so much scoring you can enjoy thinking about whether your team can catch up.

If you think hockey is a bad sport for television, try listening to it on radio sometime.

—A lot of men turn to the sports pages of their paper first, but that doesn't mean they think sports are the most important thing in the paper.

THE FOLLOWING THINGS ARE TRUE ABOUT HOT WEATHER

—Very little work gets done in hot weather. Everyone accomplishes more when it's cool or even when it's cold. This is true of whole countries, and accounts, in part, for the Third World.

—Even when some work does get done, it isn't usually good work.

—I would not buy an expensive Swiss watch made by someone working in a factory where the temperature was more than 90 degrees.

—When it's too hot to walk barefoot on the sand at the beach, it's too hot to go to the beach.

—Food doesn't taste as good in hot weather.

—People who say they don't like air conditioning—and there are a lot of them—are crazy. I don't know how the human race survived before air conditioning was invented.

—A car is the perfect sized space to air condition because it's so small.

—I do not really understand how air conditioning works. I suspect I am not the only one who doesn't. As far as I know, gas is compressed and as it becomes liquid under pressure, all the heat is squeezed out of it. The cold, liquid gas is passed through pipes and air is blown over the cold pipes at us. The stuff in the pipes becomes gas again and is fed back into the compressor, around and around. But I'm not sure.

—It seems as though the Earth would gradually get colder and colder as the sun burns down and gets less hot, but temporarily, at least, the Earth is getting warmer and warmer. I didn't think the Greenhouse Effect would be so immediate as it seems to be.

—It's cooler for a man to wear an undershirt in hot weather than to go without one.

—A swim isn't always the answer to a hot day. It usually involves some standing around in the hot sun and often you feel hotter and worse half an hour after you went in than you did before.

—The world is divided between people who look cool, collected and neat in hot weather no matter what clothes they wear, and others who look hot, sweaty and rumpled five minutes after they get dressed in the morning.

—I don't understand why car engines don't break down more often, all cooped up in there under the hood. The idea of having an air-conditioning unit in there with the hot engine is beyond my understanding. Doesn't it care?

—Neckties should be illegal once the temperature reaches 80.

—No matter how hot it is, you always see someone on the street wearing a coat or sweater.

—In the big cities, homeless men often keep their overcoats on all summer.

—In spite of all the warnings about how bad it is for the skin, you still see people lying in the hot sun all day. Craving for the sun seems almost like a sickness some people have, not unlike alcoholism. They have to have it and can't get enough of it.

—It's easier to lose weight in the summer. Not easy, but easier.

—As good as modern refrigerators are, anyone who isn't old enough to have been around when the ice man came every other day and put a fifty-pound block of ice in the ice box missed something. If you wanted a good, big, irregular chunk of the crystal-clear ice for a cold drink, you used an ice pick. If you got too big a piece, you cracked it with the heavy handle of the ice pick and put some of it back in the ice box.

—I feel sorry for hot dogs (the animals, not the food). Panting doesn't seem nearly as satisfactory as sweating. I don't know whether cats get hot or not. I don't know anything about cats because they don't talk to me like dogs do.

—People who like it hot call it "warm weather." In Arizona people who like it hot say "at least it's a dry heat." They can have it. In New York it's usually too hot in July and August and part of either June or September, but at least it rains once in a while and cools off the sidewalks. Barry Goldwater once told me the desert gets in your blood. I've spent some time in Arizona and it never got in mine.

—It always seemed to me that the world would logically end when the fire went out and the earth got stone cold. Now it looks as if the end might not be cold but hot.

—Too hot is a worse way to go than too cold.

C'EST LA VIE

It's too bad that:

—Our clothes don't get bigger when we do.

—People aren't as nice as dogs.

—Yelling at a television set doesn't help.

—There isn't a way to pipe information directly into the brain without having to go through the time-consuming process of learning.

—You can't tear a twenty in half when you need a ten and they don't have change.

—There isn't a lock that opens when you say a code word.

—The best things in life aren't free.

—It isn't always winter when it's supposed to be winter and summer when it's supposed to be summer.

—There's no tomorrow.

—The President we elect isn't always the smartest man in America.

—People don't practice what they're preached at to practice.

—Newspapers don't print the names of people with gun permits.

—It's olive oil, not heavy cream, that's good for us.

—Someone doesn't invent an automatic bedmaker.

—They don't publish the names of all the people who buy lottery tickets and lose.

—They don't print a dictionary where you could look up how to spell a word without having to know how to spell it first.

On the other hand, it's a good thing that:

—Birds can fly and cats can't.

—There are people who want to be nurses.

—We don't have to wear seat belts in our living rooms.

—"Thou shalt not get caught" isn't one of the Ten Commandments.

—More than 99 percent of the population are either honest or haven't been caught, because less than one percent of all Americans are in prison.

—Oranges look pretty, taste great, and are good for you anyway.

—There isn't much on television that's good. If it was all good, we'd never take time to do anything else.

—Grass doesn't grow when it snows or we'd have to mow and shovel, too.

—No one has come up with the idea of publishing a swimsuit edition of the Bible.

—There are people who hate Florida and California because if there were not, everyone would move there.

—Politicians usually turn out to be better and more honest after they're elected than they were when they were making campaign speeches.

—Shakespeare wrote *Hamlet* when he did because he probably couldn't get anyone to publish it today.

—We can't hear what the driver in the other car is saying about us.

IT ONLY HAPPENS IN THE MOVIES

Alot of things happen in the movies that never happen to me:

—When two men come up a long flight of stairs in a movie and stop to knock on a door, they almost always have to break it down to get in. When I knock on a door, someone usually comes to it and opens it to see what I want.

—When a lone person comes into a house or an apartment and starts looking around, he or she almost always finds a body on the floor in the living room. In all the years I've come into thousands of living rooms, I've never found a body on the floor.

—Cars in movies routinely screech around corners at high speed, spin 360 degrees, and continue on. I have never done this in my own car and I have never seen it done on any of the streets I drive on.

—The long road, winding through the woods, leading to the big house on the hill in movies, is longer than the driveway to the house of anyone I've ever known.

—When a man sitting behind a desk is confronted by someone un-friendly who comes into his office, there is almost always a gun in the drawer when the man opens it. I have seen a lot of desk drawers, but I've never seen a gun in one.

—The stairways actors go up and down are always wider and longer than the stairs in our house.

—Although I don't know anyone whose house has them, the average home in most movies seems to have sliding, glass-paneled doors leading out to a stone patio overlooking the swimming pool.

—The women around the swimming pool and lying on the sand in movies are better-looking than any I've ever seen around a pool or at the beach.

—I have never seen a fight in a bar where they threw chairs and broke the mirror behind the bottles.

—The only time anyone in a movie watches television is when there's a news show on with an item about a murder committed by the person watching.

—No one in a movie making a phone call ever gets a wrong number or a busy signal.

—Whenever a big car pulls up in front of a building, there's always a parking place for it. I haven't seen a parking place in front of any building I want to go to in twelve years.

—The cars have all been washed recently, too. You never see a dirty car in the movies.

—I've seen hundreds of them in mysteries, but I have never actually met a real, live butler, or even heard of anyone who has.

—In a picture, when someone is stranded or abandoned out in the middle of nowhere, on a road that stretches straight for as far as the eye can see in both directions, at least three cars and two big trucks always go whizzing past before anyone stops. The person who stops often has something to do with the plot.

—If a good guy in a movie sneaks into an office in the middle of the night to look for something in the files, someone always comes in and catches him.

—The average person in a movie seems to own a yacht and there's usually someone really bad on board. I have a small wooden boat but I never just barely pull away as someone runs down the dock trying to get on board.

—No one in the movies reads in bed.

—You can tell the good guys from the bad guys by looking at them on the screen a lot easier than you can in real life.

A CONN JOB

It's been almost thirty years now since the U.S. Postal Service officially changed the initials we're all supposed to use when we abbreviate the name of a state in an address, and I never got used to the new abbreviations. We live in Connecticut and I still abbreviate it "Conn." The Postal Service wants "CT." They don't use periods after their abbreviations, which is a break for us, but as far as I'm concerned, "Conn." says a lot more about my state than "CT" does.

It's not just my own state I feel that way about, either. I say the same for "MA," formerly "Mass.," and "TN," once "Tenn."

I wish the Postal Service would look again at abbreviations. Their idea was to limit them to two letters instead of three or four to make it easier, and therefore faster, for them. Have you noticed your mail getting there sooner since they started insisting on the new abbreviations? It may serve their purpose but it doesn't serve ours.

I don't know what genius worked out the new state abbreviations but they don't make sense. For example, they shortened Wisconsin to "WI" from "Wis.," but they shortened Pennsylvania to "PA" from "Penn." Now, if Wisconsin's going to be "WI," then Pennsylvania ought to be "PE," not "PA."

If they followed the pattern of using the first two letters of a state as its abbreviation, Montana would be "MO." Even the Postal Service was smart enough to know that Missouri staked out "MO" for itself years ago, so they didn't change that, but the Postal Service is at its worst abbreviating the eight states beginning with M. Montana got the abbreviation "MT." If you don't live there, however, you have to stop and think what "MT" stands for—other than mountain, and we don't have a state named Mountain.

To call Michigan "MI" instead of "Mich." is wrong. "Mich." has a sound to it all its own and, furthermore, "MI" could be anyone of three other states, Minnesota, Missouri, or Mississippi.

To further compound the problem they gave us with the M states, Mississippi was changed from "Miss.", which sounded good and appropriate for Mississippi, to "MS." "MS" makes Mississippi sound as though it had something to do with women's rights, which it hardly ever does. And, while I know you're not supposed to pronounce these abbreviations, the sound of what they look like is bound to come to your ear, so it's "Jackson Mizz."

Alabama was "Ala.," but the Postal Service changed it to "AL" without our permission. The trouble with "AL" is that it could also be Alaska. Alaska is now "AK." Arkansas might have been assigned "AK," but instead, Arkansas drew "AR." What does "AR" bring up in your mind when you read it? Probably Arizona, but Arizona was assigned "AZ."

California was shortened from "Cal." to "CA" and "Neb." to "NE." I prefer the old abbreviations in each case and still use them.

There are some Postal Service abbreviations that I concede may be an improvement. For instance, "OK" in place of "Okla.," "KY" for "Ken." and "VT" in place of "Ver." seem good.

Some state names simply don't take kindly to being abbreviated at all and never should be, no matter what the Postal Service says. How much time or space is anyone going to save abbreviating Ohio, Utah or Iowa? There's no good way to abbreviate Hawaii and it should be spelled out every time. The Postal Service's designation for Hawaii is the ridiculous and demeaning "HI."

Four of our states are "New": New York, New Jersey, New Mexico and New Hampshire. There isn't much you can do with those in two letters except "NY," "NJ," "NM" and "NH."

I like the names of a lot of our states. In a few cases the abbreviations are good enough so you don't need the whole name but, generally speaking, I think it would be best if we all took the time to spell out the whole name of most states when we have occasion to write them down. "WA" does not begin to say what a good state Washington is.

The beautiful state of Maine is listed as "ME." Not good enough. When I want to write to someone in Maine, I'm going to spell it M-A-I-N-E, no matter what the U.S. Postal Service wants.

part eight

THE ABSENT MIND

THE ABSENT MIND

The following went through my head as I was lying in bed, not sleeping. I play both parts in the conversation.

"That woman I saw from behind at the museum the other night was an attractive, intelligent, college-educated woman about fifty-one years old."

"Are you sure?"

"Yes, I'm sure."

"If you were behind her, how do you know she was attractive?"

"I don't know. I just know."

"How do you know she was fifty-one?"

"You know, just the way she was. The way she walked. I don't know. You can tell."

"How can you tell? Can you even be sure it was a woman you were behind?"

"Listen, I know a woman when I see one."

How do we decide these things in our little minds? There's something going on in our brains that we don't know about. I'd hate to have to put down on paper the reasons I know I was walking behind a woman in the museum, but I know I was. She looked like a woman, that's all . . . but what exactly does a woman look like that a man doesn't?

Furthermore, why did I decide she was fifty-one and attractive? I'd be willing to bet ten dollars she wasn't more than a year off fifty-one. Someone fifty-one looks just slightly different from someone either forty-nine or fifty-three. What that difference is, I can't say.

We have these little computers in our heads that riffle through a million impressions stored in our brains and the brains end up pointing at a sign that says to us "Woman, good-looking, smart, educated, married, kids." We call it instinct sometimes, but instinct is too vague a word for what it is. It's better than instinct.

Our brains often come up with the right answer from very little evidence. When we come into a restaurant we've never been in before, we can tell within the first thirty seconds whether it's any good or not.

It would be difficult for any of us to say exactly how we know. We just do. It's experience gained when we entered all the other restaurants we've ever been to in our lives. That's the way it is with everything. Our sense of things is sharper than a razor's edge—including our sense of women we see from behind, walking in museums. That computer in our head with a memory for everything we've ever known, goes to work and hands us our opinion on how old she is with a little bit of her probable history.

The thing that's too bad is that we can't direct this cognitive power better than we do. It works but it works at random, not necessarily at our bidding. Thoughts come into our minds we wish we didn't have and we can't always call up or focus on the ones we want to have. I imagine even the Pope has thoughts come into his head, unbidden, that he wishes he wasn't having. But he has them.

The thinking we want to do is as hard to control as the thinking we don't want to do. I just get my mind going on something and it wanders off. The other day I was talking about measuring lumber and I wanted to figure out what percentage $2\frac{3}{8}$ was of $3\frac{3}{4}$. I could not force myself to do it. I knew the knowledge of how the mathematics should be done was back there in my mind someplace, but I couldn't make it go to work on the problem.

We read Shakespeare or we read about what Einstein discovered, and even though we couldn't have done what either of them did, we understand it. We say, "Hey, yeah. Great! Why didn't I think of that?"

If we can say, "Hey, yeah. Great! Why didn't I think of that?" on reading a passage from Shakespeare, it must mean the thought was already somewhere in the recesses of our brains but we had never bothered to call it forward.

It's why, when I write something like this, I don't worry about whether readers will understand it or like it. I have the same attitude toward everything I write. If it's true for me, it's true for everyone. If they don't get it, I didn't say it right.

THE NUMBERS GAME

While I'm nervous about the possibility I'm wrong, I'm determined not to feel inferior to the people who do numbers. By "do" numbers, I mean people who understand numbers and keep track of the ones that are important to their lives.

The numbers people know to the penny how much they have in their bank accounts. When their checks come, they look at them and know what all the deductions are for.

These numbers people pay their bills on time, answer their mail, keep dates on their calendar for months in advance and the rich ones among them understand the difference between a money market fund and a tax-free municipal bond. I have to think about which is which when a financial reporter on television talks about a "bull market" or a "bear market."

No matter how superior I may feel in my own mind to people with the bookkeeper mentality, I'm afraid the people who know about the numbers in their lives are winning. Everything that happens suggests they're taking over and, to make things even harder for the rest of us, there are more numbers in our lives every day and more forms to fill out. The numbers people make sure of that.

I just hope I can make more money working than they can save during the time they spend checking all the numbers.

Someone does my taxes for me. If there were a law saying every citizen had to fill out his own forms, I'd be in prison. There are other bookkeeping chores that I can't hire someone to do and I'm failing these.

My car is due for its ten-thousand-mile inspection but I can't find the certificate that came with the car providing the inspection free, and the cost of materials like oil. I guess I'll have to have it done and pay them.

There was a meeting of the Directors Guild, of which I'm a member even though I don't direct anything. If you don't attend the meeting, write them an excuse or send them someone's name as a proxy to vote for you, you're fined fifty dollars. I didn't write to say I was on vacation. I guess I'll have to pay them the fifty dollars.

I forgot to pay my VISA bill before I left the office and I just got another notice with finance charges. I know the bank makes its money on those exorbitant finance charges and I try to beat them by always paying on time. I blew it this month.

The small computer I've been writing on has some problems. I got a two-year warranty when I bought it six months ago, but I can't find the warranty and anyway, I never mailed in all the papers I was supposed to. I'm sure I'll have to pay for the repair myself. Score another one for the bookkeepers.

The only grocery store within twenty miles of here has automated its checkout counters. Monday I bought $43.10 worth of meat, chicken, vegetables, soap, paper towels and soft drinks. If any grocery store wants to cheat me, they could do it without any trouble at all. I cannot, nor do I bother to try to, read their tape printouts of what I've bought and how much it cost. I do not stand at the cashier's counter checking each item as the cashier rings it up. I know numbers people who do that and they often catch cashiers in mistakes. While I don't think cashiers deliberately cheat, it's strange that when there's a mistake in a bill, whether in a grocery store or a restaurant, the mistake almost always favors the establishment, not the customer.

People who do numbers well get places on time. They read directions first before they go someplace or try to put something together. They plan their lives. They can set their VCR for next Tuesday at nine-thirty. They know by heart their bank account number, their Blue Cross Blue Shield number, their cholesterol number, their Social Security number and the license plate numbers on both their cars.

I hate these people and I wish I were one of them.

VERY TRULY NOBODY'S

By strange coincidence—coincidence is always strange—I got two letters on the same day, each from a very different part of the country, complaining about conventional ways of starting and ending letters. The two who wrote didn't approve of starting every time with "Dear" or ending with "Sincerely."

Mark Stuhlfaut of Plymouth, Minnesota, wondered how truly yours someone is who signs a letter "Yours truly."

He envisions a scene where he comes home from the office and greets his wife.

"Oh, honey, I brought Jane home. She wrote me a letter saying she was very truly mine. Can I keep her?"

In the second letter, Bernard Brener of Sherman Oaks, California, says, "I wish you could do something on the nonsense involved in 'proper' letter writing where the polite forms of address are: 'My dear Mr.:,' 'Dear Sir:' etc., etc., and ending letters with 'Sincerely yours' or 'As always.'

"Very few people I write to," Mr. Brener says, "are 'My dear' anything, nor am I 'Sincerely' theirs.

"These high school proper-letter-writing formalities should be put to rest," Mr. Brener concludes.

I have a question for both my correspondents: How would you two suggest we start our letters and end them? Would we have to scratch our heads and think of a new and original way every time? Or would we start simply "Ed" instead of "Dear Ed"? Is this really a big step forward in human relations? Will the world get better and all the people in it happier, if we stop beginning all our letters with "Dear" somebody? And ending them "Sincerely"? I don't think so.

Even if you don't like the person you're writing to, and even if you haven't laid everything on the line in your letter, it's best to address the person as "Dear" and end it with "Sincerely."

I personally never go any further than that. I mean, I don't begin "My dear Mr. Smith" or end "Very sincerely," "Most sincerely," or "Sincerely yours." Just plain "Dear" and "Sincerely" does it for me.

The tradition among journalists is to conclude with "Regards." I don't know where it came from, but I observe it with my newspaper friends.

One problem bigger than the dear-and-sincerely one is whether to call a person "Mr.," "Mrs.," "Miss," "Ms.," or call the person by his or her first name. It often seems friendly and nice to use the first name, even when it isn't really proper because you don't know the person you're writing to.

The simple fact is, there are certain conventions that save a lot of time in almost everything we do. We have to take advantage of these conventions or we'd never get anything done. You can't start at the beginning every time with everything and establish a new form. We know which side of the road we drive on and we do it the same way every time. We know the big hand points to the minute on our clocks and watches and the little hand to the hour. Convenient convention.

The civility of starting our letters with "Dear" has been a satisfactory arrangement over the years. Civilization is always in danger of falling apart and being taken over by the boors and the uncivil know-nothings. Every little tradition we can maintain that makes us more civilized is worth preserving. The loud and public use of foul language is objectionable for this reason. We all know the words, but it is agreed, among civilized people, that we don't use them in public conversation. We have to work at being civilized. It doesn't come naturally to us.

I agree there's something a little strange about "Dear" and "Sincerely" if you take them literally but they've been civilizing and convenient tools. We don't have to think about them when we write a letter. We know how to get started and know how to end and all we have to do is fill in the middle part.

A VOYAGE AROUND
CHARLES DARWIN

The writers are writing it faster than the readers are reading it. Every year tens of thousands of new books are written and published. The tens of thousands of books written last year and the year before that and ten years ago and one hundred years ago are pushed farther back on the library shelves, some never to be opened again.

I suppose that, as a book writer myself, that may seem worse to me than it does to you. Still, I can't help thinking that book publishers ought to regularly look through their library of previously published books and choose a few of the best ones to reissue. Is everything written this year better than what was written last year? Has everyone already read the old books? I don't think so. It seems too sad to let a good book die just because it wasn't written this year.

We inherited a fourteen-volume set of books by Charles Darwin written in the late 1800s. I only know Charles Darwin for his great work *The Origin of Species*. It's one of the classic "100 Great Books" and, while I'm familiar with its contents in a general and superficial way, I've never read it.

Everyone who believed the literal truth of the biblical story of Adam and Eve as the first man and woman on earth was angry at Darwin when he proposed the theory that man evolved from the apes through millions of years of gradual improvement in a process he called "natural selection." Even his wife, Emma, was critical of him. Today no one with minimal education or intelligence accepts Adam and Eve.

A few months ago, I was looking over the rows of books on our shelves when my eyes lit on one of Darwin's red-leather-bound volumes. It was called *Voyage Around the World*. I took it down and started reading and I've been embarrassed ever since by how little I knew of the greatness of Charles Darwin as a writer. I'm going to read all of them. There's another called

The Expression of the Emotions in Man and Animals, in which Darwin analyzed things such as why it is the corners of the mouth turn up when we're happy and smile, and down when we're displeased and frown . . . for about five hundred pages.

Quite aside from his brilliant scientific mind, Darwin wrote beautifully and was a fascinating reporter of small details of his five-year trip around the world.

"After having been twice driven back by heavy south-western gales," he begins on the first page, "Her Majesty's ship Beagle, a ten-gun brig under command of Captain Fitz Roy, sailed from Devonport on the 27th of December, 1831."

After stating the purpose of the trip, he writes of first landing in the Canary Islands after more than a year at sea.

"On the 6th of January, 1833, we reached Teneriffe but were prevented landing by fears of our bringing the cholera."

Ten days later, the *Beagle* arrived at a Canary island called St. Jago and they were allowed by the natives to get off the boat.

"The scene, as beheld through the hazy atmosphere of this climate, is one of great personal interest," Darwin wrote, "if indeed, a person fresh from a long voyage at sea, and who has just walked, for the first time in a grove of cocoa nut trees, can be a judge of anything but his own happiness."

He drops little gems like that in everywhere among his scientific observations about the plants and animals.

I'll bet that a paperback edition of any of Darwin's books would sell today. One thing's certain, Darwin would make a great guest on one of the morning television shows. Maybe they could talk him into coming on to plug his book, *Voyage Around the World.*

THE LOVE THAT'S
EASY TO HATE

The good word "love" has been watered down and almost ruined by our repeated use of it in situations where love is not really what we mean.

"I love chocolate ice cream."

Really? In what comparative amount do you love it? Do you love it as much as you love your mother, your children, your husband, your wife?

"Ruth loves a good laugh."

"Ed loves baseball."

"I'd love to know who does your hair."

What we mean most of the time we use the word "love" is "like." We LIKE chocolate ice cream. Love is an emotion that should not be wasted on ice cream. It should be saved for more important occasions.

The standard wedding ceremony uses love in another way that has seemed wrong to me since the first church wedding I ever went to ended in divorce two years later.

"Do you, Jonathan, and do you, Ellen, promise to love, honor and obey until death do you part?"

"I do."

"I do."

Do you really, children? Do you know what you're promising? It's possible that you can promise to honor and even possible you can promise to obey, but love is not something you can promise. You can't discipline yourself to feel it. It is not an emotion that can be called forth on command or dismissed at will. You feel it or you don't and no amount of willpower can produce it if it doesn't come unbidden.

No one who ever married could honestly promise to love his or her husband or wife for the rest of life. It is a ridiculous promise for a clergyman to ask a couple to make under threat of not performing the marriage if they refuse.

To "make love" seems like a bad use of the word love, too. It's another example of diminishing the importance of a good word by using it as a euphemism for an act which has no socially acceptable word to describe it. "Love" is not usually what two young people who hardly know each other are making at all. They are satisfying a basic urge. They are scratching an itch. What they are doing has nothing whatsoever to do with love.

Love of a country seems more acceptable and probable than love of chocolate ice cream. I have felt love of a country most often when I've been farthest from it. If you saw the Star-Spangled Banner in Berlin in 1945 or over the U.S. Embassy in Moscow and felt that tingle down your spine, it would be hard to deny love to even so inanimate an object as our flag. Love of home, school, hometown are in the same category and might be said to have legitimately elevated themselves beyond the category of "like." This might be an argument, but you'd have to concede that using the word in relation to your country is less objectionable than using it for how you feel about the taste of chocolate ice cream.

For the most part we save love for the things that give us the most satisfaction and comfort. As soon as they don't, love wanes. Bye-bye, Miss American Pie. This accounts for love of country, the love of newlyweds, the enduring love of some lucky married couples and the love of a child for its mother—and to some lesser extent, its father. The kid has been fed and kept warm by this person. Forget the romance, being comfortable with someone is what produced or perpetuates true love.

It's interesting that we use the word "hate" as loosely as we use "love."

"I love chocolate ice cream but I hate whipped cream on it."

Even though we use "hate" casually like that, when you tell someone you hate them, it's irrevocable. You may have said "I love you" a thousand times, but those words roll off like rain hitting a tin roof. If, on the other hand, a woman looks a man in the eyes and says, "I hate you," there are not enough "I love yous" in life to make him forget you said it.

You Can't Miss It

The newspaper editors and television producers who have to fill space and time on the slow news days around Labor Day usually tell us to drive carefully.

I'd be curious to know how many lives have been saved or how many people drove more carefully because someone on radio or television told them to. None, do you think? That's what I think. People drive the way they drive.

Years ago, I got some statistics that fascinated me, although no one else seemed interested. Overall deaths in the United States tend, for some unexplained reason, to be lower on both the Fourth of July and Labor Day than on other days and the number of traffic accidents and the number of deaths on the highways are lower on those two days, in relation to the number of cars on the road, than on normal summer weekends.

In pure numbers, there are more highway accidents on those days but only because there are more cars on the road. Fewer people are home so fewer die falling off ladders and from other accidents around the house. This more than makes up for the number of fatalities on the road.

Getting good directions is harder than staying out of trouble on the highways. It would save a great deal of trouble if all of us were taught in school how to give directions and how to read a map. It would be best if we could be taught how to read a map while driving a car but I don't suppose they'd do that.

A typical exchange goes like this when a driver leans out the window of a car to shout a question:

"Pardon me. Could you tell me how to get to Middletown?"

"Middletown?"

"Yes. I'm trying to get to Middletown."

"The best way?"

"Sure. Shortest way."

"Gee, I really don't know."

Couldn't this fellow have told me right up front that he never heard of Middletown? I could have been a mile down the road in the wrong direction in the time it took me to find out he didn't know any more about how to get there than I did.

Experienced travelers know that when someone tells you to turn right at the third traffic light, it is almost certainly either the second, fourth or fifth traffic light, not the third. This is because people are careless counting but it's also because we do not have any rules about giving directions that we all learn in school and agree on.

For example, when you stop for a light and ask directions and are told, "Go down here three lights . . ." it ought to be universally agreed either that you count the light directly in front of you or that you don't begin counting until the one after that.

And while they're teaching a course in giving directions in school, they might also give a course to the people who put up direction signs.

Very often there will be a sign immediately before an exit ramp that says, "MIDDLETOWN NEXT EXIT." Does the person who put up the sign mean the very next exit, the one right in front of you, or does he mean the one after the next exit? If the sign doesn't mean you should get off right there for Middletown, it should read, "MIDDLETOWN NEXT EXIT AFTER THIS ONE."

So, if you're driving this weekend, buckle up but relax. You're going to be okay. (I doubt if anyone who doesn't usually buckle up does it because he's told to by some do-good person in the newspaper or on television, either.) And if you're going to Middletown, follow this road until you see a big brick house on the left and then . . . wait a minute. That's Middleburg. I don't know how you get to Middletown.

THE DEMON BEHIND
THE WHEEL

It was warmer than usual in the Northeast Saturday and, driving along a residential street near our house, I saw a small boy, no more than six years old, careening along the sidewalk on a tricycle. He was going as fast as his little legs could push the pedals, his head bent low between the handlebars, his elbows sticking out like wings.

This little demon wasn't going anywhere except to the corner so he could turn around and come back, but he was getting there as fast as he could.

There's something about wheels that turns a lot of us into demons. It's a disease. I was in Savannah recently, driving a rented car. As I came up to a light, there was a car stopped, but the driver had left enough room between himself and the curb for me to squeeze in. I squeezed in and, when the light changed, I took off. At the next light, the man in the car pulled up next to me, looked over, and obviously recognized me as lovable old Andy Rooney.

I was embarrassed. Why in the world had the fact that I was on top of four wheels turned me into a child on a tricycle? Where was I going in that much of a hurry? At this moment, I can't recall where I *was* going. All I know is, I was in a hurry to get there.

If I'm walking down the street with someone in front of me, I don't have any great desire to break into a trot so I can catch and pass whoever it is. When we get to the corner, I don't wait until the light changes and then try to beat him off the curb so I can get to the other side first. What happens to me when I'm on wheels? Did the genius who invented the wheel build this demon into it?

Why is everyone the enemy when I'm rolling? Why do I feel such a great competitive urge to pass everyone in front of me? In the summer, I regularly make a drive of 150 miles twice a week and I stay awake because I get a little thrill of victory each time I pass another car on the road. When I reach that highway, I see in my mind one stretch of road 150 miles long, filled with cars from here to there, each one of which I want to pass. I feel as defeated when some idiot going faster than I am passes me as I feel victorious when I put someone behind me.

I wouldn't be writing this if I thought I was the only man in America who drives like that. There are millions of us and I don't believe the devil comes with the invention because women, generally speaking, are not possessed by him behind the wheel and above the wheels, as men are. (As all we demons know, women drivers can't get out of their own way.)

I don't try to beat anyone to an empty seat in the theater as I would try to beat them to a parking place in the mall. Day after day, I am a normal, average, everyday kind of law-abiding citizen . . . except when I get behind the wheel of a car.

The 55mph speed limit is nothing more than a mark on my speedometer several notches below the speed I'm traveling. When I pass it, I start dividing my attention between the rearview mirror, looking for cop cars, and the windshield, looking for cars to pass.

The first time I ever thought much about wheels was when I went to see cowboy movies at the Madison Theater. The stagecoach, with the new schoolmarm inside, was often racing to get away from the bad guys who were trying to hold it up, and the wheels on the stagecoach always appeared to be turning backwards.

I didn't think much about wheels after that until I read where the American Indians didn't have wheels. Even though the wheel was invented so long ago that no one knows who did it, North American Indians didn't have wagons or wheelbarrows when the Europeans arrived. They were still using sledges to move anything heavy.

It sure would have been a different world if the wheel had never been invented. For one thing, someone I cut off in Savannah wouldn't be hating me today.

NOTHING COMES

Things don't come, we all know that. A check in particular never comes, or at least when it finally does come, you've waited so long for it that you've already spent it. The amount of the check, and more, is in bills or on your credit card. It's as if you never got the check. It's gone before it comes when it comes late.

A letter from someone you'd like to hear from doesn't come. There are all sorts of letters and bills and advertisements in the morning mail but the letter you want is not there. A good letter comes by surprise. It never comes if you're waiting for it.

Our mailman is very good, but don't wait for him because he comes only when you don't care whether he comes or not. Sometimes he even comes when you'd rather he didn't come.

One of the great mysteries of life is why things don't come. You hear people refer to "The Second Coming" but even that doesn't come.

I learned early in life that things don't come, and knowing it has saved me a lot of unhappiness. I protect myself from the disappointment that comes with things not coming by saying to myself in advance, "It probably won't come." And, of course, it doesn't, so at least I have the satisfaction of knowing I was right.

When my mother bought me a new suit or a coat or a pair of pants at McManus and Riley's clothing store, the salesman always wanted to send it but I wouldn't let him. I took it with me. The man would say things like, "The pants are a little long. We'll have our tailor shorten the pants and send them to you."

I wouldn't stand for it. I took the pants with me even if they were a little long. I knew that if I didn't, the pants would probably be too short by the time they came because I'd be older and taller.

Carpenters, plumbers, electricians, washing machine and television repairmen never come. It doesn't matter how many times you talk to them on the telephone about when they're going to arrive, they don't show up. I don't know what it is about repairmen. They're often good, hardworking, honest people but it takes them longer to repair things than they ever anticipate, even with their long years of experience. They have to stay longer on one job than they thought they would, so they're late for the next. One job runs into the next until, by the end of the week, they're a month behind.

You'd think that painters, after painting all their lives, would know how long it takes them to paint something, but they never do. I think they forget that it takes time to get ready to paint. They only remembering painting, and preparation takes longer than painting.

Each of us has lived all our lives with things that don't come. In college I had a chance to go to New York City with a professor and a bunch of the guys one winter weekend. We were going to do all sorts of great things like stay in a hotel, go to museums and go hear Eddie Condon at his jazz place on 52nd Street. All I needed was twenty dollars by Thursday. My father sent me the twenty dollars, just as he promised he would, but it didn't come until Saturday and the other fellows had already gone to New York. That twenty dollars was one of the worst things that didn't come in my life.

In the Army, things didn't come. Letters, cookies, the hometown newspaper . . . nothing ever came. When we all rushed to the company street for mail call, lots of names were called but my name wasn't among them usually. I'd get tense when it got near me:

"ROBERTS, ROCHE, ROCKHURST, ROMNEY . . . STRAVLAKAS . . ." Skipped me. It didn't come again.

When the war ended, I looked for my discharge papers. Do you think my discharge papers came? Of course not. I waited week after lonesome week and they didn't come. When they finally got there, they were supposed to be accompanied by a check for two hundred and thirty dollars, but that didn't come, either.

No problem is more pressing than the problem of things that don't come. I've thought of writing the President to ask for an explanation of why nothing is being done about it . . . but even if he sent me one, it wouldn't come.

NEW YEAR'S REVOLUTIONS

New Year's resolutions don't work so this year mine are revolutions. Resolutions don't work because we can't change ourselves by deciding to. It's depressing but true. Resolve is a wishy-washy verb that doesn't stand up to any kind of opposition. Resolve gives in every time.

For these reasons, I've given up on resolutions and switched to revolutions. I'm revolting against the way I am. For example:

—For years I've been the last one to get there. No longer. I'm looking at time a whole new way. I'm being realistic about how long it takes to get ready to leave. I'm not going to underestimate how long it takes me to get from where I am to where I'm going. I'm not going to fool myself about the time it takes to find the place I'm going, either. This year I'm going to be there on time, or perhaps, even a little early.

—I'm not going to lose any weight again. After years of resolving to lose weight in the coming year, I changed. Last year I was determined not to resolve to lose any. I didn't try, and for once my resolution in regard to weight was successful. I didn't lose any.

—There'll be a revolution in my pockets. I'm going to make sure I have the proper change. I'm tired of not having dollar bills and having to pay for a newspaper with a ten-dollar bill. I'll always have quarters, but I'll regularly clean out the pennies from my pockets because, as we all know, pennies are worthless weight. I may even clean out the nickels every night because nickels aren't worth much anymore, either. Name me thirty-seven things you can buy with a nickel.

—In the new year I'm going to be more careful with my fingers. Sometimes when I'm writing, I'll spend more time correcting typing mistakes than I do typing in the first place. I'm tired of hitting the ; key when what I want is a p just because the p is directly above the ;. To tell you the truth, I wouldn't care if there wasn't any ; on a typewriter at all because I don't use a ; twice a year. I do occasionally use some :'s.

It's even possible I'll learn to touch-type this year, so I won't have to look when I write. That would be good because sometimes I can't stand reading what I write.

I'm going to be more careful about my fingers in the workshop, too. I've never had a major accident, but I must have gone through a box of Band-Aids last year binding up little cuts and scratches. I use more Band-Aids than aspirin.

—For years I've tried to make myself read the newspaper in an orderly fashion. I haven't read it the way I wanted to, I've read it the way I felt I ought to. No longer. Beginning this year I'm going to the most important pages, the sports pages first, and gradually work toward the front of the paper to see what's going on in the rest of the world.

—My attitude toward prejudice for the year is revolutionary. I'm tired of fighting my prejudices. I'm going to relax and enjoy them. If I haven't been able to get rid of being prejudiced about some things by now, I never will.

—In the coming year I'm going to be nicer to my boss. A little kindness won't hurt. I realize I've treated him miserably for years now. After all, it isn't his fault he's my boss. He can't help it because he got me when he took the job. He's not responsible for the fact that he's the ninth boss I've had in fourteen years. I'm going to be nicer to him because if I'm not, I know I'll regret it when he's gone. Bosses don't last.

—Not once in the coming year am I going to wake up and decide it won't do any harm to go back to sleep for a little while. A person isn't thinking well when he or she first awakens, and the resolve to get up must be firm and unshakable, because if you decide to go back to sleep, you don't know how wrong you were until later.

IN THE BREAKFAST RUT

There are people seventy years old who have eaten the same thing for breakfast, morning after morning, since they were twenty. They'll try anything for lunch and wouldn't dream of having the same thing for dinner two nights in a row, but don't ask them to experiment with their breakfast. They ate cornflakes as kids and they have no intention of changing to Froot Loops. Americans are more rigid about their breakfast habits than about any other meal they eat.

Fortunately, this doesn't mean that the kids who are eating Fruity Yummy Mummy, Cap'n Crunch or Cocoa Puffs today will be eating them all their lives. The cereal market for kids these days is faddish. A cereal like Nerds, Smurfberry or Pebbles can be here today and gone tomorrow from the grocers' shelves.

There are almost 175 cold-cereal names on supermarket shelves now, more than five times the number available just a few years ago. The candy kind, with funny-paper names, is on the lower shelves where kids can see them. They're put there to attract kids who come to the store with their mothers to drive them crazy asking for things.

Most cereal boxes are from seven to nine inches wide, and if a grocery store carried all 175 brands, they'd take up a whole aisle. If you're a store manager and you give cereals an aisle, you have no place to put the peanut butter, the soap, the puffy paper towels and about 24,000 other items your store should carry. A supermarket store manager is faced with 11,000 new products a year and 80 percent of them fail.

As a result of the competition for space in supermarkets and the ephemeral nature of new products, there's a system of payoffs that's common. In the industry, it's called "new-product introductory allowance" or, more often a "slotting allowance." Paying for shelf space in a supermarket is so common that it's not considered unethical by grocers although it would seem dishonest to most of us.

Ready-to-eat cereal sales have soared because adult Americans are eating more of what used to be thought of as kid stuff. Adults have been sold on the idea that for life everlasting, they ought to eat more cereal-grain products that are heavy in carbohydrates and devoid of cholesterol and less food that's full of protein and fat. For the first time in their lives, some people are changing what they eat for breakfast.

The health kick that followed the fiber fad that began in 1986 was oat bran. Claims were made that bran actually absorbs cholesterol. Bran is the outer part of the grain, just inside the hull and getting it off to put in cereals isn't an exact science. Often there isn't much of it in a cereal that claims to have a lot of it.

Breakfasts are changing though, little by little. I know someone who had two soft-boiled eggs for breakfast every morning of her life for thirty-five years until she switched to granola. Now you can't get her off it. I'll bet that even the Marlboro cowboys don't sit down in the local café with a cigarette, a cup of coffee, a rasher of bacon and three fried eggs for breakfast anymore. The he-man cowboy is more apt to have a bowl of Froot Loops with skim milk. He's probably more apt to have it back at the ranch than in the café in town, too. People aren't eating breakfast in restaurants as much as they once did. I don't know who started that idea about "a good breakfast" sticking with you all day. A good breakfast always makes me hungry at lunchtime.

Some of the cereal companies are suggesting you can get healthy by eating their product. I don't know, of course, but I have always thought that a good, healthy breakfast which would get you going and eliminate the need for two cups of coffee would be a bowl of chicken soup with some rice in it.

While I like the idea, theoretically, I wouldn't dream of having chicken soup for breakfast in real life. Why is that? Like everyone else, I've been eating the same thing for breakfast for fifty years and have no intention of changing now.

LEAVE A BRIGHT LIGHT IN THE WINDOW

When some people come downstairs to the kitchen in the morning, they start getting breakfast in the dark. The only light they have is what comes in the window . . . which isn't much if the sun isn't up yet. When I come down in the morning, I hit every light switch in the place including the little one over the stove.

You'd think, or I would anyway, that everyone would want about the same amount of light in his or her life but the fact is, the amount of light people want varies greatly from one individual to the next. It has more to do with taste than eyesight.

The people who start slowly in the morning want the least light when they first get up. They pull down all the shades when they go to bed at night so the sunrise can't get in the following morning. If it's light out, slow starters don't want to know.

When they realize, by the alarm or the soft glow of the numbers on their electric clock, that it must be morning and time to get up, they prefer to feel their way to the bathroom rather than turn on the light by the bed so they can see where they're going. The last thing they do is turn on the overhead light so they can really see.

I wake up and hit the floor running. I turn on the light by the bed and when I get over by the switch on the wall by the door, I flip that. In the bathroom, I turn on the overhead light, the small one over the shower and the ones that surround the mirror. I leave no light unturned on.

The shady people accuse those of us who like plenty of light of being crude and oblivious to the subtleties of shadow. They want to warm up to the activities of the day slowly, increasing the intensity of light gradually.

Different restaurants appeal to different clientele. There are restaurants for diners who like soft candlelight and restaurants for those who like a daylight atmosphere even inside at night. They like to be able to read the menu. I'm one of those. I hate to go into some cute little place with the tables all jammed in together and be seated at a tiny table with one lone candle in the middle of it. The waiter comes along and hands you a menu eighteen inches tall and a foot wide. As soon as you open it up, you're sitting there with the menu between you and the only light source and also between you and whoever you're with. It obliterates the few dim rays emanating from the flickering flame in front of you as well as the face of your companion. You can't read. You can't talk. To make a selection, you have to turn in your chair, with your back to the table so the light from the candle hits the menu. Deliver me from candlelit restaurants.

I feel the same about those ultra-modern designer reading lamps with the long arm that extends and bends in all directions. They're ingenious, but when it comes to light, they don't pay off. At their extremity they have some kind of toy bulb that doesn't throw enough light to illuminate one whole page of a book. If I wanted a flashlight, I'd use one. If you take the newspaper to bed and have one of them over the headboard, it's like trying to read with a match. The price of a replacement bulb suggests the lamp has a solid gold filament.

The only time I'm slow turning on lights is when I'm driving. On a long trip, the first headlights begin to appear on the cars coming at me shortly after three P.M. The cars behind those lights are driven by the same Nervous

Nellies who lock their car doors when they put their cars away in their own garage for the night.

At dusk on a highway, I often begin counting the number of cars coming at me with and without their lights on. When it gets down to where I'm only passing one in twenty-five or thirty without lights, I figure it's time for me to put mine on. I don't want to be last, just close to last.

The type of person who turns his or her lights on at four o'clock in the afternoon, while it's still broad daylight, does it not because it's safer, but because he's just naturally nervous about everything. He lives his life that way. The same person who puts his car lights on in midafternoon, reads by a 60-watt bulb because he doesn't want to waste electricity.

When these people go out at night, they leave a light on in their house. It's always the same small, dull light and they never turn it on, except when they're not home. It's like having a blinking neon sign over their front door that reads NO ONE HOME! NO ONE HOME! NO ONE HOME!

THE ART AND SCIENCE
OF WASTING TIME

Wasting time is one of life's great pleasures. Maybe "wasting time" is a bad phrase because some of the best time we all spend might be called "wasted." Wasting time is as necessary as sleep. And more fun. You can't get up in the morning and just start accomplishing things without ever taking a break. Goofing off is a pleasant way to spend part of our days.

The trouble with wasting time is that too often it's forced on us when we don't want it. If we only wasted time when we felt like wasting it, that would be okay.

There's a lot of time I object to wasting. For instance:

—Standing in line at the supermarket checkout counter and getting behind a woman with a handful of coupons taken from newspapers. I feel like throwing sixty-seven cents on the counter and saying, "Here. Now will you get out of the way? You're holding up nine people behind you."

—Having to wait twelve minutes at a bank to get some of your own money.

—Being behind a driver who's fussing with something on the passenger's seat when the light turns green.

—Waiting on the phone for some big-shot executive to get to the telephone after his secretary, sitting right outside his office, says, "Just a moment, I'll see if he's in."

—Waiting in line at an airline ticket counter to pay too much for a ticket for an uncomfortable trip to someplace you don't really want to go anyway.

—Trying to find anything in *TV Guide*.

—The five minutes between when you first see a driver starting to get into a car in a parking space you want, and when the driver actually leaves.

—Getting on an airplane and having to stand in the aisle while someone with too much carry-on baggage tries to stuff something that doesn't fit into the overhead compartment.

—Having to wait in line at a store while the cashier calls an assistant manager over the public address system to get him to okay a check.

—The time it takes to find anything in the Yellow Pages. If you look up "Car Repair" it says "See Automotive Repair." If you look up "Airlines" it says "See Air Lines." Whenever I look for a doctor, I forget they're listed under "Physicians." Whatever you look up, it isn't there. It says "See Something Else."

—In the morning, when my mind is on getting to work, I hate to take the time to cut my toenails, even though they're too long.

—Waiting for the water to boil for coffee is one of life's most constant time-wasters. What we need is for someone to invent water that boils faster. I don't care what old sayings say, I can't stop watching the pot.

—In a restaurant, after you've eaten, it's usually too long before the check comes. When I finish dessert, I'm ready to go.

—It always seems like a long while between when one television show ends at about five minutes before the hour and the time the next one really starts at about five minutes after.

—The washer is doing real work and I don't mind waiting while that's going on, but the drier, which isn't doing anything nearly as hard, seems to take forever.

—I still have one watch left that I have to wind and I must be less patient than I was when I always wound my watch. Winding that watch now seems like such a long, tedious waste of time that I often let it run down.

—No matter how much faster it may be than walking up, I always resent the time it takes for an elevator to come.

A WORLD-CLASS SLEEPER

We are all proud of the things we do well, and I'm reluctant to take advantage of being in print to brag about something I do well, but I'm a great sleeper. I challenge anyone to prove they sleep better than I do.

People tell me they toss and turn for hours after they get into bed at night. Not me. I doubt if I'm awake on the average of more than a minute and fifteen seconds.

When I go upstairs to bed, I usually take something to read. It may be part of the newspaper, a book or a magazine. Whatever it is, I put it on the table next to the bed. I get in, pull the covers up, fix the clock/radio and close my eyes. End of day. The reading material waits patiently, unread, by my bedside.

It's not that I merely sleep well at night when I go to bed. I nap well, too. I can fall asleep in my office after lunch for six to eight minutes and awaken as fresh as though I'd had a night's sleep. I guess if I had to choose between my ability to sleep at night and my ability to nap, I'd take napping. It's such a good, quick way to revive yourself.

Some sleep must be better than other sleep and I get the best kind. Six hours is plenty for me and if I get that eight-minute nap during the day, five is enough. I don't have any patience with people who go to bed and sleep a lot because they can't think of anything better to do. I'd like to have the life they waste.

Once in a while, usually after I've been drinking white wine on a Saturday night, I awaken at two A.M. and can't get back to sleep. Sometimes I'll swear I've been awake from two A.M. until five and yet I have the sneaking suspicion I was only half awake. Or was it half asleep? Insomnia is terrible, but insomniacs sleep more than they think they do.

There's only one place I tend to fall asleep that worries me and that's driving. If I start a two- or three-hour drive in the afternoon with a bright sun staring me in the eyes, I invariably start to nod. Nothing helps. I sing to myself, turn the radio way up, open the windows, put my head out in the breeze, slap myself in the face or punch myself until it hurts. My eyes still tend to close. Fortunately, I can pull off the road, turn off the engine and nap for five minutes and awake ready to drive for hours.

I dream some and don't like dreaming because it's spooky. I like to be able to understand things and it isn't clear to me how dreams come about. Everything in life should have an explanation and no one can explain dreams. It seems strange that any kind of mental life goes on when we're unconscious.

Last night, I dreamed I wrote a play. The director and all the actors were ready in the theater. I was late getting the play written and didn't get it to them until the afternoon before opening night. The actors had to memorize their parts between the time I got there and when the curtain went up at eight P.M.

Lucky for me, I woke up before curtain time.

When they first announced the idea of learning something like a foreign language by having a recorder play quietly under your pillow while you slept, I was excited about the possibility of putting all that wasted time to some use. Unfortunately, they've found it doesn't work. You can't learn French while you sleep, after all.

More research should be done on sleep. We should know how much sleep we need. We should know when we're being lazy when we stay in bed another hour, and when it's necessary. Do some people need more sleep than others? Why? Do we need more sleep when we've worked hard than when we haven't? When we get sleepy, do we really need sleep, or do we sleep when we don't have to, just as we eat more than we should?

AGAINST WHISTLING

Whistlers are a little crazy. They're nice and I like them—but they're batty. They don't have both oars in the water. They live in a world of their own.

Do you know any whistlers? They pucker up and start blowing between their lips, to make what they consider to be music, at the strangest times. I don't believe they ever say to themselves, "I think I'll whistle." It comes from their mouths unbidden by their brains. They do it unconsciously.

Whistlers are divided into several categories. The worst of them, and the most common, is the nervous whistler. Any tense situation causes him to whistle until it's over. I say "him" because I don't offhand remember knowing a woman whistler. Whistling is a fault women don't have.

The sound coming from the nervous whistler can scarcely be categorized as music. While there may be some pattern to it, it's often more like the sound of steam escaping from a radiator but with a slight tune to it. It's annoying to be around one of them. As a matter of fact, it's annoying to be around any of them.

There's always been a rumor that a whistling worker is a happy worker. He may be happy but he's annoying to anyone trying to work near him. I don't want to be reminded of how happy someone else is all day. What if I feel lousy that day? Do I have to endure having it rubbed in by a joyous whistler?

In the newspaper business, there always used to be a sign hung somewhere that read NO WHISTLING IN THE CITY ROOM! I'd like to see that extended to read NO WHISTLING IN THE CITY! To me the sound of a whistle is as irritating as the sound of someone else's radio playing music I don't like. I'd rather be in the same room with a cigarette smoker than a whistler.

There's a strong old tradition of not whistling on board naval vessels. Anyone caught whistling on board a battleship could get drummed out of the Navy. An old book I have quotes a 1920 memo from a Navy captain named W. W. Gilmer. "The practice of whistling is an entirely unnecessary and irritating noise which must be discontinued," he wrote. Right on, Captain Gilmer. Make them walk the plank . . . whistling.

You could say this is sour grapes because I can't whistle worth a darn, but it isn't. I don't have any great desire to know how to whistle. I wish I could play the piano and I once took trumpet lessons, but I never studied any whistling techniques. I'll take that back. I do wish I could put my two little fingers in my mouth and make that loud, shrill sound that lets a taxicab know you're after him or calls your dog's attention to the fact that you want him to come.

The loud, shrill mechanical whistle is even more irritating than the man-made sound. Every once in a while I stay in a hotel and get a room above the front door. At about seven A.M. the doorman starts whistling for cabs. The doorman's whistle is designed more to call the hotel guests' attention to the fact that he, the doorman, is getting a cab, in anticipation of a fat tip, than it is to attract the cabdriver's attention. Cabdrivers come to hotel doors whether they're whistled at or not.

The early Disney film *Snow White and the Seven Dwarfs* was a setback for those of us who can't stand whistlers. The song "Whistle While You Work" gave whistlers the idea that whistling was a jolly pursuit that made all whistlers lovable to the rest of the world. It encouraged people to make that intrusive noise while they went about their jobs.

I don't want to incur the wrath of all whistlers, but, to tell you the truth, I've never seen anyone do a very good job on anything while he was whistling.

HOW TO BE

W hen I was young, I secretly thought that the kid in my class who got the best marks wasn't the smartest kid. I also suspected myself of thinking that as an excuse for not getting the highest marks myself. Now I know I was right in the first place. I needn't have suspected myself of duplicity.

Ever since fourth grade I've been puzzled about what smart is and it still concerns me in relation to myself and others.

Why are some people who seem smart dismal failures? Why are some people who seem dumb so successful? Why isn't the smartest man or woman in America the richest and most successful? Why isn't he or she President?

A psychologist at Emory University in Atlanta developed a test for some things no one ever considered testable before. Dr. Stephen Nowicki studied one thousand kids between the ages of nine and eleven for what he called "non-verbal skills." Dr. Nowicki thinks the problem a lot of kids have is not being able to get the message.

Messages, or information, are sent among people a lot of ways that aren't verbal, Dr. Nowicki contends. If someone makes a face after drinking something, it means that person didn't like what he tasted. Apparently, a lot of people aren't able to understand this kind of message. They don't get the message from someone's gesture or from the position of their bodies.

The friends I've had who have trouble relating to other people don't seem to know how to be. Knowing how to be doesn't come naturally to them. They *think* about how to be and almost always come up with the wrong answer.

Some people aren't good at understanding the meaning in the tone of voice someone uses or they don't even know how close they should stand when they're talking to another person. They don't know where to look. Other people who don't know how to be, can't judge how loud or how soft they should talk.

Everyone reading this must know people who stand too close when they're talking to someone. You keep backing up and they keep moving their face closer to your face. People who stand too close when they talk to you don't know how to be.

In some cases, it's almost as if a person mentally stutters or stammers through life. He or she is uncertain about how to act, so he thinks about how to act all the time. When he finally acts, it is jerky, unnatural and wrong.

In high school, I remember there were boys who were good dancers and who seemed to hear and feel music more than the rest of us. They snapped their fingers to the rhythm of the music and danced with gay abandon. There were other boys who wanted to be that way and failed miserably. They looked silly doing the same things because they were trying too hard. I was one of those.

The problem of not having things come naturally to you manifests itself in unnatural speech, as when a person picks up the jargon of a business, a hobby, a game or a fad too quickly. The person uses slang phrases that he's heard other people use in an attempt to be one of the boys, but they don't come naturally to him. From him they sound forced and dumb. To other people, the jargon of a fad comes naturally.

A second cousin to the person who stands too close to your face when he's talking to you is the person who forces you over to the building line when you're walking down the street together. Or, if he's on the inside, he forces you over to the curb by the street. He is unaware.

Awareness is a natural sense that some people have a lot more of than others. People who are aware sense a social situation quickly. They're more apt to say or do the right thing.

The smartest kid in our class that year never knew how to be. He was twice as smart as I was and half as successful. No wonder he was never President . . . of the class, even.

STUPID IS IN

You know the story. Our schools aren't working very well. Everyone, from the President to the mothers and fathers of the kids, is worried about how little kids are learning in school. All kinds of studies show that, in spite of the increased amount of money being spent on education, children aren't getting much of it in most schools in the United States.

The big reason a lot of kids aren't getting an education is they don't want one. It doesn't seem important. "None of the others kids has one, why should I?"

Ignorance is in. It's smart to be dumb if you're a teenager. The occasional good student is dismissed as a freak. How do we make the smartest kid in the class more admired than the prettiest girl or the best athlete?

Taking pleasure from not knowing anything is popular with adults, too. I noticed myself bragging this morning about not knowing one Chinese leader from another. Does this make me special? Why don't I find out who's who?

"Gee, I don't know" is a phrase we use with pride and satisfaction. It has a ring to it. We take smug pleasure from being honest without being embarrassed at being dumb.

If you talk to someone about their income tax, they're quick to tell you they're not good with numbers.

"I can't even add."

Go to a good restaurant and friends proudly display their ignorance of a little basic French on the menu.

"What is all this stuff?"

Many Americans don't know what's going on in the world.

"I don't read the paper or watch TV news. Too much bad news."

People are proud of themselves for not remembering someone's name.

"I'm sorry. I'm terrible with names."

Or, "I was never any good at spelling."

Not knowing is popular at election time and probably accounts for why about half of us don't vote.

"They're all the same. It's all just a bunch of politics."

The know-nothings excuse themselves from finding out about government by dismissing all politicians as corrupt.

One of the most popular answers to any question asked by the people who do the professional polling on a wide variety of subjects is "DON'T KNOW."

You run into the happy dumb everywhere. If you drive into a strange city and lean out the window to ask someone on foot where Main Street is, you give the pedestrian an opportunity to be pleased with himself.

"Sorry, I can't help you," he says. "I'm a stranger in town myself."

There's something about the way the person tells you he doesn't know that makes you know he's happy about it. He has no responsibility. He doesn't have to think about how to tell you to get there. He's ignorant. He's absolved of the problems attendant to knowledge.

Honestly not knowing is a lot easier than knowing. This probably accounts for its popularity. It's the people who know who bear the burden. It's the experts like doctors, lawyers, engineers, architects and even journalists who get in trouble by answering questions. Who has ever been sued for malpractice for saying, "Gee, I don't know," or "Sorry, can't help you."

Educated professionals who try to answer hard questions with knowledge are the ones who get in trouble by making mistakes. Ignorance is safe and easy. Maybe this attitude has rubbed off on the kids. Until knowing is fashionable again, there isn't any hope for education.

part nine

FIRST THINGS, LAST THINGS

What Every Kid Should Have Growing Up

Don't tune out at the mention of the name "United Nations," but the U.N. had what it called a World Conference on Children a while back. One of its conclusions was that 177 million children of the world suffer from malnutrition.

Malnutrition isn't usually the problem in our country. Not many children die because they don't have enough food; they suffer from having bad parents. I wonder if the United Nations has a solution to bad parents?

Millions of American children die a death of the spirit at an early age because their parents don't give a damn. The children get older without ever growing up. They're alive but living outside our social system. The kids feel no responsibility toward their family, their neighbors, or their country.

I know what I think every child should have growing up to become a responsible, honest, producing member of our society instead of a sad welfare case or a prison inmate.

He or she should have:

—A home with one mother and one father.

—At least one brother and one sister. A boy should have a sister and a girl should have a brother. The girl's brother should be older if that can be arranged. As a matter of fact, every kid should have an older brother, which, unfortunately, is impossible.

—A family that eats dinner together.

—A room of his or her own, even if it's tiny. The room should have the things the child wants, not what the parents want, in it. The room need not be neat.

—A good night kiss until it becomes apparent to both the parents and the child that the child is too old to be kissed good night.

—A warm bed with a blanket or a quilt that has its own character, under which the kid can hide from the world and worry about his or her problems in cozy privacy.

—A young girl should have a doll and roller skates. A boy should have a bike and a baseball bat. There's nothing wrong with a boy having a doll or a girl having a bike.

—A costume at Halloween and a cake with candles to blow out with a wish on every birthday.

—A child should have a sweet, motherly kindergarten teacher to help make the transition between home and the cold, cruel outside world.

—A friend to whom he or she can tell secrets.

—A place to swim in the summer and a place to sleigh-ride in the winter. If the child lives in the South, his parents ought to send him or her to some relative or friend in the Northeast during the winter where there is snow.

—Some minor illnesses to let the child know that life isn't always a bowl of cherries. The flu or a broken arm is okay for this purpose.

—A rich kid on the block who has everything the child would like to have.

—A rich uncle or a doting aunt.

—Talent. Every child should be encouraged to be good at something, no matter how minor a talent it is. (On my block, Billy Tanner was a wimp kid who none of us would play with until the year of the yo-yo craze. Billy Tanner, it turned out, could do 'Round-the-World and Walk-the-Dog before the rest of us mastered just plain up and down. Making a yo-yo go was Billy Tanner's talent and we never treated him like a wimp again.)

—Discipline. Along with love and enough to eat, every child should have plenty of it.

—Someone to read aloud to him or her when the kid is too young to read himself.

—A mother and father who let the child get into bed with them when there's a thunderstorm.

If every child had these things while he or she was growing up, there would be nothing to worry about the future of the world.

FEELINGS LONG FORGOTTEN

I remember:

—Not being able to reach the pedals comfortably on a new two-wheeler that was a little too big for me.

—Stubbing my toe while going barefoot in the summer.

—Getting a noseful of water swimming in the lake on a rough day.

—Coming to the top and starting down the steepest part of the roller coaster.

—Sucking up the last of an ice cream soda until it started making a loud noise.

—Jumping in a pile of leaves before they were burned.

—Being pushed on a swing until I was going so high I was scared.

—Having to take castor oil.

—Thinking that if I stepped on a crack, I'd break my mother's back.

—My father's cigar smoke in the car on a long drive.

—Keeping the turkey wishbone.

—Having a sty.

—Erasing a blackboard.

—Having to be home for Sunday dinner at one o'clock when all the other kids were out playing because they didn't have dinner until six.

—Being given five dollars by my uncle.

—Sitting in line at the barbershop waiting my turn to get a haircut.

—Sleeping in a tent when it was raining outside.

—Having to worry about bringing home my report card to get it signed when my marks weren't very good.

—Having a sliver taken out of my heel with a needle.

—The excitement of putting a three-inch firecracker under an empty coffee can, lighting it and watching the can go four feet in the air with the explosion.

—Wearing a pair of shoes two sizes too long because I was going to grow into them."

—Having to eat things I didn't like because they were good for me.

—Visiting relatives in Troy on Saturday when I wanted to be playing football in the back lot.

—Being given a brand-new, big-league baseball by my father's friend with the big, bushy eyebrows, Mr. Bernard.

—Walking on stilts or jumping on a pogo stick.

—Waiting to get out of knickers and into my first pair of long pants.

—Getting the high boots with the little pocket on the side with a Boy Scout knife in it.

—Putting potatoes down among the coals of the fire we started up behind the garage and eating them an hour later, all charred and black outside and steamy delicious inside.

—Lucy Buckley.

—Making a slingshot out of rubber bands, a little piece of leather and the crotch of a small tree.

—Buying a double-decker chocolate ice cream cone for ten cents.

—Bubble gum, pea shooters, Hula Hoops and yo-yos.

—Belly-whopping on my Flexible Flyer.

—Getting some maple syrup in every hole in the waffle.

—The weird feeling I had coming out into the daylight after being in the Madison Theater for three hours Saturday afternoon watching a double feature featuring stars like Randolph Scott, the Cisco Kid and Hopalong Cassidy. And hating it when the cowboy hero wearing his white hat started singing on top of his horse.

—The starving Chinese who would be glad to have what I was leaving on my plate, according to my mother.

MULTIPLICATION MEMORIES

We all live our separate lives, divided sometimes by age, sometimes by job, by geography—divided by a thousand things. We pass the brick walls of a hospital and perhaps think compassionately, for a few seconds, of all the troubled people inside, pinned to their beds with tubes or just weakness. We know because we have been there and we feel sorry for them and lucky for ourselves . . . but we drive on, the thought is gone and we're on our way, out of the hospital world.

Driving to work Tuesday, I passed a school. It was the day after Labor Day and young mothers were leading their younger children to the door.

My memories of what a hospital is like are fresher than my memories of school. Memories of my first school year are sketchy.

I do recall my mother bought me a box of crayons and a lined pad. I remember that pad well enough to realize now that it was very poor quality paper. She must have known I wasn't going to scribble anything worth saving on it. She must also have recognized what kind of a student I was going to be because she bought me three brand-new Eberhard Faber pencils with erasers on them and a separate red, rubber eraser. The wooden ruler wasn't much different from the one on my desk this minute.

The little pencil box contained my first woodworking tool, a pencil sharpener. It was very small but perfectly efficient and I sharpened my pencils a lot more than was necessary for the amount of writing I did with them.

I do recall being afraid to go to kindergarten. My mother had to take me by the hand and lead me the one long block down Hamilton Street to School Four. The designation "School Four" seemed more like a name than a number to me.

The builders of the school had made the same mistake so many builders make of carving in stone a legend or sign that should never have been so permanently put there. One side of the building had, carved in stone with letters a foot high, the word B-O-Y-S. The other side was as indelibly marked G-I-R-L-S. Nothing should ever be carved in stone on a new building; that's one thing I learned that year.

In the third or fourth grade, I recall trembling when Miss Rose sat and shared my small chair with me while she guided my hand in "The Palmer Method." I remember, too, learning the multiplication tables. It was a great source of pride to my section of the class that we had mastered everything up to 12 times 12 while Miss Dempsey's class was still struggling with 9 times 8.

The blackboard is much clearer in my mind now than anything any teacher ever wrote on one of them. Some teachers were very good at writing on the blackboard and others were poor. I was critical, too, of the erasing done by teachers, although I realized by the time I got to college that the best teachers often did the worst erasing. Good teachers, as a rule, do not give erasing high priority. Miss Boyd, for example, wasn't a good teacher but she often went into the girls' bathroom to wet a cloth to clean the blackboard with.

For most of my early childhood, I thought all teachers were women and all of us in my class were fascinated by the novelty of having a man as a teacher when Mr. Crowe was assigned to us. (Mr. Crowe further distinguished himself by whirling around from the blackboard where he wrote and pitching his eraser, full speed, at any student he caught talking. We loved Mr. Crowe.)

Returning home later the other day, I saw some older kids peddling home on their bikes with books strapped to the little holders over their back wheels.

I passed them as they were passing the hospital.

GET LOST,
CHRISTOPHER COLUMBUS!

They're planning to rewrite the history books for New York State schools and when they do, kids growing up in New York are going to end up with a different view of how our country got this way than kids from the other forty-nine states.

A panel of experts has recommended revisions in the books that would put more emphasis on the part non-white Americans played in building our country. Their report is called "One Nation, Many Peoples: A Declaration of Cultural Independence." Just as soon as I saw them use the word "peoples," I knew the panel was in deep trouble.

In the history books in most places in the United States, Columbus will continue to have discovered America in 1492. Not in New York. There won't be a chapter on how Columbus sailed here and discovered America. Instead there will be only a few lines mentioning Columbus as someone who came to a land that was already settled.

The panel thinks this will pacify Indians who get mad when they read where Columbus discovered a place they'd lived in for hundreds of years. You have to admit, it was a little overbearing of the Europeans to make the claim that "Columbus *discovered* America in 1492." If the Indians had paddled a birchbark canoe to Rome that year, could they claim they discovered Italy?

I don't know what we'll do with Columbus Day. The Italians have taken it over as theirs and they won't like this new deal. I don't want to get in bad with a lot of Indians myself but they didn't do much with the country before the English, the French, the Italians, the Germans and the Scandinavians got here.

Who knows how long it would have taken the Indians, left on their own, to replace smoke signals with the telephone or campfires with light bulbs. The Indians hadn't even touched the ozone layer.

The idea this New York education committee seems to have is to make history fairer and put less emphasis on the part European immigrants played in making the United States of America. That's okay where those groups, or individuals in them, really did do good things we don't know about. There have been some great black leaders left out of history books and it's wrong, but I hope the committee doesn't make up a lot of stuff as if every ethnic group and both sexes had equal parts in the development of our country. There are a lot of reasons why they didn't and those should be explained—but they aren't.

The fact is, that for all the greed that motivated it and all the bloodshed that resulted from it, the early colonization of foreign lands by Europeans produced most of what's good now in the civilization that the whole world recognizes as the best on Earth.

It's going to be difficult to get impartial writers to do this rewrite job properly. Different ethnic groups are going to be arguing about how important their forefathers were in building America.

As a person of Scotch-Irish ancestry, I'm going to be hopping mad if they don't give a lot of space to the part my people played. There wouldn't be a St. Patrick's Day parade every year if it hadn't been for the Irish. It was the Irish who brought potatoes to Idaho and George Bernard Shaw to America. You talk about important!

The Scotch have never gotten a fair deal in the history books, either. Remember! Among other things, they brought Scotch to America.

So let's get with it, New York State! If you're going to rewrite the history books, you're not going to satisfy everyone with one book. You better plan on having one history book for women, one for men, one for each European group, one for African-Americans, one for native American Indians—and one for the road.

And one last suggestion, New York. Remember, first you better teach the kids to read or what you write won't matter.

SLEEPING ARRANGEMENTS

I watched our good friends' son Tommy grow to be fifteen years old. He used to rake leaves around the house and do a few other odd jobs. When he came over Saturdays to make a little spending money, we talked about school and things like whether he was going to make the cross-country team or not. He was a good kid.

Two years ago Tommy went off to college. He's twenty now and I've talked to him a few times when he's answered the telephone but I haven't seen much of him since he went away. The other day I saw his mother for the first time since last fall.

"Where's Tommy?" I asked, figuring he must be home from college. "He got a job this summer?"

"Tommy's in Montana," his mother said. "He's having a great time. He stopped off to see my parents in Minneapolis and now they're painting her mother's house in Missoula."

"HER mother?" I said. "WHOSE mother?"

"The girl's mother. Tommy's traveling with this girl. She's real nice. They put their bikes on top of the car. Every once in a while they'll stop and first she'll ride for eight or ten miles and he'll follow her in the car. Then she drives and Tommy rides . . . like for thirty miles. They're having a ball."

"He still had his junior license and couldn't drive after dark last I knew," I said.

"Yeah, well, he's got his senior license now," she laughed. "They bought a small tent and a sleeping bag so they don't spend much money. They're seeing a lot of the country."

What struck me was not how much of the country they were seeing, but how much they were seeing of each other. "A" sleeping bag?

The last time I'd really seen Tommy, he was a big, good-looking, gawky kid. It didn't surprise me that he liked girls, but somehow I wasn't ready to hear he was taking a cross-country trip with one and sharing a sleeping bag.

"How'd that go at your mother's?" I asked Tommy's mother.

"Oh, listen," she said, "people are used to that now . . . even my family. They stayed with my parents for three days and everything was fine. You know, they didn't sleep together there or anything, but my mother liked the girl."

Well, we didn't have television or atomic bombs or cars that shifted gears by themselves when I was young, either, so I'm used to the fact that everything has changed. Still, it's been easier for me to get used to television, automatic shifting and nuclear weapons than it has been to get used to the sex habits of young people. You're probably not going to believe this, but there was a time when people got married before they'd ever slept together.

The world hasn't come to an end because young people do a lot of sleeping around, but it doesn't seem to be any better for it, either. Young people who live together without getting married have often suggested it's really a public service they're performing. They call it a "trial marriage." They tell people they're seeing whether it will work or not before they make that final commitment. It used to be called, more realistically, "shacking up."

Two University of Wisconsin researchers have announced the results of a survey of 13,000 people that's going to make it harder for unmarried people living together to justify it on grounds it will have any good effect in the long run.

The study shows that within ten years of their wedding, 38 percent of those who had lived together before marriage were divorced.

In the same group, a smaller number, 27 percent of those who were married without living together first, were divorced.

Those figures prove what a lot of old fogeys like me thought all along. That story about "trial marriage" is baloney. Most couples who live together without getting married do it because the guy doesn't want to be tied down or because neither of them gets at doing things. They just let it ride. They're probably behind on their rent for the same reason.

GRADUATE FIRST, THEN LEARN SOMETHING

There are so many college graduates these days that a lot of young people with diplomas are taking jobs that aren't traditionally held by college graduates.

This information comes from officials at the Labor Department in Washington. College graduates, the Labor Department says, are taking jobs as cooks, salespeople, secretaries, bookkeepers and factory supervisors.

There's something funny about that. Why would a factory hire a college graduate as a "factory supervisor" if that person hadn't worked in a factory? No one wants a supervisor who doesn't know more about the job than the people being supervised do. No one wants a supervisor who got the job because he or she went to college.

The Labor Department also says that companies want college graduates and pay them more money than high school graduates.

The trouble with this Labor Department announcement is that it assumes, as a lot of college students assume, that there are jobs for college graduates and jobs for people who never went to college. The Department also assumes that the purpose of learning is to turn knowledge into money.

These assumptions are each wrong, not true and dumb. Very few people learn how to do anything in college well enough to make a living at it. If you want to be an engineer, a scientist, a doctor, or a lawyer, you need a basic education in those specialties, but I've seen a thousand college kids come to work at a job they'd studied and most of them couldn't find their way to the bathroom, let alone help with the work.

As far as the preference companies show for hiring college graduates over high school graduates, all that means is that kids who go to college are, generally speaking, smarter, more ambitious and better workers than those who don't. It doesn't mean students learn how to do the jobs in college.

The way you learn to do a job is to do the job. Sometimes college can teach what the problems are, but every job is so different, specifically, from what's taught, generally, that an education isn't much help.

The medical profession learned this years ago. A doctor needs to go to medical school, but the profession recognizes that medical graduates don't know what they're doing and requires that the neophyte doctors spend two years practicing the practice as an intern and resident at a hospital, actually doing the work under supervision.

Going to a liberal arts college means having four years free to learn. You never have another four years like it in your life. There are books you'll never read if you don't read them in college. There are subjects you'll never know anything about if you don't take the time to find out in those years. In college, everything about everything is laid out and available to you. It's like a buffet table with good food. You can take what you want. All you need is the appetite. There's always time to learn how to make a living.

I'm always surprised that more college people don't get into manual labor. How did we ever decide that being an accountant, a teacher or a vice president was a job for a college graduate, but that being a carpenter, a plumber, or an electrician, was not?

Where is it written in stone that people who do manual labor aren't college graduates? Where does it say real estate agents have to be better educated than the people who built the houses they sell? Who says the person with a necktie selling cars from the showroom floor has to be better educated than the person out back, under the car, fixing it?

College ought to be for learning all the wonderful things in the world that have nothing to do with making money.

COUSINS

Some families are more serious about cousins than others.

We never made much of them in our family. I can't even remember exactly how many I have. They were nowhere near as important in my life as uncles and aunts.

You're more aware of cousins when you're young than you are later in your life. When I was little, I knew some of my cousins pretty well, but in our family we treated cousins more like friends. If we liked them, we saw them. If we didn't like them, we hardly ever saw them.

One of the first questions I recall having about cousins is why boy cousins and girl cousins are both called just cousins. It's as if uncles and aunts were both called by the same word. Cousins are the only relatives the word for which does not have distinguishing gender. And, come to think of it, English is probably one of the few languages in which the word for boy cousins or girl cousins is the same. In French, it's *cousin-cousine;* in Spanish, *primo-prima*.

Southerners make more of cousins than people from other parts of the country. They talk of second cousins and third cousins and cousins twice removed. Most of us don't have them, as far as we know. I couldn't give you the definition of a second cousin ("kissing cousins" I understand).

It doesn't make sense to be best friends with every cousin you're born with, but there is some value to the permanence of cousins. They remain your cousins no matter what your social relationship is with them. Friends can drift apart by accident. You move to another city or get a different job and make new friends. You still like your old friends, but you never see them and pretty soon, even the Christmas cards stop. They're gone as friends.

Cousins are forever. You always have them, even if twenty years go by without any contact. It's still possible after a lapse of any number of years to get together with a cousin and share stories about how Uncle Herbert drove his car through the garage door. Cousins are like glue in the small cracks that hold big families together.

Our twin daughters, Martha and Emily, live five hundred miles apart but they see each other twenty times a year. Martha has two boys and Emily has one daughter. It appears to me as though Justin, Ben and Alexis are going to be close cousins. Ben and Alexis are within a few months of being the same age and they are clearly closer than they'd be if they were only friends. There's an affinity between them that age and friendship alone doesn't explain. The only answer is, they're cousins.

In the South, everyone knows their second and third cousins. I hardly know what a second cousin is and I know darn well I couldn't give the definition of a third cousin. Whatever it is, we didn't do third cousins in my family. Just plain cousins were enough to deal with.

Jack Prescott was my closest cousin. He was just the right age, four years older than I was, so I looked up to him. He let me help him with his paper route, which I thought was great until I read about Tom Sawyer letting his friends help him whitewash the fence.

Strange things happen with cousins in relation to age. If your mother has a brother ten years older than she is and he has children early in his marriage and your mother has you late, you can easily end up with a cousin twenty-five years older than you are. My cousin Bob was more like an uncle than a cousin to me because he was about fifteen years older.

Cousins are a great reminder of genes and inheritance. You can know a cousin for years and never give much thought to what he or she looks like, and then one day the cousin will turn his head or pick up a glass or a shadow will fall across the forehead and, in a flash, you see the whole family in his face. There is something about the way the cousin held his chin or something about the position of his thumb that reminded you of your father or your mother or yourself. You see some minor gene you have in common and wonder what major genes you share.

Cousins, for better or for worse, are forever.

LIFE, ONE DAMN BIRTHDAY AFTER ANOTHER

Someone said to me this morning, "I see you celebrated your birthday yesterday."

Wrong. I HAD a birthday yesterday. There was nothing even vaguely celebratory about any part of the day. I hated it from beginning to end. The only worse thing would have been not having another birthday.

You never get used to your age, no matter what age you are. The trouble is, you're that age for such a short time. Just when you begin to get used to it, you get a year older.

It's hard to say at what age you reach the top of the hill and start down the back side. You reach the top physically and start downhill much sooner than you reach your intellectual peak. Or, at least that's what people my age like to believe, because evidence of our physical deterioration is evident to everyone while any mental decline is not so apparent.

I often try to assess my intellectual powers, now that I've passed seventy, and compare them with what I had when I was twenty, fifty and sixty. I don't notice any diminution in them although I realize I'd probably be the last to notice. There are some small indications from the people I work most closely with that they think I might be losing it a little bit, but I dismiss those. They are based on minor memory lapses on my part and I don't deny those. I don't worry myself with petty details like that. Forgetting a few things doesn't bother me. I have filled my life very full and have a great deal to remember. It's no wonder I forget a few.

Life, it turns out, doesn't slowly wind down at all. That's what I can't get over. I hope that, before I die, my memory goes, my ambition to get up in the morning and go to work diminishes, my appetite for life becomes less voracious than it is today. I'd like to care just a little bit less about what people think of my work. I'd prefer to be not quite so sad at the death of a friend. Why do I still dream of becoming a better tennis player? It would make getting old less painful if my memory of the good times I've had were not so vivid, too. Why doesn't my memory fade just a little?

The clearest evidence of age is how eagerly I look for evidence that I *haven't* slipped. I relish the newspaper story reporting the success of the eighty-four-year-old scientist, the ninety-year-old novelist or the aged marathon runner. At football games, I cheer for the oldest players even though that means thirty-four.

There has always been some propaganda in favor of the idea that wisdom comes with age, but you can bet no one young ever says or thinks it.

The truth is that a person of seventy is a totally different person than a person of twenty. A comparison of their intellect is impractical. If the young person makes the mathematical calculations quicker, the old one may understand what the numbers mean better.

I look back with some satisfaction on an idiot I was when I was twenty-five, but when I do that, I'm assuming I'm no longer an idiot. That's the part that satisfies me even though it almost certainly isn't true. Were I to live another seventy years, I'm sure I'd look back at 1991 and wonder how I could have been so stupid when I was the age I am now.

If there is one sign of age that bothers me more than others, it's my tendency to become more conservative in political and social opinions. I admire liberals more than conservatives and am somewhat concerned to see myself, more and more often, in agreement with the conservatives I've always disagreed with.

There is nothing good about birthdays and true friends would ignore them. I think I detect a certain gloating in the voices of the people who say "Happy Birthday" to me.

There are quite a few surprises about being old, or at least getting old. The surprise to me is that I don't feel a lot different from when I was young. Of course, it may be that I've forgotten how I felt when I was young. When I was young, I used to think that old people just got vague in the brain and drifted off without knowing or caring much about life. Boy, was I wrong!

I am absolutely as interested in living now as I was when I was twenty. I am not tired of life. I have not had enough. I am not ready to fade away. I don't think I'll be ready twenty years from now either, if I live that long.

It's widely assumed that age is a defect and if that's true, it's one from which no one ever recovers. I don't feel physically or mentally infirm and the only thing I reluctantly concede about my age is that I am, statistically speaking, closer to death than someone younger or than I was a year ago.

When I was in high school, I could get all choked up reading the lines of the poet Edna St. Vincent Millay:

> *"I only know that summer sang in me*
> *A little while, that in me sings no more."*

Pardon me for saying so, Edna, but now that strikes me as pretentious hot air. Life—summer, winter, fall or spring—sings to me as it always did, and I hate birthdays because I don't want the music to stop.

AGING BACKWARDS

I think I'll go into town this afternoon and get me some of those growth hormones that turn your age around and start it headed in the other direction toward younger instead of older. I don't know how they come, but I'll take two.

The report in the *New England Journal of Medicine* said that twenty-one men between the ages of sixty-one and eighty-one were given a growth hormone for six months, and when they finished, their bodies were twenty years younger than when they started taking the hormones. Twenty years younger sounds good to me. Even five wouldn't be bad.

There are some things I'd be looking for to improve if I can get hold of some of this new stuff.

You can bet I'll be walking up the three flights of stairs to my office instead of taking the elevator the way I have been the past few years. And it's going to cut down on what I spend for gas, too, because I'll be walking just about everywhere.

I got down on the living room floor to play with Alexis, my grand-daughter, the other day and it was harder getting up off the floor than it used to be. Half the time when I drop something and it rolls under the bed, I leave it because I hate getting down on my hands and knees to look for it. Actually, it isn't the getting down part I mind as much as it is the getting up part. I guess I'll be able to jump right up off the floor the way I used to after a few growth hormone injections.

Sometimes I hate the idea of making two trips when I have to carry those grocery bags in from the car to the kitchen. Margie often says, "Will you carry those in for me?" If we can both get some youth hormone shots, she'll be able to carry the groceries in herself the way she always did when we were thirty.

There's a fellow down the hall in the office whose name I can never remember. I imagine if I get a couple of shots of this stuff it'll come right back to me.

If I sit in one position for a long while, for instance on a long car ride, my back gets stiff and my legs feel funny when I get out. That'll certainly clear up because I never remember car rides bothering me when I was younger.

For the last few years I've usually had to get up in the middle of the night to go to the bathroom at three or four o'clock. This is a pain in the neck and interrupts a good night's sleep. I guess this new potion will enable me to go back to my old ways when I hit the pillow, fell fast asleep, and didn't wake until the alarm went off.

I blame needing glasses on wearing glasses. I never needed glasses until I started wearing them and now, when I'm reading or writing, I can't do without them. I won't ever have to worry about where I put my glasses again because my eyes will be rejuvenated and I won't need them once I start taking this hormone.

I have most of my hair but there is one small bald spot gaining some ground at the very top of my head. The growth hormone will almost certainly produce a new and luxuriously thick head of hair. When I was a small boy, my hair was blond. That'll probably come back and if you see me on television, I don't want you to think I dyed my hair while on vacation. It's what I'm taking.

The researchers who developed this genetically engineered growth hormone say that the skin of the men in the experiment regained a youthful thickness, too. I could have used a thicker skin a few years ago when I got so much criticism.

One of the best things that happened to the men in the experiment was that they lost an average of 15 percent of their body fat and gained 9 percent in muscle. That's for me. I'm not looking to be another Arnold Schwarzenegger, but I think you probably won't recognize me when you see me again after I've taken those hormones for a while. I'll be lean, mean and thick-skinned, as opposed to the overweight, thin-skinned writer you're used to.

If you do recognize me, wave.

A VANISHING BREED

If it's true we're all born equal, we certainly don't die equal. My friend Bob Freihofer died last Friday. He had done so many good things with his life that, by the time he left us at age seventy-one, it was hard for his friends to think of anyone who was his equal.

Bob and Terry were a close couple, you just knew it seeing them together, even if they were arguing. Last week I phoned and asked Terry if she thought I should come to see Bob. You never know for sure whether to bother a sick friend or the family with a visit. Bob had cancer. He had it bad and Terry was being inundated by well-wishers. She had been living on the edge of tears for three months as she watched her guy slip away from her.

"Here," she said. "I'll put him on."

"Don't come over," Bob said. "I'm just trying to curl up and find a comfortable place. You're on vacation. Make something out of wood." He knew my hobby and it was the kind of funny, offhand remark he'd make.

I couldn't get Bob off my mind that day or in the ten days since then, but I didn't go to see him.

Last Saturday morning I decided to do it whether he wanted me to come or not. I wanted to see him. As I pulled into the driveway about nine o'clock that morning, his boy Al came out.

"Should I go in and see him?" I asked.

"Dad passed away last night at eleven o'clock," Al said.

I have always been surprised at how little we can anticipate our emotional reaction to any situation. Tears come unbidden and unexpectedly sometimes. Our hearts often know something our brain hasn't told us.

Bob Freihofer was the kind of American that all American men like to think they are. He was bright, handsome, masculine, quick with humor and successful in business. He became president of one of the most successful baking companies in the U.S.

Bob was one of a vanishing kind of American businessman. His first concern was the quality of his product. He was proud of everything his company made. At dinner in a restaurant, he'd start telling you how good their chocolate chip cookies were. We all laughed at him, but the cookies were good.

Bob and I went to college together, and at reunions he'd have a truck sent to the campus loaded with enough cakes, cookies, donuts and bread to feed several thousand returning alumni of all classes.

He worked to keep it a successful family business. He didn't want to do it with the kind of advertising that promises more than it delivers. It broke his heart several years ago when his board of directors decided, over his vote, to sell the company to one of the industry giants.

Bob and I lost track of each other after college, but I found him again a year later. It was 1943 and we were both in England. He was a B-17 pilot bombing Germany. That's what a lot of the most capable young American men were those days, bomber pilots. I was a reporter for the Army newspaper, *The Stars and Stripes.*

One day I went out to Bob's base to talk with him and get a story when he returned from a bombing raid. Bob and his crew never came back. They had been shot down over Germany. The ten-man crew had all parachuted to the ground safely and were prisoners of war.

After the war, Bob told great stories of his two years in prison camp. His waist gunner, a nonconformist—there always was one on every B-17 crew—had refused to wear a parachute. Bob argued with him but, like the person who doesn't wear a seat belt, he wouldn't put it on. When the others jumped from their burning plane, the waist gunner was last seen struggling to get into his parachute.

He didn't show up in camp and his friends sadly concluded he had gone down with the ship. Three days later, the waist gunner showed up in the Stalag, black and blue and battered around the head and shoulders.

"We all thought those bastards beat him when they caught him," Bob said. But their friend had not been beaten. In haste, he had hooked the parachute straps behind his legs at the knees and floated to earth that way. He landed on his head and shoulders. Bob would rock with laughter telling the story.

Maybe the best thing Bob Freihofer was, was a human being. There haven't been many as good in my life.

DEATH OF THE HANDYMAN

L ast weekend, we returned to the house in the country one last time to close it for the winter.

The house has stood for seventy years and I guess it'll still be there on that windy hilltop looking out onto the Catskill Mountains when we get back in the spring, but there were a lot of things left undone. One storm window was missing, I never got to clean the leaves out of the gutters and I couldn't find any insulation to stuff under the door of the little building I write in. I'm sure some snow will drift in.

Those things are minor, though, compared to the big problem.

Lloyd Filkins has been shutting off the electricity and the water and draining the pipes and the radiators in the house every fall for about forty years. In the spring, he's been turning on the water and reconnecting the electrical system.

Lloyd knew where all the pipes and valves were because he put them there.

Lloyd knew which switches to throw to cut off the furnace and the electricity to the house and in my shop. He knew because he wired the place, too. Lloyd knew where everything was and no one else but Lloyd did know.

Lloyd died three weeks ago and took 1,000 secrets with him.

We often said we couldn't do without him and now we're having to do without him. Lloyd was a wonderfully dependable old grump. You had to be careful who you mentioned in his presence, because there were a lot of people he wasn't speaking to and if he wasn't speaking to them, he didn't want you speaking to them either.

It wasn't that he held a grudge for long . . . maybe fifteen or twenty years at the most.

He was more like a country doctor than a handyman. He knew the medical history of just about every house in the village and made house calls when things weren't going well. He had the keys to fifty of them.

Lloyd thought of it as his town. The rest of us lived there by the grace of his beneficence.

Just about everyone in the village had some job that Lloyd had started and were waiting for him to come and finish. He had so many emergencies that he usually couldn't come to do those ordinary jobs . . . sometimes for years.

Lloyd loved an emergency best. You could call him any time of day or night with an emergency. He'd grumble at you over the phone and he'd tell you that whatever had happened was your own fault . . . but he'd be there in no time.

When Emily and Kirby were married in the little garden by the side of the house, someone parking their car up by the garage, hit the standing hose connection. The pipe broke and water gushed out. The well pumps only three gallons a minute, so it's quickly emptied if someone in the upstairs bathroom takes a long shower at the same time someone is doing the same thing in the downstairs bathroom . . . or if there's a broken pipe.

The pump cuts out automatically when there's no water in the well and that means no water for washing dishes, cooking, showers, or flushing toilets. With sixty people at a wedding party, this is bad news. When I called, Lloyd dropped whatever he was doing and came. His routine never varied. Without looking or speaking to anyone, he'd go around to the back of his truck and pick out his tools for the job. He spent a lot of time at the back of his truck.

He fixed the broken pipe that day, restarted the well pump and grumped off without saying a word. Lloyd took some perverse pleasure in not giving me the satisfaction of thanking him. His visit that day of the wedding showed up on some bill with other items later in the season. FIX PIPE it said. "Labor . . . $8.00. Parts . . . gasket $.12 . . . Total $8.12."

There were people in town who said Lloyd had a heart of gold and others who were not sure what his heart was made of. He never spoke to them unless they called him in the middle of the night with an emergency.

WOOD MUSIC

Wally died.

Wally wasn't just a friend, he was a pal.

When you're four, you don't play with two-year-olds because the age difference is too great. When you're fifteen, you don't hang around much with the kids who are twelve. A difference in age seems to disappear when you get older, though. You like being with someone for reasons that don't have anything to do with age.

Wally must have been eighteen or nineteen when I was born, and I didn't meet him until fifty-some years later, but age was never a factor in our friendship. Wood was what brought us together. Wally's hobby was making furniture and so was mine.

If I had to name the American who had most of the virtues Americans like to think they have, even though not many Americans have them, I'd name Wally. Whatever it was, he could do it. He assumed there was a solution to any problem that arose, and he'd set out to find it.

Wally was a big, good-looking guy, too. He was six-feet-five inches tall, about 240 pounds, with a big jaw and prominent cheekbones. Even in his eighties, he was a powerful man. When we went out to get lumber together, Wally always lifted his end of the board.

We both spent our summers in a tiny village in upstate New York, and the most fun we had together was going out into the countryside looking for small sawmills that might have some wood we could use. We bought a lot more wood than we had time to make anything out of.

Wood is sold by the board foot, which means a foot long, a foot wide and an inch thick. It's tough to figure when a board is seven-eighths of an inch thick, nine inches wide and ten-feet-two inches long. Wally could do it in his head.

Wally's house was on the main street, right in the middle of our little village, opposite the pretty white-steepled New England church. Wally and I didn't go to church. We were in our workshops Sundays, praying to other gods.

One very hot Sunday morning, I came to Wally's shop and asked him to run some rough board through his thickness planer for me. The planer is one of the noisiest pieces of woodworking equipment. It starts up with a high whine and ends with a loud grinding noise as the blades cut into the surface of the wood.

The job took us half an hour and, while we were vaguely aware of the pleasant sound of familiar hymns emanating from the open church doors, we were oblivious to the fact that the racket we were making was going back through those same doors.

Wally's wife was furious when she came back from church. An attractive, usually soft-spoken, sweet-tempered woman, she was neither of those that morning. From that day forward, she dressed Wally in his Sunday suit and led him by the hand across the street and into the church every Sunday where he sat like a good little boy throughout the services, not making a sound.

Three years ago, Wally and his wife moved permanently to an apartment in Washington, D.C. That was the end of his woodworking. I often talked to him on the phone and I hated to think of him being cooped up there without his tools, without his stacks of lumber and without sawdust in his shoes.

Wally's funeral service was held Tuesday in the magnificent National Cathedral in Washington. The Episcopal canon referred to him as "Wellington."

"It was a beautiful service, wasn't it?" I heard a woman saying as she left. It wasn't, though.

I guess the Episcopal service is designed to be cut-and-dried and unemotional to make it easier on the family, but it didn't have anything to do with the Wally I knew and I wished I hadn't gone.

All during the reading of the prayers and the sorry singing of the hymns, I hoped someone across the street from the cathedral would start up some heavy woodworking machinery and put a few boards through a planer. I'd have thrown open the cathedral doors to let that music in.

MY FRIEND, THE STAR

If you have a clear impression of what Harry Reasoner was like from having seen him on television, I can promise you, you are wrong. Whatever you think he was like he was not like that. I could not possibly explain to you what Harry really was like, even if I was sure I knew myself. He wasn't like anyone you ever knew.

Our careers in television were inextricably mingled for twenty-five years. I wrote hundreds of scripts for him and always labeled his part "THE STAR." I was needling him, but he always was The Star to me.

We first met when we worked on a morning broadcast called *Calendar*. From those early days our little joke was to greet each other "Good Morning," no matter what time of day or night we saw each other. "Good morning," we'd say when we met for dinner.

Simple is the last thing Harry was, and if I told you everything I know about him you would, in all probability, not like him as much as I did until you got to know him better. Then you'd like him a whole lot. He was the most difficult person to be good friends with that I ever knew.

Harry was, in pure intellect, the smartest of all the television correspondents—but he did more dumb things than any of them. He would not have died at the age of sixty-eight if this were not true.

He smoked three packs of cigarettes a day. He drank martinis, a lot of them. Four years ago he had his cancerous left lung removed and continued to smoke heavily.

"I can stop drinking if I have to," he said to me quietly one day two years ago, "but I can't stop smoking."

That was the last time I ever said anything to him about smoking. He died of almost everything. His other lung, his liver and his kidneys had deteriorated, and in early June he had brain surgery. I hope the surgeon knew this was a special brain when he operated on it.

When he was in his twenties, Harry wrote a novel called *Tell Me About Women*. It said a lot about Harry's attitude toward both women and life. He was a romantic. He liked small, dark, candlelit restaurants and dinner with beautiful women.

Kay Carroll of Minneapolis was beautiful. They were married in 1946 as soon as Kay graduated from law school. After thirty-four years and seven children, they were divorced because . . . well, because they were Harry and Kay. Kay died three years ago and Harry remarried.

Harry was born in Dakota City, Iowa, and grew up in Humboldt, right next door. His father was a school superintendent who died in a fall off a cliff in Harry's presence. Harry told me that just once. He didn't offer any details and made me feel I shouldn't ask for any.

In 1972, we went to Humboldt to make a film called *A Small Town in Iowa*. Those two weeks in Humboldt were a happy time for Harry. I remember wondering if he might not have been happier if he'd stayed there and not left to become famous.

Harry was good to talk to. He liked the bond established between people who understood more than they were saying to each other. He loved humor and used it frequently with his good, quick laugh.

In the hospital one night, there were tubes and dripping bottles hanging over him everywhere. I held his hand. His eyes were closed. They said if I spoke loud he might recognize that I was there.

"Harry!" I said in a loud voice. "Good morning!"

He'd have smiled through his pain if there had been any of his great cognitive power left. He did not, and while his heart beat for three more weeks, I knew then that he was gone. My life is riddled with holes where great friends once were.

When I first met Harry Reasoner, he was forty. He liked working in New York and living in Connecticut but even then he was uneasy about being so far from home. I remember him saying that a person should be buried in the ground where his roots were. For Harry, those are in Humboldt and that's where he'll be buried.

I am a writer who tries to put down one word after another in a direct and logical way. I often fail to say precisely what I mean. I have failed here if you don't know that I am writing with tears in my eyes.